P. M. H. Atwater

Coming Back to Life

The After-Effects
of the
Near-Death Experience

Dodd, Mead & Company
New York

*To Terry Young Atwater who taught me the meaning
of tomorrow while lighting my path with
gentleness and love.*

Library of Congress Cataloging-in-Publication Data

Atwater, P. M. H. (Phyllis M. H.)
Coming back to life : the after-effects of the near-death
experience / P. M. H. Atwater.
Bibliography: p. 204
Includes index.
1. Near-death experiences—Psychological aspects.   2. Atwater, P.
M. H. (Phyllis M.H.)   I. Title.
BF1045.N4A87 1988   87-33086
155.9'37—dc 19   CIP
ISBN 0-396-09219-5

Contents

My deepest thanks to:

The forty near-death survivors who participated in the last phase of research for this book. Scattered across the United States and Canada, these people had the courage to openly speak out about their pain and joy, revealing intimate facts about their personal lives—sometimes at risk to their reputations and family relationships.

Merelyn McKnight and Charles C. Wise, Jr., editors during different stages of production; and Liz St. Clair, who rescued me from "mountains" of typing and last minute corrections.

Arthur E. Yensen who first introduced me to what heaven might be and became a treasured friend and a beloved member of our family.

M. Elizabeth Macinata, Thomas More Huber and Terry Macinata, three strangers who came to my aid, nourished and guided the babe I was while I struggled to relearn and redefine life.

William G. Reimer, the one who taught me what real health is and, in so doing, illustrated what holistic medicine and natural healing are all about.

Kenneth Ring who suggested I write this book and then guided me through the scientific labyrinth of statistical facts to help me discover my own worth and trust my own insights.

Tam Mossman, the one who finally located a publisher; Sallie Gouverneur, whose foresight in tossing the first two versions in the wastebasket prompted me to do better.

My three children, Kelly John Huffman, Natalie Gae Huffman Rowell and Pauline Ann Huffman Carter, who put up with me and loved in spite of all, at a time when I was barely functional and had nothing left to give.

Introduction

Several years ago, when I still engaged in my early research into near-death experiences, I came across a reference to a book with a title so unabashedly straightforward that it stopped my usually nystagmic gaze in its wobbly tracks. *I Died Three Times in 1977*, it declared. Well, if a title is supposed to make you curious, this one had certainly hooked me, so I found myself writing straight-a-way to the author—one P. M. H. Atwater—for a copy. I couldn't help wondering about the author's name, too: all those initials tended to conjure up an image of an Englishman of rather pronounced reserve. When I received my copy of the book, however, I learned that I had been wrong on all three counts. This was hardly a reserved Englishman—it wasn't even a man living behind all those initials. To the contrary, this was friendly Phyllis from Idaho (of all places!), and she was (as I was later to learn when we met face to face) as warm and delightful as a ray of sunshine on a cloudy spring day. I *was* right about one thing, though: Phyllis did have a forthright style, as her book title had suggested to me. Her use of language is spare, to the point, and full of zip. And her tone is always intensely practical. As Phyllis says, "If you can't scrub floors with what you know then it isn't worth knowing."

And so, in that same style of pith and verve which has been her journalistic trademark, Phyllis Atwater speaks to us in *this* book on a subject which she has made her specialty over the last few years: What it is like for a survivor of a near-death experience to *come back* to "ordinary life" after having glimpsed the realm of "the eternal." On this matter, Phyllis is, I believe, uniquely qualified to address us. Not only has she had her own near-death experience (actually, *three* of them, as you will recall), but since 1977, she has spent countless hours talking in-depth with hundreds of near-death survivors about how they have dealt with the aftermath of their own experiences. In addition, she has for several years now been writing a regular column, called "Coming Back," for the Magazine, *Vital Signs*, which is a periodical sent to all the members of the International Association for Near-Death Studies, an organization dedicated to the exploration and understanding of near-death experiences. Finally, and especially for this book, Phyllis has carried out a systematic questionnaire study with forty more near-death experiencers that focuses on issues related to problems of coming back. As a result of her personal experiences in coming to terms with her own near-death episodes and her wide-ranging exploration of others' coping with the same problem, Phyllis has amassed a wealth of knowledge and insights on this subject that is, I am convinced, unsurpassed by any other researcher in the field.

Furthermore, beyond the sheer amount of information Phyllis has compiled on this question, she brings a new and fresh perspective to it as well. For in Phyllis' case, she can obviously speak not merely as a researcher, but also as an *experiencer* herself. As such, she knows directly and intimately certain aspects of the process of coming back that may elude or be misunderstood by reseachers who have not had this experience. And more than this, because Phyllis is not constrained by the usual caution of academicians, she is not able to probe fearlessly into controversial areas of this experience that more conventional investigators are inclined to bypass or overlook altogether. In this connection, it is worth noting here that *Coming Back to Life* brings to light two related aspects of the transformative process following near-death experiences that earlier research tended to gloss over or miss completely. The first is Phyllis' attempt—and to me it is a very persuasive one— to show just how long and difficult the process of psychological integration following this experience can be. Ultimately, that process can lead to enormous fulfillment and expansion of consciousness, but the road to that end is lined with a multitude of ditches, obstacles and blind alleys which Phyllis manages to illuminate brilliantly. A second point here is that though the near-death experience may well involve an experience of Light, it does *not* make for instant enlightenment. A near-death experience *is* or can be an awakening of sorts, but it is only a beginning in the arduous task of *full* awakening and should, she cautions us, be regarded by experiencers and others as only an *opportunity* to grow into greater awareness.

Now, one might well contend that however intrinsically fascinating this process of coming back may be (and few will be bored with the dynamics described in this book), it must be of decidedly limited interest because, after all, how many people have actually had near-death experiences? Such an objection, at first hearing, seems cogent enough, but it turns out to be totally misguided for several reasons, as we shall see.

First of all, according to a recent survey conducted by the Gallup Poll, it is estimated that perhaps as many as *eight million* adult Americans have already had at least one near-death experience! Not a trivial number—and one that excludes children, who have also reported experiences of this kind. We have learned that near-death experiences occur in other parts of the world as well and that at least in Western countries they take the same form described by Phyllis, so presumably we are dealing with a phenomenon that has been experienced by many *millions* of persons across the globe.

Second, as Phyllis points out, with the spread and increasing perfection of resuscitation technology, it is proba-

ble that the incidence of near-death experiences throughout the world will increase substantially in the short-term
future. On this assumption, Phyllis appears to be treating a
phenomenon that is not only widespread but destined to be
even more pervasive before the end of this millenium.

Third—and in this interpretation Phyllis stands in
accord with most other researchers of the near-death experience—the process of change and transformation that she
describes for us here is NOT limited to persons who have
had a near-death experience. There are many *other* ways
besides coming close to death by which people can have
this same kind of experience and can be catapulted into a
similar process of spiritual growth. Thus, the near-death
experience is simply one currently publicized example of a
more general type of transcendental experience leading to
a profound alteration of one's somatic, psychological, and
interpersonal functioning. This book, then, is by no means
merely about what happens to near-death experiencers
only; it deals with the much larger question of the effects of
transformative experiences *in general*, many of which, like
the near-death experience, involve a death and rebirth
motif.

This leads us to the fourth reason this book has a
much wider scope than might be supposed. What Phyllis is
really delineating here is not just the difficult process of
psychological and social integration following a near-death
experience, but a pattern of *evolutionary change* that
humanity is now about to undergo. In agreement with other
researchers of the near-death experience—though Phyllis
reached her own conclusions independently—Phyllis sees
in this experience and its transformative effects a possible
evolutionary catalyst for the next stage in humanity's
psycho-spiritual development. In making her argument
here, she, like several other researchers, draws our attention back to the pioneering work of the Canadian psychiatrist, Richard Maurice Bucke, and his book, *Cosmic
Consciousness*. Modern research into the near-death experience is doing much to bring this book back into promi-
nence, for it was Bucke who helped to popularize a similar
hypothesis at the beginning of this century. In this respect,

then, Phyllis Atwater is dealing with matters of the widest possible scope and relevance, as the destiny of our entire species is her central issue.

In any case, I hope I have said enough to indicate to you that *Coming Back to Life* is a book that all readers interested in the process of human transformation should find deeply absorbing. And though I have insisted that the range of this book takes it far beyond the realm of near-death experiences and their after-effects, it is also the case that researchers in this field will find it a rich trove of testable insights and provocative interpretations, consideration of which should further advance studies in this area. It goes without saying that those to whom this book may prove most *personally* meaningful are those millions of near-death survivors, and their families and friends, for it is to them that the findings, advice, and wisdom of *Coming Back to Life* are especially pertinent. In writing this book, Phyllis Atwater will have helped many to come back more easily, with deeper self-understanding, and with a greater capacity to contribute to humanity's continuing evolution. For this all of us stand in debt to the author of *Coming Back to Life*.

Kenneth Ring, Ph.D.

Opening Statement

This is a book about after-effects, consequences, if you will; what happens *after* surviving the worst of all possible outcomes. You will recognize some of it, even most of it, for there are many ways to meet death and many types of dying. It is about what happens when known worlds collapse and belief systems collide, when in place of darkness there dares to be light—literally light—which shines like no other.

Using the near-death experience as its premise, this book examines the consequences of such an event. It contains within—the rest of the story!

Another Definition of Death

The Aramaic word for death translates:

*not here
present elsewhere.*

This ancient concept of death best describes the near-death experience and what happens to those who go through it.

These people were present—elsewhere!

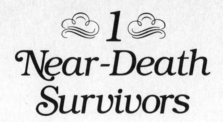

1
Near-Death
Survivors

"On the day when death will knock at thy door, what will thou offer him? I will set before my guest the full vessel of my life. I will never let him go with empty hands."

Sir Rabindranath Tagore

I am a near-death survivor. That means I am one of those people who died but didn't stay dead. I came back. While "dead," I experienced something quite extraordinary, something far beyond my understanding at the time it occurred, even beyond my ability to articulate or believe. I experienced "The Other Side." I passed *through* death.

Much has now been written about people like myself and what happened to us, for to have experienced anything at all after dying has always seemed impossible, absurd, an infantile projection of wishful thinking, or some kind of hallucination. What happened to us seems to contradict death's finality. For this reason we have been studied, researched, interviewed, and analyzed by all manner of professionals.

Elisabeth Kübler-Ross, M.D., was the first to publicly speak out about the existence of the near-death phenomenon, a unique situation where people who revive after being considered "dead" give detailed accounts of leaving their body, passing into a light and, in some cases, visiting "heavenly" realms. Raymond Moody, M.D., further explored this phenomenon, writing *Life After Life* to describe his findings. In this book, which became a global best-seller, Moody outlined a repetitious pattern to the event as revealed by the stories of survivors. This pattern was later verified scientifically by Kenneth Ring, Ph.D., and reported in his book *Life at Death*.

The work of these three pioneers set the stage for all that followed—all the research, experiments, and scholarly writings—all the magazine and newspaper headlines. Many were the professionals who, convinced they could easily discredit the whole thing as a hoax, proved it very real and very credible, regardless of whether the death event was clinical or an unverified claim. So far no one has been able to disprove any of the original findings; yet, by the same token, no one has been able to fully explain any of them, either.

A 1982 Gallup Poll survey indicated that about eight million Americans believe they have experienced the near-death phenomenon, either as a result of brushing close to death, nearly dying, or after being pronounced dead. George Gallup, Jr., admitted the estimate conservative, with perhaps twenty-three million being a more accurate figure. And that is just in the United States. Far from being some short-lived novelty, reportings are on the rise, both in this country and throughout the world. Better resuscitation methods and more effective medical care are turning more and more people from the brink of death and reviving some who were "lost." And more and more of these people speak of being quite alive *after* they died. Latest estimates figure forty percent of all resuscitated patients will have a near-death experience.

Thanks to the media, scientific assessments of this puzzling enigma are well reported. But is there more to the story? What about the survivor's view? What do these people have to say—about what happened, about death, about life after death? What about afterwards, when they return to society? Are there after-effects?

This missing element constitutes the rest of the story, for there *is* more, much more—and plenty of surprises, as well.

To begin with, there are two near-death survivors who conducted their own original research on the subject *inde-*

pendent of other findings and unknown to each other. One is Margot Grey, a British psychologist, who based her masters thesis on such material and then later wrote the book *Return From Death*, which wound up further validating Kenneth Ring's work, including his more current ideas about various types of transformational experiences which he detailed in *Heading Toward Omega*. The two psychologists had met each other once, but they never discussed each other's projects. Margot's focus was British cases and what could be learned from them, then how such cases compared with those reported in the United States. Although her work is of her own doing, what many people do not realize is that her efforts were fueled by the fact that she, too, is an experiencer.

The other one is me. Both Margot and I began writing our books in 1983 and finished in 1984, but she published first, undoubtedly because her approach to the subject was more professional academically. *Coming Back* was different, perhaps too much so to be taken seriously, so I wrote it again and again, searching for a way to make it more acceptable without compromising what it contained. The book you are reading at this moment is version seven, a product of five years and more work and determination than I care to recount. I am not college-trained, except for one semester of beginning drafting and illustrated geometry at Boise State University in Idaho. I did not set out to research anything. I just wanted to survive.

What this book contains is an "accident," a by-product, if you will, from the experiences I survived in 1977 that so radically changed my life and me with it, that life "as usual" became impossible. I had never heard the term "near-death" until Elisabeth Kübler-Ross used it. Raymond Moody and Kenneth Ring were unknown to me. All I knew was that I had to make sense of what had happened to me. Although the experience itself was important, I instinctively knew that what came after was more important.

A passage from the Christian Bible showed me the way out of my dilemma. It read, "For those who knock the door is opened." I took this passage literally and began my "knocking" by accepting a request to share the story of what I had experienced while at the "edge of death." Certainly the sharing was sincere, but my real goal was the hope that such a public appearance might attract other near-death survivors. I had a lot of questions I wanted to ask of such people. It worked. Two other experiencers came to that first talk. This began a quest that led me through ten states to speak with several thousand people and to find over two hundred other survivors. Once met, we would cry, kiss, and hug each other, and share more deeply than I have ever shared with anyone. I asked my questions, more than I ever dreamed I would, and the answers I received enabled me to rebuild my life with renewed faith and joy.

Nothing more would have ever come from all that "research" had it not been for Kenneth Ring who, after tracing me through a small publication I had written, asked that I write magazine articles about what I had learned, then later suggested that I produce a book. Writing such a book would necessitate "real" research and more leg work, but the idea that others might benefit from what had once helped me spurred me on. Yes, I would write such a book. It would be for the purpose of helping others to help themselves. This is the result.

The bulk of material contained herein came from my original quest. No one else influenced that acquisition, for the only need that seemed important at the time was pure survival. I did not have benefit of learned advice then, nor was I privy to any kind of material that might have made a difference. I was on my own. Expenses came out of my own pocket except for occasions when donations were offered. Skills of observation and listening were the tools I used, for I am analytical by nature, curious by choice.

Even though most of my attention focused on the aftermath of surviving death, enabling me to isolate a pattern to the after-effects, I first want to briefly share a few things I noticed about the event in general and about those who experienced it.

The Universal Experience

Historical precedent offers a wealth of documentation to validate the near-death experience. Even Plato wrote of such phenomenon in his story of Er, the soldier, whose dead body laid in waste beside his fallen comrades for ten days. When at last help came many were puzzled, for the body of Er had not decayed as had the others. Confused, his relatives took him home for burial and upon the funeral pyre he revived, stood up, and recounted for all to hear what he had learned while on "The Other Side."

Throughout recorded history there are such writings, and the connecting threads between them are the same as those found today. Revelations, like those of Er, are as incredible now as ever before and just as accurate, impossible revelations which could not have been known in advance. And each is coherent, lucid, detailed, consistent and sound, unlike mere dream images or hallucinations. People of different religions and of different cultures report the same basic phenomenon in much the same manner, even children, and those I met were no exception.

But recently, a startling discovery, was made. Tiny babies can have a near-death experience, too!

Reportings are few, but enough have been made to confirm that small infants who brush death, nearly die, or who revive after death seemed final, can not only experience the same near-death pattern as adults, but they can remember what happened long enough to describe it clearly once they are older and attain proficiency with language. This startling discovery makes it even more important that serious scientific studies of children's experiences be conducted, and that the surgical techniques and the treatment of tiny babies in crisis be rethought because of later implications from memory.

During my own quest to understand, one question I often asked was, "How long were you dead?" Time estimates are difficult, of course, because the death event requires immediacy plus the undivided attention of any attendant who might be present. People in such situations seldom check a clock. But as near as anyone could guess, the average time "out" was thought to be five minutes. Many were "gone" longer, one for over an hour.

Before exploring what I found any further, allow me to review what is now considered the universal prototype of the near-death experience. This pattern consists of eight basic elements:

1. *A sensation of floating out of one's body*, often followed by an out-of-body experience where all that goes on around the "vacated" body is both seen and heard accurately.

2. *Passing through a dark tunnel* or black hole or encountering some kind of darkness. This is often accompanied by a feeling or sensation of movement or acceleration. "Wind" may be heard or felt.

3. *Ascending toward a light at the end of the darkness*, a light of incredible brilliance, with the possibility of seeing people, animals, plants, lush outdoors, and even cities within that light.

4. *Greeted by friendly voices, people, or beings*, who may be strangers, loved ones, or religious figures. Conversation can ensue, information or a message may be given. Activity such as this is referred to as a "scenario."

5. *Seeing a panoramic review of the life just lived*, from birth to death or in reverse order, sometimes becoming a reliving of the life rather than a dispassionate viewing. The person's life can be reviewed in its entirety or in segments. This is usually accompanied by a feeling or need to assess losses or gains during the life to determine what was learned or not learned. Other beings can take part in this judgment-like process or offer advice.

6. *A reluctance to return to the earthplane*, but invariably realizing either their job on earth is not finished or a mission must yet be accomplished before they can return to stay.

7. *Warped sense of time and space*, discovering time and space do not exist, losing the need to recognize measurements of life either as valid or necessary.

8. *Disappointment at being revived*, often feeling a need to shrink or somehow squeeze to fit back in to the physical body. There can be unpleasantness,

even anger or tears, at the realization they are now
back in their bodies and no longer on "The Other
Side."

This, of course, is a general pattern. Few episodes contain
all eight elements. Most have about half; some two or three.
All manner of variations can occur. In talking with other
survivors and hearing their stories in detail, I can attest to
the fascinating variety of accounts; and, although similar
to the overall prototype, each individual case has its own
particular difference. For instance, one woman I spoke
with saw herself encased within a blue bubble which floated over her lifeless body pinned by twisted steel in a car
accident. Hers was a typical out-of-body experience, yet it
had features unique to her (the "blue bubble"). Here are
more examples of what I mean: a man in a respirator saw
and felt himself held by "a giant hand," a younger woman
described "straddling a light beam and touring the universe," another man saw nothing at all but heard "a thun-
dering voice" speak to him giving specific instructions for
a job he was to perform once he returned to the world of the
living.

I noticed that some fellow survivors would describe
the presence of a broad field of steady light that held
constant throughout their experience while others saw
smaller, flashing lights of various colors. There were out-
of-body experiencers who left the location of their body and
went outdoors or traveled to see friends or relatives who
lived far away. A few of these "travelers" were *physically
seen and recognized* when they "arrived" at their destination, appearing as usual in every way, even though their
"corpse" remained at the sight of the death event, unmoved
and unmoving. No one had any explanation to offer as to
how such a "bi-location" could have happened. It just did.

Some scenarios told to me involved huge cities of gold
and temples of rare beauty with inset gems. There were
survivors who claimed to have met with historically famous religious leaders while others were greeted by a next-
door neighbor or loved ones who had recently passed on.
Survivors would descibe those on "The Other Side" as
appearing human and wearing modern clothes, though

some witnessed these people in historical raiment, without clothes, or angel-like in shape. Others observed these people as "beings of light," without any recognizable shape at all except globular, cylindrical, or a glowing mass. Lengthy dissertations ensued in some cases or there would be question-and-answer sessions, revelations of life's secrets, tribunal judgments, or trips to a great hall to consult "The Book of Life." Animals were often seen, especially household pets who had previously died and lions.

Regardless of how simple or complex the near-death episode, the vast majority of survivors commented *most* about the incredible, overwhelming love they felt, the peace, the feeling of total acceptance, and the Presence of God.

Individuals can have more than one experience. A woman I contacted had six experiences spread out over twenty-nine years of living. One man with astronomical health problems claimed to have them about every couple of years or so. "It gives me the strength to keep going," he said. It is not at all uncommon to hear of someone having had at least two.

There seems no rhyme or reason for multiple cases unless it is because the average near-death experience emerges from conditions involving severe or extreme trauma, such as an accident or life-threatening illness that can leave the survivor weak and in ill health, vulnerable— sometimes for long periods. Relapses do occur or perhaps another life-threatening illness comes. Death can be faced yet again, but repeated crises are no guarantee another near-death episode will happen. Case in point: one man had two near-death scenarios within one month, recovered, but several years later almost died again from another condition brought on by the first. This time, however, he did not have a near-death experience of any kind, encountering instead only darkness. The following year, he again nearly lost his life but this time he had a third scenario. Four times he barely survived death, yet he had only three near-death events. Still another man almost died eight times during his lifetime before he experienced near-death with crisis number nine.

In cases where more than one is experienced, the scenarios can lead into each other, that is to say, one can set the stage for the next to come and it can begin where the previous one left off; or the next episode can be totally unrelated to the first. Additional scenarios can be more *or* less important than the original, as there is not necessarily any progression. So far, I have yet to find multiple cases from one individual that were all identical in content; but I have met *different* people who seemed to share the *same* experience, or at least what appeared to be the same experience. This peculiarity happened in two ways: they were either all at the same hospital within the same timespan, or they were miles and years apart.

In my own case, two of the events happened in January, the other in March. I have since met three other people whose experiences were so much akin to my first one, that it is as if we both lived through the same thing. Later, I met twelve other people who also had three near-death experiences in 1977, with before and after conditions similar, although we "died" in different months and had different scenarios.

There was a time when I felt uniquely alone because of what I had survived. I was convinced no one else could possibly have seen what I saw and lived to speak of it, that somehow I must have been "chosen," but dialoguing with other people like myself quickly dispelled such notions.

Although each case differs, some more than others, there are commonalities, connecting links, if you will, that run through all experiences regardless of the person's age, background, belief system, or nationality. We are more *alike* than different.

The Survivors' View of Death

During my search to find other people like myself I often went with notebook in hand, determined to somehow understand what seemed so confusing. At that time, I had only heard the term "near-death" once and knew little of the subject. Everything I finally learned about the phenomenon I learned by reaching out to others first-hand, then comparing what I discovered with my own experience and previous knowledge of other events that seemed related.

After many years of this, I put together a consensus of survivor comments to describe the actual moment of death and what it feels like. Although it would be irresponsible to claim that near-death experiencers have the answer to life's greatest riddle, I do believe their viewpoints are worthy of consideration and offer some degree of credibility. For this reason, I submit the following:

What It Feels Like To Die

Any pain to be suffered comes first.

Instinctively you fight to live.

That is automatic.

It is inconceivable to the conscious mind that any other reality could possibly exist beside the earth-world of matter bounded by time and space. We are used to it. We have been trained since birth to live and thrive in it. We know ourselves to be ourselves by the eternal stimuli we receive. Life tells us who we are and we accept its telling. That, too, is automatic.

Your body goes limp.

Your heart stops.

No more air flows in or out.

You lose sight, feeling, and movement—although the ability to hear goes last.

Identity ceases. The "you" that you once were becomes only memory.

There is no pain at the moment of death.

Only peaceful silence.

Calm.

Quiet.

But you still exist.

It is easy not to breathe.

In fact, it is easier, more comfortable, and infinitely more natural not to breathe than to breathe.

The biggest surprise for most people in dying is to realize dying does not end life. Whether darkness or light comes next, or some kind of event, be it positive, negative, or somewhere in between, expected or unexpected, the biggest surprise of all is to realize you are still you. You can still think, you can still remember, you can still see, hear, move, reason, wonder, feel, question, and tell jokes—if you wish.

You are still alive, very much alive. In fact, more alive than since you were last born.

Only the way of all this is different, different because you no longer wear a dense body to filter and amplify the various sensations you had once regarded as the only valid indicators of what constitutes life. You had always been taught one has to wear a body to live.

If you expect to die when you die you will be disappointed.

The only thing dying does is help you release, slough off, and discard the "jacket" you once wore (more commonly referred to as a "body").

When you die you lose your body.

That is all there is to it.

Nothing else is lost.

You are not your body. It is just something you wear for a while, because living in the earthplane is infinitely more meaningful and more involved if you are encased in its trappings and subject to its rules.

A good portion of near-death cases feature out-of-body experiencers. As I spoke with these people, they would become quite animate in their gestures of what it was like to try communicating with a nurse or loved one only to be ignored because no one heard them, or to try grabbing someone's arm only to pass clear through as if that person were so much thin air. These so-called "departed" ones would feel perfectly normal and perfectly alive yet no one else could see, hear, or feel them. The "departed" had suddenly become invisible.

This state of invisibility, they claim, is eerie and frustrating, and takes some getting used to. While loved ones are busy grieving and in shock, the dearly departed can be just as busy adjusting to a new existence, and undergoing just as much shock. It works both ways.

Death is like birth. Birth is like death. When you leave one world you are born into another. It doesn't seem to matter in which direction you are going: death means "you leave" and birth means "you enter." Each event reflects the other.

Survivors note how difficult it can sometimes be to realize you are dead. This, they feel, may explain ghosts, for maybe that is all a ghost is—someone like themselves who has yet to realize he or she died. It is easy enough to imagine why deceased "persons" would continue inhabiting familiar surroundings or would keep trying to make contact with anyone who might listen. If you didn't know you were dead, how would you know when to quit "hanging around?"

Using the same format as before, I now submit the following consensus of survivor opinions on the subject of death itself:

What Death Is

There is a step-up of energy at the moment of death, an increase in speed as if you are suddenly vibrating faster than before.

Using radio as an analogy, this speed-up is comparable to having lived all your life at a certain radio frequency when all of a sudden someone or something comes along and flips the dial. That flip shifts you to another, higher wavelength. The original frequency where you once existed is still there. It did not change. Everything is still just the same as it always was.

Only *you* changed, only *you* speeded up to allow entry into the next radio frequency up the dial.

As is true with all radios and radio stations, there can
be bleed-overs or distortions of transmission signals due to interference patterns. These can allow
or force frequencies to coexist or commingle for
indefinite periods of time. Normally, most shifts
up the dial are fast and efficient; but, occasionally, one can run into interference, perhaps
from a strong emotion, a sense of duty, or a need to
fulfill a vow, or keep a promise. This interference
could allow coexistence of frequencies for a few
seconds, days, or even years (perhaps explaining
hauntings); but sooner or later, eventually, every
given vibrational frequency will seek out or be
nudged to where it belongs.

You fit your particular spot on the dial by your speed of
vibration. You cannot coexist forever where you do
not belong.

Who can say how many spots there are on the dial or
how many frequencies there are to inhabit? No
one knows.

You shift frequencies in dying. You switch over to life
on another wavelength. You are still a spot on the
dial but you move up or down a notch or two.

You don't die when you die. You shift your consciousness and speed of vibration.

That is all death is.

A shift.

Are near-death scenarios symbolic or literal? No one can
be certain, but I honestly think both apply. Right after
having such an experience, though, survivors take what
happened to them literally, quite literally. There is no
questioning at first. Questions come later.

Regardless how much or how little happened, it is
staggering to accept that anything happened at all. We are
so programmed to believe death ends everything, or just
about everything, that anything even suggestive of continued life is a jolt. Even for those who profess a belief in life
after death before their experience, it is still a jolt, for the

enormity and diversity of what comes next stretches the imagination beyond what seems possible.

You encounter more when you die.

No matter what your previous beliefs, you encounter more.

And there is more beyond that. As near as I can tell there is no end to the "mores" and the "beyonds." Death is a shift in consciousness, a doorway we pass through. What we encounter, no matter what it is, constitutes the mere tip of a bottomless iceberg, a wink in infinity!

Negative Experiences

Thus far, I have only described positive reportings. Scenarios can be negative, too. Seven people came my way who had negative experiences. I heard of six others. Let me tell you about the first four.

It was the late sixties (long before my own episode and before I knew what a near-death experience was). The place was St. Alphonsus Hospital in Boise, Idaho. I was visiting a lady there who had just moved to Boise from southern California. She had suffered a heart attack, and because I had previously befriended her, she called me. She was chalk-white with fear when I arrived. While clinically dead, she had experienced an incident which went like this: she floated out of her body and into a dark tunnel, headed through the tunnel toward a bright light ahead; once the light was reached, she came to view a landscape of barren, rolling hills filled to overflowing with nude, zombie-like people standing elbow to elbow doing nothing but staring straight at her. She was so horrified at what she saw she started screaming. This snapped her back into her body where she continued screaming until sedated. As she relayed her story, she went on to declare death a nightmare, then cursed every church throughout all history for misleading people with rubbish about any kind of heaven. She was inconsolable.

While I listened patiently, two other people entered the room, an elderly man and woman using walking canes. Individually, both had suffered heart failure, too, and later revived after being declared dead. Both revealed substantially the same story as the lady I knew. They were equally frightened. The three had found out about each other from nurses who had been comparing notes on patients they felt were having strange hallucinations.

This was such a coincidence that I instinctively began asking pointed questions. For whatever reason, each answered my questions without hesitation. It is as if they were hoping I could explain away what they had experienced and somehow make everything okay. They seemed to "need" me there, to listen and to care.

This is what my questions revealed: none of these people had the same religion, background, or lifestyle. None had mutual friends or common interests, nor did they have the same doctor in attendance. They had never seen each other before. All had lived long lives of varying degrees of hardship and success; two were still married to their original spouses and had several grown children apiece; the lady from California had been divorced several times and had no children. The only common denominator I could find, beside their heart ailments and the hospital floor they shared, was this: all three had suppressed guilts of various kinds deep within themselves. These guilts seemed quite painful to them and the strange "vision" they experienced while "dead" only served to deepen that pain. They admitted meeting what they feared most in dying, which confirmed and strengthened their already strong belief that their "sins" would be punished.

Before I left, a nurse took me aside and said there was yet one more, a man so shaken he refused to speak with anyone but kept muttering words like "hills and hills of nude people all staring." I was not allowed to see him.

Why four people within a span of two days at the same hospital had the same basic experience brought on by the same type of ailment is a mystery to me. I could offer no consolation to any of them. I could only listen and ask questions. The whole thing was so unnerving I was shaking when I left. What became of these four people, I do not know. The lady from California became so irrational and rude afterwards, I stopped visiting her. Had I known then what I know now, I would have handled the situation differently. These people were absolutely convinced there is a hell.

Another case of more recent vintage involves a young man in his late teens who experienced near-death because of a motorcycle accident. His scenario involved good and evil depicted as an angel and the devil both battling over his lifeless body, claiming his soul up for grabs, while he watched in horror from a position above his body and to one side. Before he revived, the angel announced victory but the devil vowed revenge. Seemingly recovered from the accident, the young man swears the devil is after him yet, manifesting itself physically and in broad daylight almost everywhere he goes, peeking around corners, leering at him with fiery eyes. When I interviewed him, he readily admitted feeling guilty from years of heavy drugs and alcohol. Apparently, his Catholic upbringing had been on a collision course with his abusive lifestyle until the accident cut short what seemed out of control. His near-death experience served only to convince him that the devil would eventually punish him for his "sins." He was so obsessed with this idea that he would snicker arrogantly if anyone suggested there might be another way to interpret what had happened to him. He refused all attempts at therapy, was smug and resolute in his conviction that he and the devil were locked in a deadly game of hide-and-seek. His parents were frightened and confused.

This response might be better understood if one takes into account the fact that his case received much attention. Professional researchers and the curious came from far and near to hear his story. His growing celebrity status noticeably increased any sightings he claimed to make of the devil. It is quite clear this man needed therapy, not fame. I can only hope he finally received what he sorely needed. I was sorry afterwards that I had ever interviewed him, for I came to perceive myself as just another in a long line of curious "onlookers" who seemed to exacerbate his problems, not help to solve them.

Positive experiencers readily claim to have seen heaven; negative experiencers warn there is a hell. Research facts cannot prove either claim.

It is interesting to note, however, that negative experiences follow *the same pattern of common elements* as positive ones do. Both phenomena are identical but specifics differ. Note the following comparison:

Positive	*Negative*
friendly beings	lifeless apparitions
beautiful environment	barren or empty expanses
conversations	threats or silence
acceptance and overwhelming sensation of love	danger and the possibility of violence
a feeling of heaven, warmth	a sense of hell, coldness

Negative experiencers are relieved and overjoyed to find themselves back in their nice, safe, comfortable bodies again, surrounded by familiar landscapes and what they believe life to be. Many times they turn negative into positive by learning valuable lessons from their experience and taking steps to improve their attitudes and relationships with others. Some consider their experience a "preview" of what might happen if they do not change their ways. Invariably, negative experiences are brushed aside more readily than positive ones, sometimes forgotten altogether or remembered only from the positive vantage point.

Why there are so few negative reportings, I do not know. It has been speculated by various professional researchers that these people may be afraid to speak up publicly and report such things, especially now after thousands of positive accounts have been studied. They may fear excessive ridicule because of what their scenario may indicate about themselves and the way they have lived their lives. But, then, it could be there are few reportings simply because negative experiences seldom occur.

The Issue of Suicides

Some near-death episodes emerge from the trauma of suicide. On the average, these suicide scenarios are positive and uplifting but lack much of the complexity and involvement of those resulting from other forms of death. Still, these near-death scenarios are important, perhaps doubly so, because each tends to confirm the importance of life and illustrate for the confused victim how truly loved and special he or she really is. Like any other survivor, the suicide victim often returns with a sense of mission, a sense of a job yet to be accomplished, and often that job turns out to be a desire to inform other potential victims that suicide is not the answer. Case in point, a young man:

> "Since then, suicide has never crossed my mind as a way out. It's a copout to me and not the way to heaven. I wish you luck in your research and hope my experience will help stop someone from taking his own life. It is a terrible waste."

Near-death episodes of this sort can lay to rest problems and conflicts, explain away confusions, and emphasize the need to remain embodied. These survivors usually return with a feeling that suicide solves nothing, that it is not yet their time to die—and they are invariably renewed and refreshed by that feeling. They resolve to stay alive and often use their near-death event as a source of courage, strength, and inspiration.

Not all suicide scenarios are positive, however.

Some are negative, and these can be so negative they upset the individual more than the original problem. This kind of devastation *can* be transforming if used as a catalyst to help him or her make changes that comprise constructive, long-term solutions. Such changes can come from an inner awakening, or from the fear that what was experienced may indeed herald the individual's ultimate fate if something is not done to turn things around.

But there is another aspect to the suicide issue.

Just because an individual has had a near-death experience does *not* prevent him or her from considering and perhaps attempting suicide at a later date. I am aware most researchers claim the opposite to be true, but I cannot substantiate their claim. The near-death experience, especially if positive, *can be* a suicide deterrent, but not always. We are not "saved" by having one, not even from ourselves.

One woman who contacted me spoke of being hospitalized twice for attempting suicide—*many years after* her near-death episode. She had formerly experienced a scenario that was indeed soul-stirring and uplifting; but, with the passing of years and a life filled with tragedy and pain, the positive upliftment she had previously received seemed to fade. Memories of how wonderful it was on "The Other Side" prompted her to try killing herself so she could return. She failed both attempts and caused herself even more grief. When last I heard from her, she seemed reasonably back on her feet and more sensible, stating that she now realized there was no escape and she had better get busy and solve her problems herself.

Another woman who repeatedly brushed death and had a positive near-death event each time seriously considered killing herself so she could escape her horrible life and return to the wonders of life after death. Although this woman did not follow through on her threats, neither did she follow through on advice to seek help. What has become of her I do not know.

I can personally relate to both of these cases for my third death experience was what I came to call an "emotional suicide." I willed myself dead and my body was too exhausted to argue. Whether or not I physically died is debatable here, but as far as I am concerned, I did die. This happened two months *after* an incredibly loving and wonderful near-death scenario in which I was overcome with forgiveness and joy.

Regardless of how meaningful a near-death experience is, it will not necessarily protect or shield you from the realities of life. *The experience is not magic. Surviving does not make you enlightened or superhuman.* Life goes on. Your problems do not stop just because you did. They are still waiting when you get back. You may regain your health but deep inside you can still be a mess.

After-effects from the event can be severe or at least so unsettling as to cause some survivors to disassociate from normal living habits. Your brain can shift and personal skills may alter, leaving you disoriented. Certainly, the near-death experience can be a source of strength and guidance, but its impact may tend to fade as years pass, perhaps not so much in memory as in importance. Depression and a sense of hopelessness may ensue if needed help is not received. The vast majority of survivors heal successfully and restructure their lives in a positive fashion— but not all of them.

Not all survivors are survivors!

I heard Elisabeth Kübler-Ross once explain how near-death experiencers secretly hope their final end hurries so they can return to stay in the "other" world they had previously visited. Even if active and reinvolved in earth-life, their greatest joy and satisfaction seems to come from the memory they cherish of a time when they once had a "peek at heaven." It's almost as if they fully consume life so they can hurry up and die.

If the "The Other Side" is so great, why stay here?

Why does anyone bother living on this plane at all?

We stay because it makes sense to stay.

The vast majority of near-death survivors have come to realize that hurrying your death is no escape and guarantees nothing. If it isn't your time, you will either cheat yourself out of what might have been had you stayed, or you will not stay dead regardless of what method you use to kill yourself. For instance, your body might continue living, even if doing so makes medical history, with you "trapped" inside, unable to animate the uncooperative hulk—technically alive, but more vegetable than human. I know a man this happened to. There was no possible way he could have survived his violent suicide attempt, but he did. The physical complications that resulted were beyond belief, making his original problem scarcely worth mentioning.

It is not worth it.

No matter how wonderful "The Other Side" seems, you cannot stay if it is not your time. And timing seems to be the key. Real progress, real learning, real growth is done here in the earthplane.

No matter what instructions you receive "over there," the real curriculum is "over here."

One survivor put it quite succinctly, "I think of life as school. I think of death as recess." I agree. If you opt out too soon you will be back, one way or another. It is better to stay with the program—AND GRADUATE!

Talking About It

The typical near-death survivor wants to talk about what happened. The typical concerned bystander does not want to listen. The typical survivor has a story to tell. The typical bystander thinks the survivor is nuts.

The typical near-death experience is positive and up-lifting. Even a negative experience can have redeeming aspects. The typical response from bystanders is to: call a psychologist, alert a psychiatrist, tell the person to shut up, or somehow try to convince him or her it is only a dream or a vision or a hallucination.

The survivor is told to forget it.

But it cannot be forgotten.

It won't go away.

It is too real to be either dream or vision.

It makes too much sense to be a hallucination.

Without exception, every survivor I have spoken with or heard from expressed the same sentiment: if only some-one had cared enough to listen, what a difference that would have made. There is pain in that statement, real pain.

Certainly, some survivors were able to find caring listeners, and they healed and resumed constructive life-styles more quickly because of it. A few were not only heard but believed, and that invariably fostered a transformation of all concerned. But the great majority were either ignored, made fun of, threatened, and in some cases physically abused because they dared to tell their story. This simple act of communication was considered a "crime" because it either created a scene, received "undue" attention, or was somehow thought "weird."

The survivor became a family embarrassment.

One woman spoke of being threatened by all her rela-tives, including her parents, and told to shut up and forget everything she had seen or they would have her committed to a mental institution and labeled insane. A man told of being immediately wheeled around and forced to see a psychiatrist while still hospitalized from the medical cri-sis which had spawned his near-death experience to begin with, and all because he had told his doctor what he had seen on "The Other Side" while dead. That psychiatrist told him it was just a dream and to forget it, which only made matters worse for the survivor. Against his will, he was transferred to the mental ward for observation. There was both anger and sadness in his voice as he described this incident.

You have to talk about it.

Even if it means you may be branded a "lunatic."

The crucial factor is—will anyone listen? If you do find a listener, what kind of listener have you found? Will he or she condemn or give you the benefit of the doubt?

Predictably, survivors often retreat and withdraw.

Either you cannot find the right words to describe your experience or you cannot find empathetic listeners. Sometimes all you can do is cry. This silence, this withdrawal stage, can last for months, years or even decades. As one survivor, Lucy B. Ater of Decatur, Illinois, puts it:

> "It would mean so very much to find someone and/ or an opportunity to express my experience. It seems so restrictive to try to write about it, and for approximately thirty-seven years, any mention of it seems to bring rebuke to me on a personal level."

Well over half the survivors I contacted want to write a book about their experience. Each feels his or her story remarkable and any "message" received important enough to revolutionize society. Most of these people are sincere in their desire to spread the word—that death does not end life and that God is no myth. They are imbued with a sense of "spiritual mission" and a desire to help others. Once in a while, however, you run across one or two whose only thought is for fame and fortune with their blockbuster story, and these few are almost paranoid lest anyone steal their details of what happened to them and violate their copyright.

But the fear of being labeled insane is the main reason for silence, especially for those who were unattended at death and have no witnesses to prove what happened. The fear of insanity is a haunting, gnawing kind of thing. I know only too well how it can cloud your mind and fill you with doubt, how it can rob you of vitality and hasten further illness.

That was my problem, and the reason for my compulsive search for others like myself. Before I could "come back," I had to first make certain I could survive.

≈ 2 ≈
One Woman's Experiences

"This is the state of death. Now I know I am a soul, that I can exist apart from the body. I shall always believe that, for I have proved it."

Paul Brunton

Research is tricky. Statistical data provides indications and trends but misses underlying causes. Scientific research builds diagrams, but only individual cases supply color and design. For a more meaningful opportunity to understand the near-death phenomenon, I believe we need to go beyond statistical renderings and view what happened *in context with the lives of those who lived it.* You cannot realistically separate the experience from what caused it. To treat it only as an external event is to deny internal realities and miss important clues.

It is helpful, I think, to realize that not all survivors respond to the experience in the same manner. Some are relatively unscathed by what they went through. Others change to some noticeable degree, and a few are so deeply shaken that life for them can never again be the same. Most of those so deeply shaken experienced long, complex scenarios and because of this, they are classified as the "core" group.

Individual response to what happened makes more of a difference than the event itself.

Sometimes it takes years to assess impact and recognize what changes have been or are being made.

At this point, I believe it would make sense to examine one experience in more detail. This way a generalized life pattern of the individual can be seen in context with the near-death episode and its more immediate aftermath. Although objectivity is often difficult to maintain when relating personal issues, I will be as honest as I can while using myself as an example. Naturally, much detail must be forgone to save time and space.

As you read what follows, I invite you to put yourself in my place. What would you have done if such a thing had happened to you? What would have been your responses? Do you think there is a cause-and-effect relationship between the life lived and the resulting near-death experience? Was the scenario literal or symbolic, or both? Are there underlying causes, connections? Would you have told anyone about it or remained silent? Do you think you could have resumed normal lifestyle habits after such an event? What, if any, changes would you have made in your life had it been you?

The more questions you ask and the more answers you search for, the more you will begin to appreciate what a near-death survivor goes through.

Before, During, and After

I had been dying for some time; at least, carbon copies of letters I had written reveal such thoughts, although I honestly do not remember writing any of them. It was 1975 in Boise, Idaho. My husband had left on the pretext of looking for work in the state of Washington, but the truth is we were both destroying each other and neither of us knew how to stop. The period between 1975 and 1977 is like a dark fog. A family tragedy involving the youngest of our three children facilitated our divorce after twenty years of marriage. It was the last straw.

Mine had been a disruptive and unhappy childhood, but my husband's had been protected and steady. He expected traditional compliance in our marriage, but I had grown in life without such role models. So, not knowing any different, I "assumed" the role I thought he wanted of me, that lasted until I had a nervous breakdown eleven years later at the age of twenty-nine.

During those eleven years every possible hardship and loss occurred, including farm failures, the birth of a child with a serious deformity, near-bankruptcies, and the forced sale of our home to satisfy tax payments; yet, we all chipped in and made the best of what life offered, calling ourselves "The Happy Huffmans." I learned to recycle everything and waste nothing, to raise and can most of our food and to bake everything from scratch. I came to live by the clock in order to balance heavy workloads with full-time secretarial employment and dedicated Sunday School teaching at church.

Of interest is the fact that during this time my husband turned an old hobby of flying into a profession. He excelled as a pilot and came to specialize in crop dusting, flying mostly night jobs. Because his work was so dangerous, we made it a point to joke about dying and even sat a place for "DEATH" at many a supper table with the hope our children would grow up without fear of their father's familiar consort. The lives of many a friend ended in fiery crashes or mid-air collisions.

After the nervous breakdown, I began an intense exploration of metaphysics, psychism, Eastern religions, and altered states of consciousness. The more I learned about levels of mind, the more I learned how to better use my own. From then on there was no stopping me. Being practical and insistent upon demonstration, I put everything I learned to work. In a very short time, I went from being a secretary to employment as a professional writer for the state of Idaho, and won award after award for innovative achievement. Miracles then came daily and with them a rediscovery of God as a valid and vital force in my life. I meditated conscientiously.

My husband left flying after a near-miss, but the reality of personality changes and glandular deterioration from years of exposure to toxic chemicals could no longer be denied. In an effort to regain self-esteem and self-worth, he tried his hand with insurance sales. The more successful I was, the less successful he became. I skyrocketed, while he turned rude and sullen. When he gave up and left for Washington, I was unable to understand why. I felt betrayed and cheated. So did he.

During the dark days that followed after my husband's exit and our later divorce, the family began to drift apart. Kelly, my son, borrowed money and left to attend a cruise school aboard a square-rigger in the Atlantic Ocean. Natalie, my oldest daughter, started college at Boise State while still living at home. Paulie, the youngest, somewhat numb from her family's collapse, began junior high. After a siege of unemployment and living on food stamps that followed the premature demise of my writing career, I found a position as technical manuals writer with a large bank and was later promoted to forms analyst.

I was thirty-nine years old at the time and thought myself and my life a failure. My search for spirituality seemed more a path of escapism than a way to God, and that bothered me. My achievements no longer brought satisfaction. The idea of being single again after a lifetime of marriage terrified me; dating felt somehow obscene. With a flood of unexpressed emotions locked tightly inside, I became like a "bomb waiting for a place to explode." It wouldn't take much.

Into this cauldron went the decision to attend college and get a degree, but then a man I met while holding weekly public meetings in my home changed everything. We simply enjoyed each other's company at first. He possessed a gentleness I found fascinating. One night he missed the regular meeting so I went on to bed, exhausted from studying for my first college exam. After midnight, Natalie shook me awake saying he was here but something was wrong. Half asleep, I found him more incoherent than I, mumbling something about an accident on the Interstate, totaling his car, police and paper work, no one hurt but the car was a rental. I did what I could to help, then invited him to spend the night as I had several empty beds. After I returned to sleep, he chose my bed.

There is no blame, really, in what happened. Neither of

us were thinking clearly. But I became pregnant and he went half-crazy. He would stage dramatic shouting matches with himself and demand I have an abortion. Try as I may, I could not understand his behavior. I loved children and the idea of having another child, though embarrassing, was rather delightful. His peculiar tirades continued off and on for nearly two months. When the business assignment that had brought him to Idaho ended, he flew back to his home in California, pledging to come back when I needed him. Once he was gone, there was again peace and quiet, I turned to God in prayer, asking that if the baby was not to be born it should leave nature's way. Although I would defend any woman's right to choose abortion, my choice was not to have one.

Three days later on a cold and snowy Sunday morning, January 2, 1977, I was suddenly wracked with pain and began hemorrhaging. The girls had not yet returned from overnight visits and I was alone. I made it to the toilet and filled it with blood, passing a very small, somewhat whitish-looking sac. I stood to have a look, never having miscarried before, and, as I did, a sharp pain squeezed my gut and stabbed my chest. I screamed.

That scream exploded all around the bathroom like a Gatling gun, bursting out what seems a million centuries and a million different forms of me all screaming and all suddenly seeking to converge as each "voice" added to the reverberation of the other until the very shrill of it pierced the house and clawed the heavens. My body fell away. And there was silence.

You don't always know you are dead when you die.

It can happen so suddenly and unexpectedly that the thought of death simply does not occur to you. For this reason, I did not recognize death. I only recognized myself as floating next to the bathroom light bulb with the ceiling scarcely an eyelash away. There was no darkness or distortion of any kind; if anything, my surroundings were even brighter and more distinct than normal.

As I looked around, distance relationships differed. It was now a long way down to toilet, sink, and bathtub surfaces. Although I felt no discomfort, the distance change was disorienting and confusing. I began to bump into the brightly glowing light bulb like some kind of moth, yet it did not seem hot when I touched it. Gradually, the confusion cleared and my mind formed lucid questions. Why was I up here bobbing along the ceiling? How was this possible? Why did I keep bumping into the light bulb? The body on the floor was a mess, so I paid it no attention. Spatial differences were all that mattered.

With the beginning of thought and question came the appearance of dark gray blobs floating around in the air beside me. With every new thought, another blob would appear. No other word seems appropriate. They were blobs, like ink blots, but fully dimensional, buoyant, and without definitive form. The more I thought, the more blobs there were, until my peripheral vision was filled with them. What were they? Where did they come from? Why were they here? They seemed an irritating mystery without solution. I did not like them.

There was an audible snap, and I was jerked like an overstretched rubber band back into the crumpled, bloody mess on the floor, entering my body through the top of the head, that area that was once my "soft spot" when a baby, and feeling the need to shrink or contract to fit back in.

I revived to the reality of blood and pain which I dealt with as best as I could, cleaning up my mess, changing clothes, stumbling into bed, propping my legs up with pillows. Sleep came. I have always been a heavy sleeper, able to easily sleep through any noise, but I do vaguely remember my daughters shaking me and asking what was wrong. Illness was feigned and they fixed their own supper. I remember feeling a sense of relief because of the miscarriage, for now I would not have to tell anyone about the baby. There would be no embarrassment. My foolishness would remain my own private affair. It was a hell of a way to learn about myself and about sex, especially at my age, but it was over and the baby was gone. I had learned a painful lesson. Soon enough, sleep returned.,

Monday morning I was still bleeding profusely, so my oldest daughter Natalie called where I worked and reported me ill. Then both girls left for school. I managed to dress, get in the car, and start it. Even though our family doctor was only about five blocks away in the same subdivision where we lived, it took me nearly half an hour to drive there. The road kept "jumping around" in front of me and sounds were different. Strange geometric figures zigged and zagged before my eyes and the houses on either side of the street kept changing shape. I was also in a great deal of pain and lacked coordination. When the office nurse saw me, she shrieked and ushered me right in. The doctor laughed uproariously when I told him what had happened. He really chortled about all that pain and blood for just one night of sex that I didn't even get a chance to enjoy. To him that was the most hilarious thing he had ever heard of; and I must admit that when I saw myself through his eyes, I did indeed appear to be a stupid, naive fool with a ridiculous story to tell.

But I kept asking him why my legs hurt so much, as there seemed no connection to me between leg pain and a miscarriage. Neither he nor his office nurse responded. So I spoke louder, asking again and again. He never answered my question but instead gave me an injection in my lower right thigh to stop the bleeding and then laughed some more. Every time he looked at me he laughed. I stubbornly kept asking about my legs but his answers were unrelated. No, he did not think I needed hospitalization; yes, he felt the worst was over: and cheer up, the shot should do the trick and I would be fine. All I needed in his view was to smarten up about sex. He sent me home. I never thought to ask why the drive to his office had been so difficult.

Again, it took what seemed forever to drive the distance but I made it back, and within a half hour of arrival all bleeding stopped abruptly, as if a faucet had been turned off. With cessation of blood, my leg pain increased dramatically, especially in the right leg. I went straight to bed, propping up my legs with more pillows. Sleep came quickly and I slept all night, which is not unusual for me. Pain and discomfort, even the labor of childbirth, had never interfered with my ability to sleep. When it is time for me to sleep, I sleep.

The next morning Natalie again called the bank to

report me ill and left with Paulie for school. It was now Tuesday, January 4, and my right leg hurt so much I would have hacked it off with a knife had one been available. In throwing back the covers, I stared in disbelief at what I saw. Encircling my leg from knee halfway to crotch was a wide band of bright crimson skin, fiery hot to the touch. Growing out the right side of that band was a huge lump, like a hot burning volcano, angry and bubbling inside. I had no idea what was wrong. I only knew I had to get help quickly. Our only telephone was on the other side of the house on the kitchen wall. My quest for that phone involved more falling and crawling than walking. I made it as far as the dining room.

The pain became so great it obliterated any semblance of reason or logic. There was just me and the pain. I came to regard that lump as my enemy and instinctively I began to fight back. The lump was killing me. At that point, I did the worst possible thing I could do, I attacked the lump, pushing, hitting, shoving, pounding, and pushing some more. The only thing I could think of was it had to go. It was the lump or me. The lump won.

This time I floated ever so gently out of my prone body, rising straight up while passing through waves of pain that appeared as heat waves on a sidewalk on a hot summer day. These waves of pain were located outside my body; and, as I floated through them, I could feel piercing, ripping power yet it had no effect. I floated on past the pain waves and continued upwards until reaching the ceiling. I stopped floating when I bumped into the light bulb.

That was funny, and in spite of everything, I laughed, appreciating that at least this time it was the dining room light and not the one in the bathroom and it was off instead of on. My sense of humor was intact.

I hovered around the light bulb for what seemed the passing of many minutes, staring at my body below. I was waiting . . . watching. I knew quite well what had happened this time, but I wasn't certain if my body was fully and completely dead. I searched and studied for any sign of life, any movement, heave, twitch, or breath. I waited, and there was silence. Nothing moved. I waited longer. Still nothing moved. When I was satisfied the body below was truly dead and nothing more could be done for it, I felt an incredible sense of relief. I felt relief at being freed from the heavy, burdensome mass and weight of that body; I felt a sense of having been released from prison. My body was not me. I was me. A body was something I had once worn, like someone wears a jacket or an old coat. It was gone and I was free, and in my freedom I shouted, "I'm dead, thank God, I'm dead."

There was no sorrow, remorse, or even the slightest concern for anyone or anything, including my children's welfare. There was no thought of needing to live again, to finish unfinished business, or of anger or pain. It was completely natural and comfortable not to breathe and I could see everything distinctly, colors and all. I could hear, feel, move around, think, remember, reason, and experience emotion, only all this was different because I no longer had a physical body to filter and amplify sensations. I did not need that body any more.

I was free! I was free!

So great was my joy in my newfound freedom that I danced and whirled around and around the light bulb as if it were a May Pole, and chanted with unbridled glee, "I'm free, I'm free, I'm free." Everything was bright and there was no fear. I was my true self at last. I was me and nothing else mattered. All my obligations, responsibilities, and duties were over. It was all over.

Soon, enough, though, I bored of twirling around and began to ask questions. Each question was asked "out loud" in the hope of attracting "someone's" attention. What happens next? Isn't an angel or being of some kind supposed to come and take me somewhere? What happens now? Where is everybody? Am I supposed to do something or say something? Hey, anybody, somebody, what comes next? Where do I go? What do I do? Hello? Hello?

As my thoughts produced questions, blobs began to form around me. Blobs again, only this time they were more like shimmering pastel bubbles, fully pliable, transparent, and translucent. This time they were pretty and I liked them. I finally recognized the blobs to be my thoughts jelled into substance but devoid of specific direction, size, or shape. This being the case, I decided to experiment with them (experimentation being a favorite hobby of mine). I wondered what would happen if I could concentrate deeply enough to bring my thoughts together into one single focus and then project that focus forward as if it were a laser beam to a specific spot in front of me. Could I purposefully solidify substance from thought alone? Could I create with it? Would such a creation continue to exist when I was finished or would it simply evaporate?

Excited about this experiment and busy fixing details in my mind, I glimpsed a peculiar shift in my environment. My dining room below was slowly but surely merging into another kind of space coming down from a source past my ceiling. These two spaces or dimensions of space were merging into each other, but I was not moving. I did not change position in any way. I was where I was, but the world around me was changing and shifting and becoming something else. My dining room faded from sight as this new space became more visible and more real. It was like nothing I had ever seen before. It encompassed me.

The new space was both totally bright and totally dark at the same time yet without shape, form, sound, color, mass, or movement. It was aglow but there was no light source. It was dark but there was no darkness. Somehow within this strange environment was the presence of all shapes, all forms, all sound, all color, all mass, and all movement. Everything that ever was, is, or will be was there, yet there was nothing there at all. It was everything and it was nothing, yet within it was a feeling, a pulse, a sensation of energy "winking" off and on—a sparkling potential which "shimmered," just as Jell-o does before it responds to touch. I called it "The Void" for lack of a better term or idea. It was comfortable enough, so within its crammed nothingness I proceeded with my experiments.

I decided to create and shape a house, a specific kind of house; and I fixed its exact details and size in my mind, clearly seeing each part, noting every proportion, then focusing all that I saw in my mind to hold it steady as I projected it out to a definitive area in front of me. I remember feeling some pain in doing this, like a throbbing ache, as if I was using muscles long dormant. The discomfort or strain I felt was like that of a new skier trying out winter slopes for the first time, pulling and stretching muscles not used in that manner before. I held my focus, though, and before me there formed an image. It happened fairly quickly and when done, I was aghast. There it was. A house.

I moved forward and knocked on a window. It seemed to be glass. I then opened and shut all doors and windows, stomped across the green floor of the front porch, fingered the large brass front door knob, inspected foundations, roof, and chimney, and gave a hearty slap to each of three white porch pillars. This four-square white house with steeply pitched roof was as solid and sound as any house I had ever encountered. It was a good house. It seemed *very* real.

This demonstration only whetted my desire to try again. The house was inanimate. I wanted now to try something animate, something alive. I chose to try a mighty oak tree. It had to have a huge, thick trunk with large gnarled roots and countless branches in full leaf. Again, I repeated the same process as before, picturing in my mind each detail of the tree and then projecting that image forward to a particular spot to the right of the house, using my mind as a laser beam. This time I did not feel the same strain or discomfort as before and my thoughts were easier to gather into one single focus. Presto, there was the tree complete with textured bark, insect holes, and vividly beautiful leaves.

It happened! It was possible! It could be done! A human like myself could create from scratch. I could bring together the tiniest of prematter, thought energy itself, and direct it to form specific objects, whether animate or inanimate. Thoughts really are things. They are powerful. All the old stories are true. Thoughts are prematter itself for they have substance and mass and thus can be shaped into form at will. It can be done and I did it. I really did it.

I was so overjoyed I went nuts.

I went on a creation binge, bringing together, creating, forming, and giving life to anything and everything I could imagine. I made cities, people, dogs, cats, trash cans, alleys, telephone poles, schools, books, pencils, cars, roads, lawns, birds, flowers, shrubbery, rain, suns, clouds, rivers; and everything had life and everything moved of its own and there was breath, noise, language and all manner of activity aside and apart from me. Everyone and everything had substance and mass and reality, and all went about their own business according to their own pleasure and perception. It was all so incredibly wonderful that I watched long with fascination, never thinking I was some kind of god, but rather with a feeling of satisfaction that I had engaged in an exercise perfectly normal for me to do and perfectly natural. I rested.

It came then to my mind to see again those family members and loved ones who had passed on before, and no sooner had I thought the thought then they were there—Mrs. Stinson, Daddy Sogn, and a whole host of people from my past including a grandfather I had never seen as he had died of diabetes when his own children were small.

Everyone who came looked as they had when last I saw them, only they seemed more vibrant and healthier than before, brighter. The grandfather I did not know bore a striking resemblance to photographs I had once seen of my natural father's sister in Montana. Next, I wanted to see Jesus, for I had always wished to thank him for the role he played in history and the example he set for others to follow. His life and mastery of being had always deeply impressed me and I was in awe of it. He instantly appeared, without any effort on my part. When he stood before me, there was no feeling to bow down or worship him; rather, I felt him to be more of an elder brother, long absent, whose return was joyous and a cause for celebration. We spoke at length and I was able to express my thanks. There was great love between us and happy chatter. Then he disappeared as suddenly as he had come and with him all my loved ones disappeared as well, leaving behind only the creations I had made. These I dissolved by thinking them away. It felt right that everything should disappear.

I was now alone in this nonplace and there was nothing.

For the first time I looked upon myself to see what possible form or shape I might have, and to my surprise and joy I had no shape or form at all. I was naught but a sparkle of pure consciousness, the tiniest, most miniscule spark of light imaginable. And that is all I was. I was content that way, without ego or identity, pure, whole, and uncomplicated. Within that nothingness I had become, I simply existed, ecstatic in perfect bliss and peace, like perfection itself and perfect love. Everywhere around me were sparkles like myself, billions and trillions of them, winking and blinking like on/off lights, pulsating from some unknown power source.

I would have existed in that state of bliss forever had an irritation not made itself known, like an old sore deep within me; then energy waves burst forth from that deep old sore, and with them came the life of Phyllis, playing itself out from birth to death. I remembered hearing stories of past life reviews, a particular feature of dying common to all, where your life passes before you at great speed for final review. Remembering this, I expected some kind of theatrical showing of my life as Phyllis or perhaps something like a television replay, but such was not the case. Mine was not a review, it was a reliving. For me, it was a total reliving of *every* thought I had ever thought, *every* word I had ever spoken, and *every* deed I had ever done; *plus* the effect of each thought, word, and deed on everyone and anyone who had ever come within my environment or sphere of influence whether I knew them or not (including unknown passersby on the street); *plus* the effect of each thought, word, and deed on weather, plants, animals, soil, trees, water, and air.

It was a reliving of the total gestalt of me as Phyllis, complete with all the consequences of ever having lived at all. No detail was left out. No slip of the tongue or slur was missed. No mistake nor accident went unaccounted for. If there is such a thing as hell, as far as I am concerned this was hell.

I had no idea, no idea at all, not even the slightest hint of an idea, that every thought, word, and deed was remembered, accounted for, and went out and had a life of its own once released; nor did I know that the energy of that life directly affected all it touched or came near. It's as if we must live in some kind of vast sea or soup of each other's energy residue and thought waves, and we are each held responsible for our contributions and the quality of "ingredients" we add.

This knowledge overwhelmed me!

The old saying, "No man is an island," took on graphic proportions. There wasn't any heavenly St. Peter in charge. It was me judging me, and my judgment was most severe. As when I previously realized my body was not me, I also came to realize Phyllis wasn't me either. She was a personality or a facade I had once projected. She was an extension of me, a part I had played, a role I had acted. She was a particular development I was engaged in, a particular focus I had become, and that focus had not developed quite as planned.

I was disappointed and saddened at this, but I took interest and satisfaction from one characteristic she had repeatedly displayed, and that was her desire to try and try again. She always did something, even if unwise. She was not one to sit back and wait upon others or capricious fate. She was relentless in her determination to make of herself a better person and to learn everything possible. She was a doer, willing and able, a person who would reach and stretch. This pleased me and at last I pronounced her personality good and the life she had lived worth its living.

During this judgment process, "The Void" in which I dwelt began to pull away and separate from my dining room in Boise. These two worlds separated as they had previously merged, but I was still next to the light bulb, having never at any time altered my location or the space I occupied. Only my environment had changed, not I. As I looked down at the body of Phyllis on the floor, I was so filled with love and forgiveness that I floated ever so gently back into her body, moving as I went on a layer of large bright sparklers such as those used on the Fourth of July. Again, I reentered through the top of the head, feeling the need to shrink and then squeeze back into the tight form Phyllis's body offered.

When consciousness returned and I was again Phyllis,

I was so stunned and shocked I was incapable of relating to anything, even the searing pain in my right leg. Instead of continuing only four or five more feet to the kitchen phone, I rolled over the other way and crawled back to my bedroom, lifted myself into bed, and remained there for two days lost in a stupor.

I did not know my two daughters. I did not recognize food nor did I know how to eat, and the bed on which I lay was a foreign object. Everything around me—clothes, sheets, newspapers, lamps, windows, clocks—nothing made any kind of sense nor did I recognize any of it. I was lost between two worlds, existent in neither, and unable to identify any sign or landmark that might stimulate memory. Both daughters realized something was wrong but since I had always projected an image of invincibility, they left me alone, figuring I'd call if I needed help.

We are all descended from a long line of independent, individualistic people who pride themselves on being self-sufficient. Add to that the typical "Code of the West" and you'll have some idea just how independent we all were. Once, when our kitchen caught fire and flames licked the ceiling, I saved the children myself, cut off the electricity, doused the fire with salt and then, when everything was under control, called first our insurance agent and then my husband at his job. It never occurred to me to call the fire department. I could take care of it myself and I knew it. So I did. Many were the emergencies, major and minor, I handled in this manner. Bearing this in mind, it is understandable why the girls were reluctant to take action.

Typically, however, I finally managed to come out of the stupor myself. Memories of my job filtered through. Since it was my only source of income, I had to get back to work. I had to. The thought of it became a driving force pushing me out of bed and to the clothes closet.

I have no recollection how I managed to dress and drive my car all the way across town, let alone safely park it. I only remember trying to walk up those two long flights of stairs in the old building where I worked so I could reach my office on the second floor. There was no elevator. My climb up those stairs was more like an ascent up a formidable mountain where I lost more ground than I gained but, at last, I reached the top just as my boss walked by. She screamed when she saw me and said I looked more dead than alive and insisted a doctor be called. With her help, a specialist was located who would see me immediately and I was whisked off to his office.

By this time, more memory was returning, at least enough for me to remember my right leg, the band of crimson skin and the hot lump. I could neither stand, sit, nor lie without excruciating pain. After a long and thorough examination, the doctor was puzzled and shook his head. He could not figure out why I was alive, for I should be dead. He said I must have had a major thrombosis in the right thigh vein which, when dislodged by my pounding, must have blocked all oxygen to my brain. The result could only have been death in his view, but since he was not in attendance when it happened, he could only hypothesize. Phlebitis was evident and severe. In his judgment, he felt the worst was over and I was no longer in imminent danger so he prescribed a potent drug labeled dangerous and sent me home to heal. The drug could not be used for more than seven days or it would kill all red blood cells; it was to be taken around the clock. The pharmacist warned a meal must be eaten before taking each dose or I would sicken. My stay at home was to be that of an invalid with legs propped up and no walking except to the bathroom. My boss granted me a leave of absence, so I settled on the living room sofa near the television for a long convalescence. A few people came to visit and the girls arranged to be home early from school, but other than that, I was alone most of the time. I never once used the television, though. I didn't need to. Strange things began to happen.

Perhaps it was side-effects from the drug; at least, that seems as good an explanation as any. All I know is three unusual incidents occurred.

First, I could hear someone's thoughts at the same degree of tone and pitch as their spoken words. Try as I might, I could not distinguish between what anyone thought and what was said. I could hear both. Since people seldom say what they think, I could not tell how to respond—neither with visitors nor my daughters. This continued the entire week I was on the drug, creating a dilemma so confusing I finally refused to speak with anyone, including my children, or acknowledge conversation.

Second, while lying on the sofa staring into space, there formed slightly above my chest an elevated "rainbow-type" arch like a misty bridge, and across that arch there began to parade a whole host of tiny people I came to realize were all my past lives parading by for review, ending with my existence as a lizard-like being from a water star which had gone nova in the Sirius System. This strange refugee to planet Earth eventually died, as did most of its kind, finding the atmosphere and living conditions here not as compatible as originally calculated. I strongly identified with the lizard being, feeling myself to be every bit the foreigner it was, and just as lost. This parade of life fascinated me and I studied each character carefully, noting the possible evolution of my own personality traits and how each came to be. These tiny characters were like fully animated holograms, totally real and alive yet like so much thin air. This parade also continued for the seven days I took the medication.

Third, I became aware of how thee physical trauma was affecting my body and quite by chance, I looked intently at the area of my female organs and right thigh. Instead of seeing the outer shape of my body parts, I was able to see with seemingly X-ray vision each individual cell and groups of cells deep inside myself. These cells were upset and they were marshalling together in efforts to fight off any further destruction and to rebuild damaged areas, moving in waves to accomplish this task as if engaged in battle. It had never entered my mind that microscopic, individual cells had any worth or value other than that of primitive organic functioning; yet, there they were, intelligent beings fully capable of emotion, choice, reason, memory, response. They were truly intelligent, not mindless nothings. To say I was surprised is hardly adequate.

I immediately desired to speak with them and apologize for what had been done. Had I continued trying to get to the phone after regaining consciousness, damage might not have been so severe. I was truly sorry. With the desire came the ability, and speak with them I did and they with me. We had quite a discussion. That experience had such a profound effect on my appreciation of intelligence that to this day I still work in concert with my body, its cells, and substructure. We are a team, my body and I, and we perform together for the common good.

My physical progress was deemed satisfactory by the doctor, so when the week was over, the dangerous drug was replaced with aspirin treatment. Since aspirin makes me very dizzy, my memory of those six weeks of treatment is a blur. I do remember the man who had impregnated me called many times to see how I was doing. He refused to fly back and help but he did send money and, between his contributions and my group insurance, I was able to keep up with mounting medical and household bills. But my morale suffered.

Healers of all sorts came to help once the word was out that I was ill. I had no idea there were so many different ways to heal and so many different people who channeled or worked with healing energy. I know these people meant well and, in their own way, they were doing all they could. But nothing worked—not laying-on-of-hands, not any kind of prayer, not "poison sucking," not magnetic healing, not burping or high energy, not anything, whether orthodox or unorthodox. Nothing worked because I no longer cared. I allowed healers to come because it would have been impolite not to but, when they left, it was as if they had never been there. Although I could converse somewhat normally by now and was putting up a good front, nothing made much sense. I functioned more from habit than reason.

I returned to work in increments of time, first for a few hours, then half-days, three-quarter days and finally full-time. It was painful to sit in office chairs and I had trouble focusing my mind. Yet, I did my best and slowly strength returned, but I could not walk properly and wound up dragging my right leg. It was unable to support weight.

More help came, and the specialist who doctored me was grand. I was just starting to make real progress when my landlord chose to raise my rent far higher than I could afford to pay, effective immediately. I panicked. Friends came to my rescue, another house was found in an older section of Boise, and my daughters and I moved bag and baggage to our next abode. The house was not as desirable as we had hoped. My daughters were cramped in a small bedroom and the junior high school Paulie attended proved to be her undoing. It was enough to watch a once strong and able mother reduced to jelly, to have her father move far away and experience the loss of all her security, but to attend a school she both feared and hated was the final straw. There were many episodes of skipped classes, drugs, sex, and drinking. I was frankly puzzled by her behavior and was without any clear idea as to how I might handle the situation.

By now it was March 29. My son Kelly had returned unexpectedly from his long voyage on the other side of the globe. He was only home three days when he decided to join the Coast Guard, a move which would enable him to pay off the loans he had borrowed for the cruise school and to pursue further involvement with the sea. The man from California finally returned to Boise and called to see if he could stop by. I said yes. It was evening. Both girls were gone for overnight visits with friends. Kelly was at a bar talking over old times with buddies from high school. When the man came, I was able to briefly state what I had been through and how it had affected me, withholding any emotion and placing no blame. He listened silently. I made one request. I asked that he hold me one more time and just let me cry, let me be a child again without any burdens or fears—if only for a moment. He jumped up, shouted "NO," and ran out the door, slamming it behind him. Almost immediately, he returned, thanked me for meeting with him, and slammed the door again.

He wrote much later to explain his behavior, saying that one of his daughters had been impregnated by a man who promptly deserted her, leaving her destitute. In coming to his daughter's aid, he had cursed and damned the man who left. After storming out of my house that night, he had later realized that throughout my entire ordeal he had in es-sence deserted me. He had become the man he had once cursed. This overwhelming realization drove him to near-suicide before he could get a grip on himself. He wanted me to know this so perhaps I could find it in my heart to forgive him so he could in turn forgive himself.

I had no way to know any of this, however, when he slammed the door that night. All I knew was that throughout my life I had never once turned down anyone in need, no matter what sacrifice or inconvenience might be necessary on my part—and now in my hour of need I was denied.

Denied.

The waiting bomb inside me, at the very core of my being, exploded at last.

It was a kind of suicide, for I willed myself dead and my body was too exhausted to argue. Getting well had proven an arduous task; life had lost its meaning; I could no longer understand my own children; and I had come to dislike my looks and body size intensely, feeling myself to be ugly, old, and fat. I knew "The Other Side" was better than this so I resolved to return there. I wanted to die so I did. I have no way of knowing if I really died or not. I only know my body dropped away, falling on a large, overstuffed chair.

This time, I moved, not my environment, and I moved rapidly, first moving out through the top of my head, then sailing up through the ceiling, out the roof, and into the night sky with a universe of stars watching. My speed accelerated until I noticed a wide but thin-edged expanse of bright light ahead, like a "parting" in space or a "lip," with a brightness so brilliant it was beyond light yet I could look upon it without pain or discomfort. I had been a meditator and teacher of meditation for nearly a decade and "heavenly" lights, white light, and all manner of etheric light were familiar to me; but this was not like any of those. It was more intense, more probing, more radiant, more powerful. It was beyond any frame of reference I had. The closer I came the larger the parting in space appeared until, when I reached its edge, I was absorbed by it as if engulfed by a force field. I cannot describe for you how that felt, except to say it was "divine."

I had succeeded. I was where I wanted to be. I was *inside* bliss.

Further movement on my part ceased because of the shock of what happened next. Before me there loomed two gigantic, impossibly huge masses spinning at great speed, looking for all the world like cyclones. One was inverted over the other, forming an hourglass shape, but where the spouts should have touched there was instead incredible rays of power shooting out in all directions. The top cyclone spun clockwise, the bottom counterclockwise, but their sides were somewhat bulgy rather than being as smooth-sided as might be expected, considering what appeared to be a tremendous rate of spin.

I was floating at a height about mid-way in relation to the cyclones yet far away. I stared at the spectacle before me in disbelief. They were so massive. And seeing them was so unexpected.

Cyclones!

As I stared, I came to recognize my former Phyllis self in the mid-upper-left of the top cyclone. Even though only a speck, I could see my Phyllis clearly, and superimposed over her were all her past lives and all her future lives happening at the same time in the same space as her present life. Everything was happening at once! Around Phyllis was everyone else she had known and around them many others. The same thing was happening to all these people as was happening to Phyllis. The cyclone was crammed full of people and I had the feeling of seeing all life. The same phenomenon was happening to each and all. Past, present, and future were not separated but, instead, interpenetrated like a multiple hologram combined with its own reflection.

The only physical movement anyone or anything made was to contract and expand. There was no up or down, right or left, forward or backward. There was only in and out, like breathing, like the universe and all creation were breathing—inhale/exhale, contraction/expansion, in/out, off/on.

The lower cyclone mirrored the upper one. My Phyllis self was there too and so was everyone else, occupying the same general sector of space as above, with the same phenomenon happening in the same manner. As above, so below. To be very honest with you I felt as if I were witnessing the wave pattern of a giant echo, and I began to wonder about life and its meaning. Was existence really just a series of echoes upon itself, spiraling forever outward from some primeval sound or explosion?

Remarkable as the sight was, I soon lost interest for I was tired of life and its struggle, and I was tired of any search for my place in it. My interest was the middle, where the spouts should have touched but didn't, where that powerful, explosive energy was, where those shooting rays originated. The force from that place was so mighty, its radiation so potent and intense, that it *was* painful to look at it straight on. What I saw of it came in quick side glances to avoid discomfort. That's where I wanted to go regardless of what such a choice might mean. I had a feeling that place, that space, would somehow lead to God. I wanted to know God, I wanted to know what God was, so I began to move toward the rays.

Meanwhile, my son was enjoying himself with his friends, drinking and laughing and talking over old times. He had a mug of beer mid-air when suddenly he put it down, faced his buddies, stood up and said, "My mother needs me. I have to go help my mother." With that, he left, surprising himself as much as everyone else with this unusual outburst.

A year later, when Kelly and I finally spoke of this night, he described for me the bar scene and how surprised everyone was at his behavior, and how it was when he entered the living room and saw my body. He said it never occurred to him to call for help; rather, after sizing up the situation as best he could, his next impulse was to sit opposite my body in another chair and start talking, not about anything in particular, just tallking in a way which would create continuous sound. That impulse seemed of utmost importance so he complied—talking and talking—out loud. To understand why Kelly would trust that inner impulse, I feel a need to explain that all three of my children were taught from infancy to trust their own inner guidance, question all authority, and think independently. No form of dependence was allowed. As everything turned out later, this impulse of his was "right on" in the sense that hearing is the last physical faculty to leave at death. Had he spent time calling for help, I probably would have been beyond assistance, too far removed to return. But because he remained true to what "felt" right and followed that prompting, I was able to "hear" him and respond.

I heard Kelly's voice just when I was close enough to the central core to feel the piercing intensity of each ray and be almost blinded by the radiance. His voice caught my attention. As I turned for better reception, I hesitated. Although no words could be heard there was something unusual in his sound. I didn't hear the voice of a son loving his mother. I heard instead the voice of one human being freely giving love to another human being because he wanted to, not because he had to or because it was expected of him. It was the sound of one human being giving full measure, without reservation, without hesitation, without expectation or need, without conditions or strings attached. There was no pleading. Just love. Love so full-bodied and rich, so warm, fresh, and joyful, so generous and all encompassing, that it seemed the greatest of all gifts. Unconditional love! I was so delighted to discover such a thing could exist on the earth-plane, I moved away from the cyclones, past the edge of this light-world that had engulfed me, and back through the night sky to my house below, descending rapidly and entering my body, again through the top of the head, squeezing to fit back in.

This time my body did not respond. It felt slightly cooler than when I left and a little stiff. I panicked.

Instantly, I assumed the role of both coach and cheer-leader, and sped from cell to cell, shouting for all I was worth, apologizing to each for what I had done. I promised never to be so thoughtless again, that I was back to stay and I would do whatever I could to regain my health and make full amends. I kept shouting at cells to wake up, wake up now, I was here to stay and we all had a job to do. The lungs were the hardest to restart. The bellows wouldn't expand, so I puffed and puffed and puffed until a whoosh of air entered; and when it did, my consciousness shifted to my head level. Physically, I blinked for a moment, then tried to stand, just to make certain "everyone" had awakened and all cells were responsive.

Standing was a real struggle. Kelly being wiser at that moment came to help, but my vocal cords would not work. I could not speak. He then put his large arms around me and held me tight. It was as if a prayer had been answered. My son supplied what the man from California refused. Tears came and then a flood. I cried silently for what seemed hours, then Kelly spoke. He told of receiving a letter from me mailed around late January, a letter handed to him after a gale had struck and they were forced to port in northern Spain. It was a dark and dismal time in his life, and he had become uncooperative in class, depressed at discovering this so-called special school was no different than regular high school and did not include oceanography classes, as he had been led to believe. He was saddled with a tremendous debt for what seemed a waste of time and he was inconsolable.

In that letter, I had described life as being an immense school, where we each study certain subjects in certain grades according to our level of understanding, where there were recesses when we earned them and time out; but essentially, the schooling was relentless as we passed up grade levels to higher and more difficult studies until we graduated. Nothing was ever wasted, regardless of how it seemed, and we were all, for the most part, headed in the same direction, back to the God from whence we came. The letter gave him hope and showed him there was purpose in everything, even darkness and despair.

As I stood cuddled in his arms, Kelly returned my words to me, words sent in a letter half-way around the globe, words that helped him in his darkest hour and were now returning to help me in mine. I saw in my mind a "circle" close and I understood. I took this gesture to be a confirmation that my choice to live was a good choice. It was okay to be back. I really could rebuild my life.

My son put me to bed. I slept long and soundly.

By morning I could speak so I telephoned William G. Reimer, a naturopathic doctor.[1] Although major symptoms had been alleviated by traditional medical procedures, I was far from well and still dragging my right leg. Something was wrong, very wrong, and I intended to find out what. I had never been a patient of Reimer's before, but I had once

defended him and several other naturopaths when they
were unfairly arrested by an overly zealous and ambitious
attorney general. Fair treatment under law had always been
an issue with me and I considered their treatment grossly
unfair. The public defense I helped arrange proved the
naturopaths innocent of all charges. They were released
and all charges dropped, but the "price" I paid for helping
them was high.

In those days, advocacy was not appreciated and
naturopaths were considered quacks.

Now my life was on the line. I wasn't certain how
naturopathy worked but I was certain about Bill Reimer's
ability as a healer. I did not want symptoms cured, I wanted
to get down to the basic cause—and this time it must be
nature's way. It didn't matter to me if Reimer could solve the
entire problem of cause or not—but I knew he could help me
begin, point me in the right direction—and that was what I
wanted. I was through dying. I wanted now to live.

My choice to explore natural healing and naturopathy[2]
as a starting point meant I would need to relearn the
definition of what constituted health. I had always thought
of health as the absence of disease, but I discovered health
is really a state of balance and harmony existing between
our physical, mental, emotional, and spiritual selves. Anything else is dis-ease (not-at-ease).

Natural healing, I learned, is based on the premise that
all parts of the self are involved in any disorder and that all
must be addressed to insure recovery. No single part can be
treated out of context from the others. In natural healing,
the patient is considered an active participant and all
treatments are geared toward that individual's own inherent rhythms of self-healing. Root causes are dealt with
rather than symptoms alone and, since disorders are
"backed" out of the body the way each entered, the patient
usually gets worse before he or she gets better. It is defi-
nitely not the fastest method for healing, but it is more
thorough and more complete.

After extensive examination and diagnostic testing,
Bill Reimer described several courses of action which
could be taken; one of which involved a thorough "house-

cleaning" going all the way back to birth to readjust anything which might be out of line. The idea of possibly correcting a lifetime of abuse and misuse was appealing but also frightening. I was about to pick an easier alternative when I remembered my vow to regain total health, so I consented to the full package. Monthly payments were arranged as my office insurance did not cover naturopathic care. What I experienced while "dead" was not discussed except in passing, and briefly at that. Of primary concern at that point was the condition of my body and my lack of physical coordination.

My health did indeed get worse during the months of treatment which followed but it plummeted farther and faster than Reimer expected. I seemed locked in a downward spiral which could only be slowed, not stopped. As Reimer searched diligently for any procedure which would prove more effective, I began to question the wisdom of naturopathic care. The biggest stumbling block to recovery, as it later turned out, though, was not the type of healing I had selected, nor my purpose in selecting it, but rather my state of mind. I was convinced I was going crazy. Yet I confided to no one my fears lest I be made sport of or condemned, for the reaction from the first physician I had seen and his incessant laughter still "burned" across my memory. It would have made a difference had I been more open—but I wasn't.

I didn't fully trust Reimer because I didn't fully trust myself.

I could not believe what had happened to me in dying nor could I forget it. I tried to tell myself it was all a dream or a vision or a hallucination, but I knew in my heart it was none of these. What I saw and experienced began to haunt me. It began to come back, replaying itself over and over again when least expected—the sparkles of pure energy, cyclones, "The Void," exercise of creation—all of it.

What does it mean? Why did it happen? What am I supposed to do about it? Why won't it go away and leave me alone?

What I experienced challenged everything I had ever read, seen, or heard, everything I believed. What I experienced was so powerful, so intense, so shocking, it practically wiped clean the slate of my mind, annihilating my belief systems with it. I had nothing left solid enough to stand on, no grounding, no foundation on which to rebuild; every step I took wavered, like trying to walk on Jell-o. Enough habit and memory returned so I appeared relatively normal and could continue limited consulting projects and various other jobs in addition to my employment at the bank—I could help others but I could not help myself.

My major focus kept centering around the experiences I had survived rather than any other issues. What if they were real? What if everything really happened exactly as I remembered it? If so, if real, then that meant there is no such thing as death. Death does not exist for it was truly just like walking through a doorway or switching states of consciousness. That was all there was to it. Death, then, does not end life, it only changes the scenery and turns life's script around.

If that is right, if my experiences were indeed real, then there really is a single, all-powerful, all pervasive Force in, through, and behind all things. God! That means, then, that God is no fairy story, no wishful thinking, no joke, no ancient legend. It means God is real. God is.

Such joy, such remarkably good news should be shared. At least, I decided to tell others what had happened to me and what I had learned from it. But when I did, they would nod accommodatingly and continue as if nothing had been said and, if I spoke louder and insisted on the importance of my message, they would withdraw altogether as if I were some kind of kook trying to get attention. I wound up awash in ridicule. If indeed I had a message to share, I certainly did not know how to share it. Whatever good news I possessed came without any instructions on what to do with it.

Silence seemed the better virtue.

I rationalized this retreat into silence by telling myself that what had happened was my secret, it was my own private affair, a special tryst between God and me, and spreading such news around would somehow cheapen or lessen its importance. It belonged to me. It was mine to keep. Others weren't interested anyway so why should I bother?

The deeper into silence I retreated, though, the more I questioned my own sanity and the validity of what I thought true. To complicate matters further, I could not relate to myself as Phyllis. Her habits, personality, clothing, possessions, and lifestyle were foreign and irritating to me; yet, when I looked in the mirror, there she always was, looking back at me, all five foot seven, one hundred ninety pounds of her. She was shaped like a pudgy balloon with a deep sadness in her eyes and a washed-out face rimmed with short wavy hair. There was ample proof in her surroundings that she had once been a happy, bouncy, spontaneous woman with a penchant for song and a lust for exploration, be it caves or ghost towns. And she adored rocks. Everywhere I turned there were rocks, even in her purse. Rocks in her head, too, I mused.

What was I going to do about Phyllis? I was wearing her body and living her life yet I did not know her. All I knew was—she wasn't me, and I didn't fit her pattern.

This schizoid behavior deepened my fear of instability and insanity.

Into this confusion came three people, all strangers and younger than myself—astute, enthusiastic, and voraciously bent on learning all they could of life and the potential of "self." These three people offered to help me and together we formed a kind of "extended family" whereby we exchanged keys to each other's homes, shared our resources, and formed a mutual support pact. Elizabeth and Terry Macinata were married then and had a young son, Daen (they are now divorced). The other member of our group was Tom Huber. I dubbed us all "cousins" as we began our year-and-a-half journey together, probing the depths of life and its living.

We would hold sessions employing various kinds of confrontive therapy. Sometimes our sessions were spontaneous and sometimes they were planned in advance, occurring daily or only once in a while. We tried out any idea that seemed reasonable, including psychological games utilizing symbols for deeper insight. Sometimes we just went about the business of everyday living, listening carefully to what each said while observing physical mannerisms. If we detected anything negative or self-defeating, we would challenge that person immediately, forcing him or her to confront the habit, where it came from, why it was there, and what might be done about it. Often we would verbally battle each other and argue heatedly. Many of our sessions were painfully unmerciful as nothing was off-limits to debate, and the more painful a session was the more successful it was considered. Personal issues of every description surfaced.

Meanwhile, my treatments with Dr. Reimer revealed a long list of problems I did not know I had, such as dyslexia (which was later confirmed by a medical physician). When I was a child, I would often feign play, sneak out to an old "milk house," and lock the door, prop up an orange crate for a stage, stand upon it, and read comic books and Sunday funnies out loud until I finally trained myself to speak correctly when I read. These "secret" sessions took three years and I never confided to anyone what I was doing or why. Dyslexia was unknown then, and there were no special classes for children with learning disabilities. My need to coordinate eyes, mouth, and brain so I could read correctly was instinctual. It was something I did because there seemed no other alternative at the time. The dyslexia condition was just one of many surprises Bill Reimer uncovered.

Since my body had always been quite sensitive, it was no surprise when I learned that many "scars" had collected from a lifetime of reactions to chemical medications. To help correct a whole host of dexterity and speech difficulties, damage from the death experience and shifts in brain/mind functioning, the doctor and my "cousins" had me do many exercises for the purpose of relearning crawling, standing, walking, climbing, running, identifying left from right, seeing, hearing, and organizing thoughts. I performed exercise drills by the hour, daily. I finally reached a point where I could run without falling and my right leg no longer dragged.

By that fall I ventured out and bought another home

with a large garden in back. This move put Paulie back in the part of town she enjoyed most, where her childhood friends lived; but, by then, her world had become rooted in rebellion. The move made little difference. She was kicked out of school repeatedly. Discontented and unhappy, Natalie deemed this a good time to leave so she rented an apartment and moved out. My overall health began deteriorating again. I suffered three major relapses, the last of which was adrenal failure. My blood pressure registered sixty over sixty. Immediate emergency treatment required my "cousins" taking over my household and my life. When I broke down my new house broke down, too, flooding out the basement bedroom three times and leaking everywhere imaginable including roof and bathtub. I missed so much work from this second round of health reversals my boss finally sat me down and made it quite clear that either I got well and stayed well or I would be replaced.

My life was out of control and I was helpless to stop it.

Everything turned into a horrible nightmare. No matter where I turned or what I did, disaster followed. All the gains previously made were lost. The only thing I could do that gave me the courage to keep going was chant the words, "GOD IS," over and over, sometimes silently, sometimes out loud, by the hour.

In early November, my extended family decided a change of scenery might help, so with Reimer's permission, I was laid snugly in a van and trucked up to Seattle, Washington, to attend the Mind Miraculous Symposium sponsored by the Church of Religious Science in the Opera House of Seattle Center. This giant auditorium was filled to overflowing with several thousand people and a roster of speakers, all famous and brilliant. The injection I had been given had taken effect by then and I was both alert and mobile. None of us knew it, but a miracle was about to happen.

The first speaker, Dr. William Tiller, physicist from Stanford University, talked about "The Eternal Now." He spoke of things like energy, mass, and interpenetration, but I only remember staring at charts and drawings projected on a huge screen behind him. As his talk ended, he stated it was his belief everything happened at the same time in the same space and, with those words, there flashed on the screen his rendition of what the physical dynamics of that phenomenon might look like. The diagram which appeared was of two spinning cyclones, inverted over each other, forming an hourglass shape, and where the spouts should have touched there was a powerful force shooting rays out in all directions.

I jumped out of my seat in shock and ran from the auditorium.

In muffled screams I cried out words like: He saw it, too. He did. I am not the only one. He knows what I know. I'm not crazy. I am *not* crazy! The cyclones are real. It all really happened. It wasn't a dream or a hallucination or a fantasy or a projection from any kind of memory. It was real. I am real. I can be Phyllis because I am Phyllis. I am me.

My heart practically pounded out of my chest as I slumped into a cross-legged position under a foyer light. I am not crazy! I am not crazy! I am not crazy!

Soon after, a medical doctor happened by, returning from a call he had made to check on a patient. He was so impressed by the "glow" on my face at that moment that he walked over and sat down beside me, then offered me a job should I ever move to Seattle. I was thoroughly astonished but said nothing except to thank him and affirm that I would consider his offer. Much later, after several more trips to Seattle, I turned his offer down, but its timeliness and impact refreshed me and gave me hope. He was never told the effect his words had on me for it seemed wiser just to savor the promise his offer implied.

He and Dr. Tiller comprised the miracle I so desperately needed. The nightmare was over at last!

From that day on my health improved so rapidly everyone was amazed, including me. The turnaround was dramatic. I now knew I could trust what had happened to me but I still did not know what to do about it. Just because I now knew my experiences were real did not mean I would have to accept them or find any place for them in my life. It was obvious my first step must be a decision. Would I accept or reject? Here is what I considered:

Accepting means taking a risk, to accept my experiences and integrate them into my daily life could well mean more ridicule and scorn from others, and facing the issue of insanity again and again. I could be labeled undesirable or a fake since I had no proof to offer, or I could be accused of trying to be some kind of holy seer or divine prophet. Acceptance would change my life completely, necessitating that I live what I now knew to be true. Since my experiences challenged the validity of everything I had previously known, accepting those experiences would mean I would have to relearn and redefine life from scratch, from breathing right on up to thinking and relating. I had already lost much, but I could lose more; I could lose everything and everyone, but in so losing, I could also gain. I could gain everything and everyone, and possibly learn how to "live" God.

Rejection would mean denial, not only of the experiences but of my own sense of integrity, honesty, and inner truth. Rejection would mean turning my back on what I knew happened and pretending it away. But it would also mean I would have to take fewer risks and could retain what security and comfort I still possessed. Rejection would be sensible and practical, all things considered, allowing me more time to concentrate on healing and the continuance of life as usual. No one would ever know the difference. There would be no further damage to my reputation or further insult to my family. My job and lifestyle could be preserved. But rejection would also mean I would have to deny what might have been a peek at God, the opportunity of experiencing creation and the discovery of divine oneness and truth. It would mean saying no when deep down inside I wanted to say yes.

It was a case of "damned if you do and damned if you don't."

Acceptance was clearly no panacea and rejection offered no escape. My decision was finally based on peace of mind. No matter what else happened in life, I still had to live with me. If I couldn't be honest with myself, who could I be honest with? I chose to acknowledge all that happened and totally restructure my life. What had happened, happened. Nobody's belief or disbelief, including mine, could ever change that simple fact.

The Quest To Understand

The near-death experience itself is just an introduction to what comes next. My choice to acknowledge my experience *and* pursue a total restructuring of my life led to pathways both magical and frightening. I will mention some of what I went through later on where appropriate, but the after-effects, the aftermath of coming back, is really the story of uncounted numbers of people, not just mine. Perhaps it is even the story of yet millions more, people who never experienced near-death but can nonetheless identify with the trauma of transformation and the struggles which follow.

Because of my confrontiveness and natural penchant for questioning and analysis, my original choice to help myself led to ways of helping others. My own need to better understand not only what had happened to me but what was *continuing* to happen impelled me to reach out and discover firsthand not only what had happened to others like myself but what was *still* happening and how they were dealing with it. I had to know. It was a question of survival.

Elisabeth Kübler-Ross was the first person I met to label what I had been through. She called it the near-death experience and described what it was like. By then, I had sold my house, quit my job, given away, stored, or sold everything I owned, and had struck out into the unknown, finding myself "led" to Shanti Nilaya, a small ranch near Escondido, California, where Elisabeth, at that time, held her Death and Dying Intensive Seminars. It was August 22, 1978. Paulie had gone to live with her father in Washington state. Natalie, although still hospitalized in Boise from recent surgery, was bent on living her own life independent of me. Kelly had been assigned to the first of several Coast Guard bases in the northeast. Now I, too, was free to leave. I did, walking out on an entire lifetime and all that I knew. I told everyone I was going to chase rainbows. I left with only what I could stuff into my little Ford Pinto.

When I heard Elisabeth speak about the near-death experience, it was as if a tiny buzzer went off inside me, affirming the legitimacy of all I had been through, and giving me the green light to seek out other ways of living wherever the unknown might lead. That unknown led me in zig-zag fashion across the United States, to Washington, D.C., and the state of Virginia. Culture shock prevented any further activity until the realization came that I could be "Idaho Phyllis" anywhere, regardless of prevailing traditions. I found a job and a place to live, then promptly devoted every spare moment to getting acquainted. Word traveled that I was willing to share my story. Invitations rolled in. I spoke at hospitals and homes, police stations and churches, libraries and funeral parlors. I traveled through ten states in short trips and long ones, meeting several thousand people and finding, sometimes most unexpectedly, over two hundred near-death survivors.

When I later moved to Roanoke, Virginia, my job as a switchboard trainer and telephone systems analyst for a commercial telephone company allowed me almost constant travel throughout northeast, southeast, and central states. I continued to meet even more survivors and their families at some of the most unlikely places, such as: Georgia truck stops, Florida beaches, Boston suburbs, West Virginia coal towns. They must have "smelled" me coming, for I met one right after another no matter where I went.

I became privy to the near-death experience as seen from differing angles of view—from those who went through it and those who didn't, from confused and frightened relatives to those who had to deal with it as professional caregivers.

During this time I began to write. A series of articles I

penned for *Many Smokes* magazine (now *Wildfire*), a publication printed by The Bear Tribe Medicine Society,[3] was reprinted in so many different newspapers and other small magazines up and down the West Coast that I finally compiled all segments into a self-published booklet entitled *I Died Three Times in 1977*. This booklet found its way around the world, selling better in Europe than in the United States, and, because of the book, surprising connections were made. One of the people who purchased a copy was Kenneth Ring. Soon after he came visiting and asked if I would represent the near-death survivor's point of view in the general interest magazine published by an organization he had co-founded with Ricky Bradshaw, a near-death survivor. The organization was the International Association for Near-Death Studies (IANDS), located at Storrs, Connecticut, and the magazine was *Vital Signs*. My advocacy column was entitled "Coming Back." In it, I first published my discoveries about the major after-effects of the near-death experience.

It wasn't until the fall of 1983, however, after several talks with Ken, that I learned of additional ways to use the material I had gathered. He urged me to write a book. But first of all, I would have to cross-check my findings. With his encouragement, I petitioned the board of IANDS for permission to gain access to the organization's archives. Permission was granted. It took the better part of a week, but I read every scrap of paper, listened to as many tapes as possible, and left nothing I could find untouched. The pattern of after-effects I had previously noted was confirmed.

To be certain I wasn't kidding myself and noticing only what I wanted to see, I selected names at random from the archives, developed a questionnaire, and sent it off. To balance that mailing, I also sent copies to some of the survivors and their families I had previously met, so I could compare answers—between those I knew and those I did not. A total of forty people cooperated. My phone almost rang off the wall. Then I asked several self-help groups (such as the Seattle chapter of IANDS) to take the after-effects material and test it out among their own members. Again and again, the pattern of after-effects was confirmed.

With the support and the encouragement of my husband Terry, whom I had married while in Roanoke, I quit all outside employment, canceled all activities, and threw myself totally into the task at hand. I became a "monk." Writing such a book, however, proved difficult. My mind was still too scattered, my ability to concentrate limited. I tried so hard to maintain a focus that thought forms spun out all over the room, looking like the blobs I had encountered in dying. The air was so thick with them I kept a fly swatter next to the typewriter so I could bat them away when it was time to type. Sensible intelligence left me when I spied one over three feet tall. Sometimes all I could do was stare at the typewriter and cry.

To make matters worse, the method I used to relive all three experiences so I could accurately describe them in this chapter of the book backfired. It backfired because it was *too* successful. In the reliving, all the conditions except the pregnancy returned—*physically*—and in full force. Hemorrhaging began, then the thrombosis in my right leg, complete with hot skin, searing pain, heart and lung stoppage. I became enraged that such a thing could happen again. Fortunately, I was able to reverse the life-threatening aspects with the same method that had brought them on, but it took nearly three months to regain full control of my health and walk again without pain.

It was my mind. I knew it was.

Reliving the events again in my mind was so emotional and so vivid my body physically recreated what I was reliving. It is eerie how that worked. I knew the mind was powerful, now I knew how powerful.

But it wasn't right; after version three was finished, it wasn't right. The manuscript was off-base, plugged, blocked. I knew it but I couldn't solve the problem. I didn't know what else to do.

Although problems with my uterus had begun again after my remarriage when another miscarriage occurred, all seemed well until I flew back to Boise, Idaho, for Kelly's marriage. After his wedding, a flow of heavy black blood gushed forth. I bled for two months, until a physician advised an emergency hysterectomy. The strange flow instantly stopped with the doctor's pronouncement, as if my uterus had heard what was said and approved. This assured me my uterus wanted to leave so I told everyone it would soon be "birthed." So total was my concept of "birthing" that on the day I checked in for surgery the hospital was so overcrowded I was assigned a room in, of all places, the maternity ward. During recovery as I was walking around, I happened to glance up at a large calendar on the corridor wall declaring the day to be May 2nd, *exactly* twenty-eight years from the day I had given birth to my first child, my son. It was 2:22 P.M. when I saw the date, *the exact same hour and minute* Kelly took his first breath. I was so stunned all I could do was stand there staring at that date and the nearby clock for what seemed a long time.

The third month after surgery while driving south on Interstate 81 to reach Blacksburg, Virginia, where I was to deliver a talk and workshop on death and dying, the "plug" within me was released—what was wrong with the manuscript became crystal clear. How it should be written was revealed, complete with chapter headings, detailed outline, and total reorganization of material.

The synchronicity of these events was peculiar to me for it was Kelly whose love had brought me forth from a life-threatening emergency only to have his wedding throw me into a life-threatening emergency; it was the third death experience where he had intervened and brought me back to life; it was the third day after surgery when I saw both calendar and clock announcing the anniversary of when I had given him life; it was during the third month of recovery that the book's format "righted" itself shortly before I was to speak of death and dying. The rhythmically logical thought-flow would not yield itself until after my physical blood-flow had ended with the uterus's need to birth itself in a maternity ward. When one flow ended the other began. The one who I had brought forth brought me forth, only to once again "be there" when it was necessary to "pull the plug." From this I finally came to realize how important the writing of this book was for my own new "birth." In helping others, I was also helping myself.

The writing of this book became the most intensive therapy I have ever undergone. To probe every aspect of near-death, I had to first probe every aspect of my own life.

Eleven years have passed now since that snowy Sunday morning in January 1977. All that I have learned since came from reaching in as well as out. Decisions that seemed so radical then have since proved wise. I am glad I did what I did. My life today is as joyfully relaxed as my previous existence was tense and stressful. What began as a quest to better understand my own experience became a quest to more fully understand and describe the universal experience. Near-death may be an enigma worthy of study, but no one who goes through it has any idea what to do when it is over. For someone like myself who chose to acknowledge what happened *and* risk a complete change of lifestyle, constructive guidance and positive role models were nonexistent. Although I do not presume to speak for all near-death survivors, I do feel qualified to share what I have learned in the hope that others will be helped as I have.

3
Major
After-Effects

"Nothing in life is to be feared, only understood."

Madame Marie Curie

Throughout my own search I could not help but notice how similar many survivors became after their experience was over; and that struck me, for, at first, I could not figure out why.

Why are we so much alike? Why are we now able to communicate, understand, and know each other so easily—sometimes without saying a word? How can this be?

This puzzle was especially important to me since most of the survivors I met were located in northeastern, southeastern, and central states and I was from the northwest. The only common denominator any of us shared was one moment in time when our lives had stopped and we had ceased breathing. We had come to "know" death and, in so doing, we had come to "know" each other as if we were all members of the same family connected by the same pulsebeat—what happens to one somehow affects all. Our meetings usually turn out to be more a time of hugs and tears than conversation. Introductions are not needed. No one is in awe or fear of anyone else. We are equal, yet joys are often bittersweet for coming back and reentering society are not easy tasks to accomplish.

Coming back can be just as traumatic as going out.

Current researchers are quick to point out that near-death survivors, to a person, lose all fear of death afterwards. They usually become more loving, more peaceful, and much more content, with a less materialistic lifestyle.

It is eeasy to report findings such as these, for the general public is open and receptive to them. These findings seem to confirm traditional religious teachings and idealistic notions of that which constitutes "good." Even if scientists deem the near-death phenomenon unsettling, its purported after-effects somehow make everything okay.

Little else is said.

Researchers usually side-step other possibilities, especially if mention is made of the psychic, religion, spirituality, mysticism, or anything "other-worldly," preferring instead to brand such possibilities as "insignificant" or "unconfirmed." For example, I was told by a former editor of *Vital Signs* magazine that if I did not play down or preferably not mention the "other" after-effects the column I wrote would be canceled. I refused, saying I would not distort facts just to satisfy editorial policy, whereupon I was instructed that I had better or the magazine and very probably the entire organization would lose much of its scientific and credentialed support. "You cannot be so honest," I was warned. "People don't want to hear what they don't want to know." The warning was delivered twice.

This "forbidden zone" of information is just as relevant and important as those facts more commonly reported. For the survivor, it is *far more* important, because coming back means facing your belief system and everything you ever knew about yourself and the world around you. It also means facing everything you have ever believed or not believed about God. This kind of confrontation covers every possible rendering of psychic abilities and psychic phenomena, immortality, mind over matter, comparative religion, reincarnation, souls, angels, and all those things termed sacred and holy or wicked and unholy. In order to understand the broader range of after-effects from the near-death experience, these topics must be broached and discussed openly and objectively. Although no one can really explain the why of it all, we should at least have some idea what constitutes factors common to the vast majority.

There are seven of these major factors or elements, in my opinion, which form the pattern of after-effects. Certainly, not everyone exhibits all seven, but the average survivor will exhibit most, some to a greater degree than others. I know of only three survivors who claim absolutely no difference in their lives before and after; the rest, whether positive or negative experiencers, encountered sometimes exciting, sometimes frightening, and sometimes just plain confusing differences. As one said:

> "I'm fifty-three years old and have been experiencing the after-effects for about thirty years now. *At first,* it was frustrating, but later it became interesting (a learning phase), adventurous (experimental phase) and on occasion downright exciting! Life is really great."

What I believe to be the pattern of major after-effects from the near-death experience are:

1. *The inability to personalize emotions or feelings,* especially those of love and of belonging to anyone.
2. *The inability to recognize and comprehend boundaries,* rules, limits.
3. *Difficulty understanding time sense,* or references to what occurred in the past or might occur in the future—a sense of timelessness.
4. *Expanded/enhanced sensitivities,* becoming more intuitive, psychic, knowing, spatial, non-linear in perceptions.
5. *A shifted or changed view of physical reality,* becoming more detached, objective, seeing "through" events and problems with a noticeable reduction of fears and worries.
6. *A different feeling of physical self,* a certain detachment from the body and any identification with it as "self," rather knowing we live in and "wear" our bodies.
7. *Difficulty with communication and relationships,*

finding it hard to say what is meant or to understand language phrasing used by others.

Each of these seven factors will be discussed separately.

It is my conviction that in recognizing what is *common* and *normal* to the experience, we can then lessen or prevent much needless misunderstanding, tension, and suffering.

Coming back need not be so difficult. It certainly does not have to become the nightmare it is for some. It can and should be an opportunity to enhance and enlarge our horizons, to relearn and redefine, to begin again. What happened can be a blessing, not a problem. But then, that depends on how we respond to it and what choices we make.

Since I am a survivor, I will speak as one in covering this material. All opinions are my own, based on the facts as I encountered them, unless otherwise stated.

Here, then, are the seven major after-effects discussed more in depth:

The Inability to Personalize Emotions or Feelings, Especially Those of Love and of Belongings to Anyone.
The vast majority of near-death survivors have positive, uplifting experiences. Theirs is both the opportunity and the thrill of being totally engulfed by overwhelming love, a kind of love beyond precedent, beyond description. There is nothing else quite like it—a feeling, a knowing of oneness and worth, of total freedom and total acceptance. No demands. No stipulations. No conditions. No criteria. Just love—boundless, infinite, all-encompassing love—a love so forgiving, so total, so immense, nothing can contain it. Love encountered on "The Other Side" makes any kind of earthly love dim by comparison.

It is God's love. You just know.

You float in the wonder of it and, when you return, you want everyone else to know about it. You want to spread the good news about love.

Love!

Over and over again, I hear survivors tell of the love they experienced and how they want now to emulate that love, to develop and expand that love, so it will become a daily reality in their lives. They want to keep it alive and growing.

Over and over again, I hear survivors describe how much more loving they are, how filled to overflowing with love they are, how much more life and its living means to them, how precious everything is. They speak of loving their spouses more, their children more, their friends and co-workers more, everyone and everything—more. Said one man in southern California, whose experience was in 1964, "I love my wife and children more than I ever thought I could. I love everyone. My experience taught me *real love, unconditional love!*"

Yet, his wife and children did not feel the kind of love he described. They recognized how wonderfully he had changed since his experience but he seemed somehow unreachable to them, as if he were "floating" around somewhere in a world of his own, out of touch with the reality of what was really going on or what their personal needs were. A gap developed between what *he felt* and what *they felt*.

The last letter I received from this loving husband and father was one of desperation. He was having tremendous difficulty holding down a job and earning a living, not to mention in his relations with his family. He just couldn't understand why people had trouble getting along with him since he was so filled with joy and love for all of them. He was generous and openly affectionate yet people seemed to turn away or back off. As a last resort, he decided to leave town and drift for awhile—until he could figure out what was wrong. That last letter was received back in 1982. I have not heard from him since.

There is no question that most near-death survivors become more loving. No question whatever. But they are not always perceived that way. In fact, many times they are thought to be either aloof and arrogant, snobbish and egotistical, or flying around on some kind of cloud—unable to "land" and be normal like everyone else. Maybe a reason for people thinking this way is because they are threatened by the overt enthusiasm survivors often display, or maybe they are jealous, or perhaps something else is involved, something deeper.

Here is an example to consider.

The Death & Dying Intensive I attended in Escondido, California, lasted for a week. It was a live-in, marathon exposure to every possible human problem, emotion, and need. Although my attention was riveted on the unfolding dramas around me, I was relaxed, at peace, and filled with an in-dwelling gratitude that an opportunity such as this was available to those who needed it. I began each day early and alone, perched on a high rock at the end of the property, in meditation and song, but I kept a low profile. During the closing minutes of the last day, after Elisabeth had introduced and shared her ideas about near-death experiences, I was moved to stand and briefly relate what had happened to me.

Afterward, I was swamped by everyone, literally swamped—*not in praise but in apology*. Fellow attendees, almost in a single voice, admitted to having avoided and ignored me throughout because they had felt I was too happy and too much at peace to be real. They had perceived me as phony. After I spoke up, they could see I was not putting on any act nor was I trying to better anyone. It wasn't me so much as what I represented that they found irritating. Just the state of my presence had annoyed them, but now they were relieved and impressed. I was okay. Certainly this need to make amends was a surprise but even more surprising was the fact that throughout the entire week, while I was supposedly being shunned, I never felt any form of negativity from anyone. I did not *recognize* their indifference or their rejection. I didn't know what was going on. I was so immersed in love and joy I simply hadn't noticed. What had been a wonderful week for me had been uncomfortable for eighty-four other people—without my knowledge.

This misunderstanding, this difference in the perception of love and joy and belonging is so important I want to spend some time discussing it from various points of view using different examples.

A woman in Bedford, Virginia, had been pronounced dead from automobile accident injuries but she later revived. Months after her recovery, her worried family asked me for help. The woman was middle-aged, married, had several older children and a younger one, and was a professional health-care giver with yet another business on the side. After hours with her and later a long talk with her family, I noticed the all-too-familiar pattern. As she described feeling so much love and joy she could almost burst, her family shuddered. Not only did they *not* feel the love she was describing with great animation and excitement, they thought she was hallucinating and out of touch with reality. She was gloriously happy. They were afraid. She was open, willing, and ready to change everything in her life. But they wanted her to be the same as always—no changes, nothing different—just "normal." While she was utterly aglow and transformed, they were bereft.

Another woman from Waynesboro, Virginia, nearly collapsed in my arms after a talk I had given because I had stated it was *perfectly normal* for a survivor to be unable to personalize love and a sense of belonging. Her story was typical. She had been sent from psychologist to psychologist and had been in therapy for over a year because she could not love her husband and children the same way any more. She loved them, but in a more detached, objective way, *which appeared to them as unloving.* She cared deeply. Her family was important to her, but she now loved each member equally with every other person she knew. The intimate bond had been broken. Love no longer had an "object," a single focus. She was filled with love for them and everyone else in her life, more than ever before, but she could not personalize it, she could not make her love exclusive. All kinds of accusations and threats had been made against her resulting in a deep, gnawing guilt. Why couldn't she love her husband and children as before? What had happened to her? She felt more loving than ever. Why couldn't they feel it? Why couldn't they see all the wonderful changes that had happened to her? What was wrong?

I would never have recognized this strange puzzle had it not been for my oldest daughter, Natalie. She brought it to my attention, quite adamantly. I, too, felt unusually loving. I felt I had finally discovered unconditional love and was devoted to sharing it profusely. But Natalie had never heard of unconditional love, and frankly, she wasn't interested.

As far as she was concerned, I had become unreachable and she felt abandoned. Both daughters claimed I was so detached nothing mattered to me any more. Yes, I was easier to talk to, and, yes, I was more understanding; but, no, I was no longer personal, familiar, or even lovable. I was a nice woman, but I wasn't Mom. They wanted Mom back, but none of us knew where to find her.

Says Joe Geraci of New Britain, Connecticut:

> "This total love and sometimes incredible sadness, on the surface, they don't go together . . . I am unable to adequately express the love I experienced. I have been told by some people they can feel the love when I am with them. That makes me very happy because then I know that I have shared the love even if it was non-verbal."

When Joe spoke more of what he went through, he explained that "I was God, God was me." That kind of experience, that kind of bond is beyond comprehension for most people. How do you bring that kind of love and knowing back to earth, back to everyday living without appearing to be some kind of Messiah?

Today, Joe speaks of living a somewhat routine life but of feeling deep inside that he is no longer the same person. He feels as if he is playing the role of two different people. He admits being frustrated in trying to find a way to live what he knows, yet he is one of the few who recognizes clearly the difference between what he feels and the way others perceive him. Also, people expect him to be above anger, worry, or unhappiness, and, even though he is happier now than ever before, he is still human, has problems, and makes mistakes. *His experience did not make him perfect*. Because of readjustment difficulties, he feels the survivor's family has the real problem, for they must reacquaint themselves with the person they once thought they knew. Joe is a little more perceptive than most. The majority cannot or will not recognize the schism which develops between themselves and those around them.

When I sent out questionnaires on the last phase of research for this book, I noticed how everyone went on and on about how much more loving they were, yet they would mention incidents where family and friends had been indifferent or unkind to them. Because of the discrepancy in answers, I sent out a second batch of questionnaires to survivors I personally know, and *this second batch was no different than the first.* Their answers were almost identical. I knew firsthand this second group *was* having problems expressing love, some even severe problems, *but they didn't know it—not even then.* They were still floating around somewhere and hadn't landed. Family members were just as worried as before, *but the survivors still couldn't understand why.*

Of all the after-effects from the near-death experience, I believe this one is the most important and the most misunderstood, for love is *the* central human emotion, and a sense of belonging is paramount to sound mental health. Perhaps we need to rethink what constitutes love, even unconditional love.

The kind of love we survivors encounter in dying is not emotional, nor is it in any way connected to emotion. It is not personal, although we feel it as personal. The kind of love we encounter is more a state of being, a transcended state of existence, if you will. It is a level of consciousness beyond human reasoning and believability. This kind of love flows *through* you, not from or to you. You cannot keep it nor can you hold it. It is impossible to possess. The only way you can even glimpse it is to give it away and watch what happens. This love, true love, belongs to no one yet is part of everyone, and exists only in complete freedom. It makes no demand and seeks no response. It welcomes all and denies none. This kind of love is the glue that holds the universe and all creation together. Existence in this kind of love *dissolves* all emotion, feelings, needs, and relationships. When you return to normal earthlife, you still exist in it. It takes a while to land, to become more involved and attached again.

In any social arrangement, we expect love to be personal, conditional, bonding, definable, limited, exclusive, sometimes sexual and passionate, very physical, and based on sense response. Our children expect to be our exclusive possessions while they are young. Our spouses expect to be our exclusive mates. Our friends expect to be intimate and privy. Each person sees him or herself playing a specific role, occupying a definite place in our lives, and expects the same from us in return for their attention and loyalty. They clearly see the role they play. Deviations are usually unacceptable.

Now, there is nothing wrong with such expectations. In order for children to grow up to be healthy and sane, they must have warmth, bonding, exclusivity. Mates come together in loving support to build homes and families. We humans have a long history of needing each other and expecting personal attention and personal interaction. We are social creatures with a herd instinct. We need emotions and feelings. We need to belong. We need *what we call love.* We thrive on it, grow from it, hunger for it. Without positive emotional interplay we either withdraw, become imbalanced, or die. Psychologically, the emotional development of a healthy individual grows in stages, beginning with primal, self-centered urges, running the gamut of passion and pleasure, compromise and sacrifice, until finally maturing into a more agape or universal sense of love for all.

That is normal.

What I have noticed with near-death survivors is that we are suddenly and without warning flung into a state of consciousness we are not prepared for. We had no opportunity to grow through natural developmental stages before instantly being catapulted from A to Z without benefit of maps, travelogue or set of instructions. We not only reached agape, but many of us slid right on past *even that* into realms and dimensions where no phrase, word or symbol is applicable. Once our experience is over, we have no innate tools or skills with which to understand or evaluate our new awareness. We struggle and stumble, sometimes alienating when we mean to inspire, confusing when we mean to clarify, threatening when we mean to soften, frightening when we mean to enlighten.

We are not perceived by others as we perceive ourselves.

The message we seek to deliver is somehow lost in the translation.

Betty Preston of Seattle, Washington, exclaimed, "The love my husband and I had shared flew out the window after I found universal love." Peggy Adams Raso of Washington, Missouri, says, "I feel like a giant mother who would like to gather all mankind in her arms." John W. Baccarini of Hanford, California, says, "Nothing can change the love I have for my wife and children but I am much more of a 'human family' person now." The list is long. We come back madly in love with all humanity, everyone, everywhere. Experiencing this state of consciousness is fantastic. It is truly universal and unconditional, yet it is not easy to grasp if you have never been exposed to it before. It is not even appreciated or wanted if you are not ready for it.

Universal love *can* cause more problems than it solves. It can hurt more than it helps. It can become just another excuse for walking out on a difficult situation instead of staying to work it through. This kind of love can be more nightmare than blessing. It can drive a wedge between people.

Let us be very practical about what unconditional love really means. *It means everyone is you and you are everyone!* It means every woman you see is your mother, sister, aunt, and daughter; every man your father, brother, uncle, and son. It means you cannot divide or separate people, that you have no expectations, no needs, no wants, no conditions of any sort in loving. Love loses its object and becomes objectless. Can you imagine what kind of world this would be if everyone loved like that? It could be glorious or it could be a disaster.

Let us be even more practical. Unconditional love means no privacy, no secrets, no keys, no judgments, no exceptions, nothing ever held back. You are not only vulnerable but transparent. Unconditional love sounds incredible, and it is, but it is not always sensible for all people in every situation.

Perhaps the wiser choice is balance—a combination of loving skills, whereby a person can be personal and intimate yet still love without conditions; cautious and discerning, exclusive to a point, yet still openly accepting and nonjudgmental. The survivor can help set a standard of behavior here, showing by example how one can be both objective and subjective, accepting and loving yet discerning—all at the same time.

One survivor I know who came to exemplify such a positive balance is Arthur E. Yenson of Parma, Idaho. Arthur died in an automobile accident in 1932 while in his twenties. He revived and recovered but was never the same again. Eventually, he married and had three sons, settling down in Parma. He loved his wife and sons dearly, yet everyone was "family," and he would go out of his way to help anyone at any time—even when it meant losing his job because he dared to openly defend American-born Japanese during World War II, and again when he dared to share his near-death experience during classroom hours as a teacher. Arthur was tossed off as a kook until he was named one of Idaho's "Most Distinguished Citizens." Then, the wonder of his many accomplishments was revealed. His life is an inspiration to any survivor.

Consider, however, the survivor's spouse and family. Perhaps theirs is the greater need, as Joe Geraci suggested. They didn't have the experience and they don't know what is going on. They have no way to fathom or understand what their loved one is going through. They are the ones, in my opinion, who need the most counseling on the issue of love and a sense of belonging. The survivor will eventually settle down some and be more capable of the kind of intimacy formerly expressed, but the family may never recover from the painful grief of feeling no longer wanted and no longer needed by the one they love. This misunderstanding can leave a deep scar.

The unconditonal love near-death experiencers bring back is ecstatically incredible—but it can be bittersweet.

The Inability to Recognize and Comprehend Boundaries, Rules, Limits. Dying has such an interesting way of blotting out nonessentials.

Coming back to life is a startling jolt.

Rebuilding with what you have left is confusing.

You deal with situations like: Who said I have to hold my fork this way? Spoons are so enchanting. Why can't I just walk up to her and start talking about what really matters? Beating around the bush makes no sense. Why can't I converse with the vacuum cleaner? It makes better noise than you do. I want to run, skip, jump rope, and climb a fence. I want to catch snow flakes with my tongue and make footprints where none have been. What do you mean I am forty-seven and people my age don't do that sort of thing? That doctor doesn't know what he is doing. Can't he see the halos of color around that patient's head and feel the pain himself? Why won't anyone listen to me? I know what I am talking about. Read the book? Why? I know what it says without reading. All I have to do is touch it. I don't follow recipes any more. I just ask the food what it wants to do and we all have fun. I don't understand why men wear the most comfortable shoes. Fashion, smashion! I'm not ruining my face with cosmetics. If I have more than I need I'll just give the rest away. Why should I charge anyone? What do you mean follow procedures and go through proper channels? Get a college degree? Nonsense.

Our life and everything in it is the same as it always was. Nothing changed while we were gone. *We did.* The biggest reason it all looks and feels so different when we return is that we now have a basis of comparison. We can now compare our life as-it-was-before with wherever-it-was-we-went. They don't compare.

Now that we are back we must do something. Life cannot proceed if nothing happens, so the most logical move is—"I'll continue where I left off." Some survivors do just that and are content. But the majority begin to deviate, usually out of a sense of awe and wonder coupled with a sense of gratitude for having been "spared" so they can search out whatever mission or goal they were spared to accomplish. There are some whose experience was so intense and so impactual that they are incapable of resuming life as always. For them the past has ceased to be and only the future remains, whatever that means.

Regardless to what extent an individual is affected, a period of time follows when readjusting is difficult and uncomfortable. Previously familiar codes of conduct can lose some relevance or disappear altogether. The loss of boundaries, rules, and limits can take on many forms such as: sensing the interconnectedness of all life while changing a baby's diaper, understanding the unified field theory while driving a truck, watching holograms bounce off soap suds, solving the mystery of resonance waves while darning socks, getting high from the hum of a food blender, conversing in archetypal symbols rather than just asking "how's the weather," recognizing synchronicity interwoven throughout all events and movements, bidding "anyone" enter as friend whether they "wear" a body or not.

Peggy Adams Raso of Washington, Missouri, admits:

> "No, I am not able to perform as before. I often become distracted and get lost in my thoughts. If I take the dictionary down to look up one word, I may lose myself in it for hours, I want to know everything. I feel I must keep myself available to those who may be sent to me at any time, and they do turn up in the darnest places. My home used to be the neatest on the block. Now, answering your questions is more important to me than doing the breakfast dishes."

John Barnard of San Bruno, California, says:

> "Even pulling weeds out of the ground seems to be more satisfying."

Betty Preston talks about how her human ego died and only her spiritual being remains. She calls herself "The Intra-Dimensional Me." Peggy, John, and Betty are typical of the average survivor. Suddenly their world has flipped over. What was once important is no more and what never was important is.

This kind of behavior can be disconcerting to family members and friends and co-workers. Such people are often quick to condemn, avoid, chide, or criticize the still very vulnerable survivor who, although healed from accident or illness, is often confused about the newness and difference of the world around him or her. Everything is the same, but they see it through different eyes, sense it through different receptors, sift it through different mental processes. It is sometimes a draw as to who gets impatient with whom first—the survivor or everyone else.

Let me give you a personal example of how ridiculous this can be. One afternoon when I realized my dearly beloved winter coat could no longer be relined or repaired, that it had in essence "died," I took it out to the trash can and held an elaborate funeral service for it. My two daughters caught me in the act and laughed uproariously, poking fun. I was embarrassed and my face turned red. I wasn't trying to be funny or pull any kind of joke. I truly considered my winter coat to be a living, breathing friend of mine fully entitled to a proper burial. I honestly could not distinguish between that which is living and that which is not. To me, everything breathed and everything was alive. Their criticism of my behavior baffled me. To this day, I still cannot always distinguish animate from inanimate.

The survivor's new frame of reference can become so openly accepting it borders on child-like naivete and, with the fading of previous norms, there also fades basic cautions and discernment. This can leave the survivor a sitting duck for all manner of negativity and harm. I am amazed at how many times survivors fall prey to repeated rapes, thefts, lies, cheating, losses of all kinds, fires, floods, financial setbacks, accidents, and to commitment to psychiatric treatment when none is really required. I myself was almost killed a number of times.

We walk innocently into dangerous situations because we honestly do not recognize them as dangerous. We see our home as beautiful, warm, and comfortable, but fail to see the leaking roof, flooding basement, and stopped-up sink. We trust everyone because we know of no reason not to. We see life as a panorama, but miss all the cracks and fissures. It is just like being a child again and having to relearn, "When you touch a hotplate you get burned." As one experiencer said:

> "I've had to undergo years of therapy. It's almost like learning everything all over again, but in a different way. It's almost like learning a new language. Every-

> thing has a different meaning for me now. I feel more
> but comprehend less."

"My experience has opened up for me a clearer sense of the meaning of life," said Dottie Bush of Roslyn, Pennsylvania. "The happenings in our lives are lessons to be learned for our spiritual growth."

High morals and the reality of truth and virtue take on new dimensions for the average survivor. In fact, such things become top priority. Fairness and a sense of excellence become quiet measuring sticks. Many take on a personal partnership with God and to the best of their ability live in accordance with what they have come to identify as Higher Laws. To this degree, they can no longer be governed or led.

Listen to this survivor:

> "What did I learn: Well, for one, I learned there are
> no limits, no time, there is only peace and love. But the
> most relevant of all is forgiveness. For forgiveness
> happens in an instant, because an instant is all we
> have. No past. No future. Only right now, this instant."

There are some survivors who cannot distinguish between work and play, and as a result, can do better work in half the time with little apparent effort and virtually no boredom. Now, be honest. Would you be willing to work with someone like that? Would you find this person inspiring or threatening?

Survivors are not saints and do not deserve to be put on pedestals. They are just people whose world and all its many parts have merged together. They are relearning life, and they need a little time.

Difficulty Understanding Time Sense or References to What Occurred in the Past or Might Occur in the Future—A Sense of Timelessness. Today's researchers have discovered poor or slowed memory responses are *not* synonymous with advancing age. They tell us a reasonably active life and a stimulating environment encourage continued if not expanded synaptic connections and nerve sprouting in the brain. In other words, the human brain is far more flexible than previously thought and is capable of rejuvenation. Yet over and over again, when I asked how their memory worked, survivors would say, "Well, you know how it is when you get older. Everything slows down and you forget." Considering that most of the people I've spoken with since 1978 were in their twenties, thirties, and forties, that excuse does not ring true. My own memory has slowed, too, and occasionally I have lapses.

Being a trained observer and analyst by profession, I began asking more pertinent, probing questions. Age could not account for what I kept noticing and, if indeed there was a slowdown, how did it work? Was it constant or sporadic? The answers I received formed an interesting pattern. In the vast majority of cases, memory of events that occurred *after* the near-death episode was sharp and clear. If anything, survivors reported how much better and faster they could remember and how much more efficient their mental processes seemed. Yet, recollection of events that occurred *before* their episode was different. They could still remember past events, for the most part, but the *process* of that memory seemed slower, somewhat impersonal, as if they could not fully identify with it.

Christy Donovan of Bennett, Colorado, admitted she "usually refers to it as *back then.* It's like one life ended, one life began."

"I say, 'before I died and came back,'" Olga S. Jensen of Millbrae, California, noted, "Although my memory seems to be slipping, I recall my near-death experience so vividly."

According to another survivor:

> "After the first death, I returned to a body with the same name, but little else in common with the woman who had died. Many of my memories were wiped out. What remained or returned seemed more like a movie."

Any number of survivors described a "line of demarcation" that seemed to have formed at the time of their experience, separating those things before from anything that came after. One man put it quite succinctly, "I truly feel as if the old me really did die and the new me has difficulty remembering what went on before." One woman said her retrieval process for accessing past memories was like rushing into a back storage vault, grabbing a movie reel on the subject at hand, running it off on a projector, and zooming in for a closer look when the missing sequence was located. This internal imagery process took her several minutes and was sometimes cumbersome around other people. Another woman said she had to first "relive" a past event in her mind before she could "remember" it.

Certainly, not everyone has difficulty remembering "past," but almost every single survivor remarked on a slowdown of memory retrieval. Only one survivor I contacted reported the opposite effect: his long-term memory heightened but his ability to remember events close at hand decreased.

I found it fascinating to listen as survivors spoke of how their memory now worked. They would invariably use impersonal pronouns when speaking about themselves *before* their experience, or sometimes they would refer to themselves by their first name as if it were another person. When they did use the personal pronoun "I," it would seem to lack importance; but, when they spoke of events that occurred *afterwards*, they would be significantly personal and animated. Their shift in speech mode was even more distinct. When I would bring this to their attention, they would act surprised, claiming they had never noticed themselves doing this before and were unaware they ever made any such reference. Often they would become flustered and embarrassed if I continued to pursue before-and-after questioning. I wasn't the only one to notice their pronoun slip. Family and friends noticed it, too.

The more I listened to others the more I realized I was doing the same thing, only I would refer to it as "before 1977" and "after 1977" as if a divider separated one version of Phyllis from the other. I could usually access more important memories, but anything of lesser value seemed inaccessible, although memory I once thought gone is now to a large extent returning.

When doing personal interviews, I kept noticing how survivors would raise their gaze above me and past me and seem to search blank space for answers of some kind. They would virtually never look me straight in the eyes if a question involved past memory. Instead, most would look upper right, gazing out into space before they would give me an answer. Some would raise their eyes to upper left.

This behavior puzzled me until I became aware that I was doing the exact same thing. Whenever I was having difficulty remembering something, I would automatically raise the position of my eye focus to upper left, bring it across to upper middle, and finally stop at an upper right position, gazing up and out into space until the needed memory surfaced. Sometimes I would just raise my eye focus to upper right and that position alone would surface some memories faster. If I lowered my eyes to look directly at anything or anyone, my memory would go blank.

I then came to associate eye movement as follows: upper right—quick stimulation of memory; upper left, then slowly moving to upper right—easing out deeper memories; eyes held in upper left position—probing stimulation; completely downcast positions (either left or right)—sensory feelings associated with past events.

These eye-position maneuvers to retrieve memories always worked, although I had no idea why. They were dependable, especially if I was in a crowd or delivering a talk. I would have to pause to use them, but my speech would be more coherent and natural if I did. People sometimes questioned why my eyes roamed around so much and why I didn't look directly at them as much as I used to, but all in all, the maneuvers became a handy new skill I found invaluable.

In late 1983, the missing logic of this eye-position process was uncovered quite by accident when my husband purchased a home study course entitled *The Neuropsychology of Achievement*.[4] Although primarily geared toward sales people, this course describes the brain as a holographic organ that responds best to visual and sensory images and, if eye focus is shifted to certain positions, specific areas of memory can be stimulated. The accompanying text has diagrams of eye positions necessary for each type of memory wanted, and the diagrams are *identical* to what I was already doing. Without knowing why, most survivors I met had chanced upon and were using the same system I was. What we instinctively used as a method to save us from embarrassment, others now learn as a maneuver to help increase business acumen.

There is something else I noticed about memory with survivors. They express more interest and concern with the present than either past or future. If they refer at all to past or future, it is seldom for increments of more than a few months or, at best, a few years. They seem to live more fully in the present and nothing else seems to matter. One man's time shift was so radical, he began to live in a heightened awareness of each single moment as it happened, refusing to acknowledge anything that had already occurred or was yet to be. Even in ordinary conversation, he came to realize that every sentence spoken had no basis in time, that past and future were nonexistent. With this awareness in mind, he initiated a lengthy period of silence where he would only listen and watch but say nothing. This "time out" proved to be immensely rewarding and helped him understand how to communicate more effectively.

This kind of intense concentration and awareness of the present moment is akin to a person high on marijuana. It is also very similar to the curiosity of a child or someone less educated, as well as to that of other drug users and the mentally ill. All these types of people have little or no concept of past or future. Needs are immediate. Once something has happened it ceases to exist and, since the future has yet to come, it, too, does not exist. For them, there is only now, right now.

Obviously, there must be some kind of chemical change within a survivor's brain, which on rare occasions might be classified as brain damage but in most cases it is rather some kind of functional shift. For those less affected, this shift may be more attitudinal than chemical in creating preference changes.

Regardless of how or to what extent individuals

change, almost every single person returns knowing time does not exist. They come back knowing time is a matter of consciousness; past and future are really qualities of perception. Once you have experienced timelessness, you can no longer be intimidated by the tyranny of time! "Time now seems to be irrelevant in the past and present sense. My memory is the same, but my scope of life has been broadened," reported Pamela Ericson of Newton, New Jersey. And another survivor said, "Past and past tense are semantic terms to me. The past, present, and future seem interrelated and I have difficulty knowing where one *really* begins or the other ends—if?"

Scientifically, we know time is a psychological standard and not an event of nature. No physical experiment has yet detected the flow of time. Space and time are both relative to who is doing the viewing and how, and from what angle. They are relevant only when recognized as so and when arranged logistically and sequentially by the viewer. Our brain, in essence, creates them both.

There are some survivors who now talk about the future as if it were already known and already lived, as if what they are now doing is an afterthought, or, perhaps, the acting out of a previously written script. For them *the present moment can be past tense*. This awareness, regardless of duration, is intense and *may appear* as precognition or prophesy when neither is the case. For them it is more a process of memory than anything psychic. *They actually remember the future*—just like they remember the past. They are not seers. They do not predict. They are just people who now live in a different reality system where the understanding of time and space has shifted from the norm. Professional researchers often misinterpret and misunderstand the phenomenon, thinking it to be something it is not.

I have come to regard future memory as part of what may be a multifaceted process whereby time and space can merge, thus creating events that are capable of being "physically lived" *before* they are physically lived. These "prehappenings" occur so often among near-death survivors that I believe the subject deserves some elaboration.

The type of events "lived" in this futuristic manner usually involve insignificant episodes but on occasion such events can be important and involve many people. These prehappenings can run the gamut from snatches of what is to come to long, drawn-out scenarios of precise and explicit detail. Individuals experience them differently, sometimes in dreams at night but mostly while wide awake and active. Little time actually passes during a prehappening although it can seem as if hours have passed by, or even days and years.

Here is one example from my own life that may help illustrate how the process works.

I had applied for a part-time position at a resort establishment where my husband Terry worked. He and I had just finished debating possible pros and cons of the job when I turned to walk into the kitchen. At that moment, everything "froze" in time and space and the air filled with tiny sparkles. Physically, I did not move, frozen as all else, yet I answered the phone, said yes to the position, agreed to meet with my new employer at seven that evening at Howard Johnson's restaurant, went there, arriving early, looked around for him, then turned to see him standing at the door after just arriving, surrounded by a bevy of women. When the scenario finished, time and space "clicked" back into place and full animated living resumed with only about a minute having passed. I vaguely "registered" what had just happened. Nothing more was said about the job as I continued walking into the kitchen to prepare dinner.

Several days later, the phone rang and I answered it. It was my prospective employer asking for my decision about the job. I said yes and agreed to meet with him that night at seven at Howard Johnson's restaurant. I arrived early and, since he was nowhere to be seen, I began to look about, feeling a strange prickling sensation as if I had already done all of this before. Suddenly, in a sparkling flash, I remembered what had happened several days before and realized I was merely acting out what had already been done. The whole thing was so funny I started laughing and, in doing so, turned around just as my new employer entered and stood at the door waiting. A bevy of women surrounded him. Recognizing the now "familiar scene," I promptly walked right up, addressed him by name, and introduced myself. He back-stepped a little as if in shock and asserted, "How do you know who I am? We've never met before!"

He was right. I had completely forgotten the fact that I had not been personally interviewed by him, nor had our paths ever crossed. My application for employment had been handled by my husband. Everything I knew about the position I had learned second hand. This man had been recently hired to initiate a new sales approach so there was no way I could have known what he looked like, yet I did. For a few seconds I was speechless. Then, tossing it off as coincidence, I sat down for our meeting, but he kept staring at me in disbelief on and off throughout the entire meeting. Our relationship was short-lived because of a disagreement he had with the resort owner but he never got over our first encounter. When we parted company, he accused me of being psychic as if I were some kind of anomaly.

When I live through a prehappening, time accelerates instantly and the air always fills with tiny sparkles, as if I were back in "The Void" of my second near-death experience. This signals for me that a future event is about to "play out." Whatever I pre-live actually happens. I have tried to cause this phenomenon to occur and to direct its activity once it did, but so far I have been unsuccessful. Visions, revelations, and precognition are familiar to me but not anything like this. This is different and somehow a "product" of the death events I survived. It is not seeing, viewing, or observing—it is a future event that is lived before it happens, then later remembered.

Because this subject is so fascinating and happens to so many, it will be included in my next book, the first of two sequels to this present one.

Expanded/Enhanced Sensitivities, Becoming More Intuitive, Psychic, Knowing, Spatial, Non-Linear in Perceptions. Oh, the stories I hear from survivors! Certainly, there are a few who claim nothing unusual happens, that they are now the same as they always were, and that their life is routine and untouched; but these people are so much in the minority that they quickly take a back seat to survivor stories that would make any self-respecting scientist or academician shudder.

Some of the more unusual phenomena involve survivors who claim they now regularly meet with the light beings or angels they saw during their near-death experience. Others claim to see and talk with departed spirits of the dead. Many claim to see plants and especially flowers undulate as if breathing, while still others claim to see a web-like substance connecting all in sight with everything else through a network of glistening threads.

One man, for instance, whose death scenario consisted of leaving his body while on the operating table, then soaring around the room and finally coming to hover over the surgeons' heads (and later accurately reporting everything he saw and heard while "out"), today still leaves his body, unexpectedly and uncontrollably. He never knows when it will occur. He can be eating dinner, smoking his pipe, shopping for groceries, driving his car, talking to a neighbor. All of a sudden, without warning, he will just float out of his body, soar around or hover, and then return. While he is out, his body seems to continue doing whatever it is doing but in a slower monotone, unanimated, as if on "automatic pilot." This happens to him so often it has become a problem. He can't seem to stay inside his body where he feels he belongs. His case is not unique.

Other stories repeated so often they have become commonplace include: knowing who is calling the minute the telephone rings, answering questions before they are asked, knowing someone's thoughts without conversing, seeing or sensing the future (regular precognition), feeling the approach of an accident before it happens, hearing plants and animals "voice" their needs, sensing life in all things, an unusually heightened response to touch, taste, and texture.

One survivor reports, "My sensitivities increased to an uncomfortable point which has made my life difficult and wearing, as I seem to march to a different drummer and am aware before the fact so often."

And listen what these others have to say:

Betty Preston:

> "I often have a visit, usually from someone who has just passed on. I have received 'messages' for someone else. I am a receiver . . . I have healing hands."

Ann Hueschen, Olympia, Washington:

> "Suddenly I stopped in my tracks. There, about ten feet from me, was the Satin Doll (a deceased cat and family pet), frolicking, running merrily, but about six inches above the old lady's pruned hedge! My only explanation—souls of all creatures, all of us, DO EXIST."

Peggy Adams Raso, Washington Missouri:

> "I have prophetic dreams, feelings of someone ill or dying (they prove to be true). Mental telepathy with my sister, children, husband and close friends. They always take me seriously. I have seen and communicated with people who are dead. My grandmother was crippled. On the night she died, she appeared to me standing straight and tall. She had that Mona Lisa smile and I knew where she was. I knew she was experiencing what I had and that our knowledge was now one. Another loved one appeared to me after his death. This was a different experience in that he was ill and suffering. He was begging me for help. I prayed intensely for him and finally he appeared again (months later) with *The Smile*."

Nina Cotton, Sierra Vista, Arizona:

> "I watched a man disappear by parts in broad daylight (head and shoulders, hips and legs, and then torso). He later reappeared as a guest on a television show I was watching. I sometimes see people in places they have no business being. How about a cross of lights floating across the sky and landing, guided by stars?"

TGST Harry Dennis USAF (Retired), Champaign, Illinois:

> "I got to see the world's future and my own future during my experience. I now recognize events and situations as what was played out before, what was revealed to me. I know people, events and places which should be strange. I have prophetic dreams, usually about two months in advance of the event."

Sharon K. Bores, Tucson, Arizona:

> "My father had a heart attack 2,500 miles away from me, and I felt it, and responded to him. I predicted my niece's and my god-child's deaths. I can feel when harm or sickness comes to a loved one in my own body. People have drained me of all my energy until I learned how to protect myself. I have through a very *scary* experience realized I have healing powers, by healing a woman of terminal brain cancer."

Legend and folk tales from throughout history, including sacred texts, claim anyone who survives death is gifted with strange powers of healing. Although this is not true of all survivors, it does seem true of many. The movie *Resurrection*, with Ellen Burstyn, clearly illustrates the joy and frustration of what happens when a near-death survivor suddenly discovers the power to heal without any explanation of why or how it happened, where it came from, or what is to be done with it. There is no easy way to handle this ability, as the main character in the movie comes to realize, much to her grief. The movie ends with the woman, Edna, fleeing an adoring public, who, without meaning to, would destroy her. She hides out in the desert at a roadside gas station and assumes a different identity, redirecting her ability into gardening and occasional "miracles." Edna shows us how fickle is fame and how empty is the "giving of gifts." Too many people want a quick fix and cry for miracles rather than having the courage to learn how to change their negative attitudes and heal themselves.

The issue of being a healer is important to survivors because it affects so many. Since most readily respond when there is need, usually feeling "led" to do so, they are prey to all kinds of misunderstandings and misfortune; and, all too often, such is the outcome of their human- itarian gestures. Survivors would do well to remember genuine or natural gifts and abilities can be improved and enhanced by training. Control and appropriate usage can be taught. The gift of healing is no exception.

Survivors who feel they have such a skill or consider themselves "channels" of healing energy would be wise to learn the dynamics involved. Faith is great, but it is even stronger when undergirded by knowledge and demonstra- tion. The process of helping to heal others can be a fright- ening responsibility, especially when you become aware of the incredible power available, how that power might be channeled or used, and what kind of connection you may or may not have with God. One woman in Canada was very troubled that she might become another Kathryn Kuhlman (a famous healer who is now deceased), and she considered that to be a curse. Sometimes our inner sense of direction and our inner awareness are developed enough to teach us what we need to know, but for the majority, help is needed in the way of books, classes, training, and teachers.

That necessary guidance, training, and study also ap- plies to the mysterious realm of psychic phenomena, for, like it or not, almost all near-death experiencers encounter this diffused arena either with new or enhanced abilities. It is as if dying opened a door that will not close. Said one survivor from Cincinnati, Ohio, "My psychic ability has skyrocketed." Another person described being very busy receiving "guidance" and "instructions" for innovative new dance steps and dance therapy techniques from a teacher on "The Other Side." A woman from Clearwater, Florida, went on to recount sixty-five years of unusual psychic events that followed her early near-death trau- ma, including physical manifestation of beings from "The Other Side," surviving death twice more, and being privy to scenes of how the world was created. Often survivors will look up into the sky and see strange objects or movements, even in broad daylight. Common are claims of people who are now prophetic and accurately so, of people who are easily able to pass back and forth between dimensions, or

live in several concurrently. Many survivors speak of discovering there are no limits in life and no need to erect any.
One woman reported kinetic experiences before and after
her surgery, where objects flew around the room and glass
shattered; and now, long after her experience, light bulbs,
bowls, or ashtrays will still break if she gets angry.

Interpretations and understandings may vary but what
happens doesn't. Most near-death experiencers automatically become more intuitive, exhibiting unusual abilities
and attracting unusual "activities." Desire and willingness seem to make no difference, nor does acceptance, as
in the case of a man who was very religious and a staunch
conservative. He begged to be told he was not psychic
because such things were against his religion. He was
psychic, however, and becoming even more so, much to his
horror.

There is no avoiding psychism.

This can be a nightmare for someone who has no idea
what is going on or who does not realize how *normal* this is.
Such new abilities and awarenesses can easily be misin-
terpreted, leading to claims of "special gifts from God" or
charges of "working with the devil" when, in fact, what is
really happening is probably more a typical result of expanded consciousness than anything else. Some survivors
go on incredible ego trips believing themselves "chosen"
and in the name of God spread a confused doctrine that
tends to be more judgmental and self-righteous than loving
and forgiving. Then, there are those accused of witchcraft
who relay dismal stories—like the woman who was forced
by her family into rigid therapy because they were convinced she had become a witch. Survivors have been beat-
en, harassed, ignored, threatened, and cursed just because
they displayed psychic abilities they could not explain.
Even scientific near-death groups avoid public discussion
of any possible connection between near-death and psychic activity as if such a reference would condemn or
nullify their credibility.

**I have not found that the near-death experience
makes a person into someone unrelated to the former
self, but I have found that it will invariably enhance and**

enlarge whatever potentials were already existent within that individual, however dormant or litte developed those potentials were.

Thus, experiencers now claiming to be psychic were probably psychic before or at least had the potential for such development. The near-death episode *did not make them psychic*, intuitive, prophetic, or anything else, but it did expand the potential for those abilities so suddenly and unexpectedly it seemed as if the impossible had occurred. *These people became "more" of what they already were.* I had many such abilities myself and a full decade of intense training in altered states of consciousness before my death experiences ever happened, yet all this did *not* prepare me for the overwhelming magnitude of what I went through, *nor* did my former training exempt me from the aftermath. Becoming "more" of what you already are is not necessarily a blessing—certainly not at first.

It maybe helpful to know that for the first time in history the American Psychiatric Association's *Diagnostic and Statistical Manual of Mental Disorders (DSM-III)*, which was approved and came into use in 1979, makes a distinction between people who are genuinely psychic and people who are genuinely disordered. Psychism does not deserve the bad press it has received and discovering you are psychic is nothing to be ashamed of. Such ability is natural to some degree and is more akin to breathing than riding a broomstick.

Survivors usually become quite sensitive to their surroundings and to other people. Everything expands while taste, texture, sounds, and feelings become unusually acute. Some sensitize even to the point of becoming empaths, taking into themselves the pain, feelings, illnesses, joys, and conditions of others. Christy Donovan of Bennett, Colorado, reported:

> "Last year, there was a little boy lost in the mountains. They found his body ten days after he got lost. During those days, I *physically* grieved for that boy—not just that he died but for the emotional suffering he went through before he died."

This absorption of what goes on around them takes on the appearance of overreacting. For one woman this became such a problem that she finally had to quit her position as an emergency room nurse. A former police officer noted the same difficulty; he could no longer shield himself emotionally or disassociate from the misery and grief which went on around him while on the job. Such people start out feeling in the same personal control as before, but quickly learn from their reactions to the condition of their fellows and from their environment that they have changed. They become living sponges, absorbing instead of discerning, joining instead of withdrawing, duplicating instead of observing. They merge with forces external to them instead of remaining separated and self-contained. Usually, this hypersensitivity will lessen as time passes or may even fade altogether but, until it does, the individual may have to make career changes and other adjustments to insure a reasonable lifestyle and self-protection.

Music changes for the average survivor, sometimes radically. Most develop a fascination with it as if a love of music becomes a natural component to death's survival. But they search for sounds which bring to mind the haunting memory of "unearthly" chords. Sometimes referring to it as heavenly music or music of the spheres, they compare it more to a rich, permeating vibration than to anything sung or created through instrumentation. Because of the lingering memory of this unusual music, experiencers are most often drawn to melodious, classical pieces, reaching heightened states of enjoyment while listening. Even though earth music is no substitute for what was heard while on "The Other Side," uplifting, flowing renditions can help to satisfy that deep longing, that certain emptiness that comes after being revived. As one person put it, "I cry when I hear some types of music or see emotional scenes." Or as Dorothy Marie Dedels of Lucan, Ontario, Canada, said:

> "I almost collapse when I hear some types of music. There are sacred, classical, and semi-classical that will start tears coursing down my cheeks until I

> sob. Music awakens in me the greatest wonder and joy.
> All the greatest of God washes through me and around
> me. I am flooded and immersed and I want to go on
> forever."

Invariably, survivors turn away from harsh music like rock
or anything excessively loud and brassy. One man can no
longer tolerate any form of earth music, claiming it all so
much noise compared to what he heard during his
experience.

      Expanded intuition and sensitivity are commonplace
after death's survival. It is interesting and sometimes sad
to note which people sharpen their new or expanded abilities and integrate them into normal daily routines, and
which either disregard such abilities or claim nothing like
that ever happened. The stigma of possible psychism can
be hard to overcome.

A Shifted or Changed View of Physical Reality, Becoming More Detached, Objective, Seeing "Through" Events and Problems with a Notice-able Reduction of Fears and Worries.
How are you
going to return to what now seems petty comings and
goings once you have experienced a perfect world and a
greater reality?

      Can you imagine what it would be like to suddenly find
yourself in another dimension or world where, like some
kind of god, you had all knowledge, all peace, all love, all
light, all freedom, all joy? Even just being able to float out of
your physical body and soar like a bird, free and unhampered, stretches the mind. You never forget it. You can't. It
leaves a mark deep and profound. Even those survivors who
staunchly insist life for them is now as normal and sane as
always, keep their experience tucked safely away inside
their heart of hearts, pulling it out for inspiration when
times get rough. Some keep the memory alive by reviewing
it over and over, or seeking out stories from other survivors, or hunting new audiences for the retelling of their
tale.

      Of interest is the fact that those who usually cling
most to their experience are for the most part those people

who cannot or will not change their lifestyle to correspond with their new understandings and insights. Such individuals usually resist or avoid significant changes as much as possible. Remembering and retelling seems to renew their vigor and give them courage.

This is not true, however, for those who strike out from former patterns of living and experiment with the world at large, exploring whatever might be found. Those more adventurous, or perhaps "driven" types, are more apt to put new awarenesses to work by testing them out in society; and, in so doing, they are much less protective of what they experienced and are less inclined to give it much attention. In essence, these survivors have decided to live what they learned rather than just "replay" the memory of it. Both types usually go through a period of evangelism, wanting the "Good News" spread to help save humanity from its own ignorance; and almost all, to one degree or another, do go through some kind of process where life and its living is rediscovered and redefined. It's just that after this initial stage, there is a marked difference in the way each type deals with his or her circumstances. While one cuts loose, the other pulls back.

Usually by the fourth year after recovery, the average experiencer will reassess the original decision to accept or reject the experience. Was it wise or wasn't it? Should the search be continued for a better way to live or is it best to settle down?

During this questioning, former stereotypes and traditions, rules and prejudices, goals and achievements are challenged, or become like so much garbage. As one survivor laughingly put it, "People are so foolish. They get upset over nothing at all and live their lives as if they were half asleep." The near-death experience brings with it an enlarged perspective, a broader view, and a basis of comparison not present before.

Because of this altered viewpoint, personalities can alter too, sometimes markedly. Survivors can become so different even their looks can change, making them appear as another person, even a stranger. Before and after photographs can be somewhat or very different. As our mind changes, so does the way we look. Such switches of character traits and appearance can be disconcerting to family and friends, creating either a nightmare or an opportunity, depending on how willing all parties concerned are in dealing with the situation.

Because our society expects men to be tough, aggressive, unemotional, and ambitious, personality changes with them are usually more noticeable than with women, although a woman's change is every bit as important. Here are some examples:

TGST Harry Dennis:

> "Before my near-death experience, I was a complete fighting man. I believed that if there was trouble in a part of the world, and they needed us, then we should go and help them out, no questions asked. But now, I believe arms and fighting will maybe settle the problem for the moment, but that isn't the way. Love is the answer to all the world's problems."

John Barnard:

> "I used to get all fired up on political issues, local and national, but they don't seem to be so important now. I take a calmer, more rational viewpoint instead of my totally conservative, loyal, all-American one. I can't seem to get myself irate or fuming angry about things not being done as promised, like the car not being ready at the garage, the plumber not showing up on time, the repairman not keeping his word, etc. They just don't seem to be that important any more."

John W. Baccarini:

> "I get more response (love) now. I am honest with people and with myself. Before, I was a self-centered person and got little or no response. My moral values changed drastically and I have a much closer relationship with God."

Bob Pinansky, Mesa, Arizona:

> "I have mellowed, from a tough businessman to a milder personality."

Dr. Patrick Gallagher, Palmdale, California:

"All the clothes I now wear have been gifts to me over the past several years. When I left Venezuela, I left virtually everything I owned there—books, clothing, cameras, and a few souvenirs and artifacts and so on; and they remain there without causing me any grief I can identify as mine... I seldom make any plans more advanced in time or need than a visit to the bathroom. Each conversation is invariably the best one I've ever had, for it is living, as yet unended, replete with authorship, possible plots ... I now seem to gradually be getting far more attention and love and approval from one and all, including many of those quite worried at first because I didn't have a hell of an office, a secretary, and my glittering Phi Beta Kappa key in focus at the right place on my vest."

In early 1983, I walked into a local Manpower Employment Agency to apply for part-time work. Back in Idaho I had often accepted Manpower assignments and enjoyed their concept of "temporaries" tremendously, but the Virginia office insisted I be tested first. They said it was a new rule. The test was in three parts—dictation and transcription, multiple-choice office questions, and a psychological quiz: the first two were timed, the third open-ended. "Don't concern yourself with the psychological quiz," I was told, "for there is no way you can flunk it." Scores ran from C-1 (someone who needs constant supervision and cannot be left alone) to C-4 (a self-starting achiever). With my résumé everyone thought I would test out a high C-4. I barely made C-2.

As it was explained to me, my scores on the first two parts were high but I had indeed "flunked" the third. According to them, those psychological questions were designed to measure the amount of stress a person stores in his or her body and since I no longer store stress but dissolve it fairly easily I had "blown" the test. This was funny—for a while. But whenever I checked in for an assignment they would claim "business is slow and we've received no call for workers," yet I met three other women who applied and tested after me and were given work right away, the very kind of work I had applied for. I quit laughing when it became clear to me that those test results had branded me unemployable. My solution was to start my own business. If I was no longer employable, then I would employ myself.

Eventually, most survivors develop the ability to see "through" worries, fears, problems, and conflicts. Even when considering their own personal history, they are often amazed at how quickly and easily all the puzzle pieces fit together and how life's paradoxes begin to make sense. One father remarked how the reason for the death of a cherished young daughter is now clear and he can understand why she came and why she left so soon. This greater objectivity and detached viewpoint allows an individual to recognize cycles, patterns, and symbolic interpretations of events. It is as if we used to view life from the level of a "mud puddle" but now we can see life from the vantage point of "mountaintops." Because of such changed vision, survivors are usually slow to anger or to get excited; petty irritations or conflicts seem almost nonexistent, and what were once significant problems and stumbling blocks now become opportunities for growth and change.

As wonderful and desirable as such changes of behavior may seem, as with anything else, they can go too far, masking concerns that really need more specific attention. Even if it does not seem so, survivors can and do worry, fear, anger, get depressed, and have problems—just as anyone else does but, unlike others, they seldom get overinvolved or negative for too long. Because they tend to see panoramas instead of details, they can appear wiser and more spiritual than they really are. It takes more than a broader viewpoint to make a saint. *Death's survivors have no exclusive rights to heaven just because they think they've been there.*

There is also a marked decrease in materialistic needs and wants. Since survivors are usually more concerned with helping their fellows than collecting dollars, they may wind up in counseling roles whether or not such was their intention. Yet even though money and possessions seem of less importance, I couldn't help but notice how affluent

and prosperous, confident and self-sufficient they appear.
When I asked more questions, a pattern emerged: if materialistic and driving before, they tended to become much
less after; if unmaterialistic and disinterested before, they
often became suddenly ambitious, goal-oriented, and more
materialistic after (materialistic in the sense of the "novelty" of ownership).

Near-death seems to level out a person's personality,
surfacing undeveloped or latent characteristics that lend
more balance to the life. I noticed that those who were
the busiest and most productive before usually became
slower and less involved after, while those whose lives were
more routine and uneventful before often returned with a
driving hunger for knowledge, stimulation, and a better
station in life.

If you were fast before you usually became slow after. If
you were slow before you usually became fast after. Pendulum swings seem to depend more on needs of the individual involved than on any uniform "magic" transforming
all survivors into nice, quiet, gentle followers of God.

Death's trauma is a catalytic event where everything
known, said, done, or believed gets shaken, rattled, sifted
around, and shifted to another position. It is the cocoon
from which a new butterfly may emerge. We now have a
basis of comparison and the right to begin again—although not everyone does. A survivor can refuse to change,
and some do just that—they remain virtually unscathed.
As one redneck truck driver from Macon, Georgia, said,
"The only thing my experience did for me was show me not
to fear death, so I don't. Other than that, I'm the same as
always." And the same as always for him meant just as hard-
drinking, hard-living, bad-mouthed, and scurrilous as ever.

Because of shifted belief systems, average survivors
appear filled to overflowing with new revelations as they
seek out other sources to verify what they learned, turning
most often to areas such as quantum physics, transpersonal psychology, the works of Tesla and Einstein, comparative religion, transformation, and human potential
movements. Others turn to traditional sources to find

multidimensional levels of truth. As Peggy Adams Raso said, "Heaven is not up and hell is not down. They are all *here*."

Experiencers speak of the soul's entry into the physical body around the time of birth and at death the soul simply leaves the body and goes on with its travels. The impact of this realization, even considering possible exceptions, is immensely freeing and joyful, helping to make life more sensible and spiritual existence more valid.

Most have a certain lightness and sense of fun about them yet they are intensely curious and determined in that curiosity. Since they are often able to understand and perform in areas beyond any previous training or expertise, they face frustration in not having acceptable credentials to prove they know what they know. Because of their broader view, they are perfect in fields such as marketing, mediation, and arbitration, but they are usually passed over or pushed aside to avoid embarrassing other employees.

And therein lies a conflict.

Even if an opportunity did come along where the average survivor could share his or her wealth of ideas and thoughts, little if anything would come of it; not just because such input would cause problems with other employees, but rather because nine chances out of ten the survivor would not be understood. *Along with the marked increase in knowledge, insight, and vision comes a marked decrease in abilities to verbalize clearly, organize efficiently, and concentrate a focus.*

Just when the survivor has the most to say, he or she usually lacks the ability to say it. It is almost as if the right-brain expanded while the left-brain contracted; hence, the survivor scatters energy in all directions, hardly knowing where to begin or what to do first. Their speeches do not always make sense, the material they write is often not worth reading. Ideas abound but the ability to express effectively does not.

Restlessness comes.

The frustrating discouragement of trying to bring back

to earth the treasures of heaven does more to silence survivors than being criticized or ignored.

A Different Feeling of Physical Self, a Certain Detachment from the Body and Any Identification with it as "Self," Rather a Knowing We Live in or "Wear" Our Bodies. St. Teresa of Avila, the great Spanish mystic and reformer, said, "After you die, you wear what you are." The near-death experience makes clear to all who survive that the human body and the human soul are *not* one in the same. The body and its ego identity slough off with death but the "I" we are continues, more alive, more vital than encapsulation inside a physical body could have ever allowed. When the experiencer revives, that realization remains.

Few survivors are relieved to find themselves once again inhabiting their well-worn, familiar bodies of solid substance. The vast majority feel more as if they have been resentenced to prison, for that shell of their former residence now feels somehow small, tight, confining, uncomfortable, clumsy, unnatural. They feel alienated—from the very body that had nourished the formation of their personal identity since birth. They now know *they are not their body!* They feel boxed in.

Invariably, survivors come to describe their physical bodies in abstract, more objective and detached terms as if it were a garment they wear or a house they reside in. Some even joke about the particular style and model of "jacket" they wear, fantasizing other designs that might be fun to try such as a classy bronze job or one of those black numbers with short curly hair. Racial issues lose all meaning and gender becomes insignificant. For some, this detachment eventually fades as years pass, giving in to social pressures of "name, rank, and serial number" and "of course you are your body" but by far the largest percentage continue to view their body differently, even after they have finally come to terms with it. One woman put it quite matter-of-factly, "My body is something I put up with. It's

the baggage I carry on my trip through life and whatever I
need to survive is packed inside."

Another woman was so caught up with her new concept of physical self that when introduced to a stranger, she
blurted out, "My goodness but it is so nice to meet the body
you are wearing this time around."

I've noticed near-death experiencers usually have a
feeling or knowing that the soul evolves and grows through
various cycles, often taking lifetimes to expand on its
experience and learning. They talk about reincarnation as
if it were an established fact and, almost to a person,
mention a *life plan* and speak of how our lives follow
rhythmic cycles of development. Survivors actually lose all
fear of death for they know it ends nothing but the physical
body and its personality facade.

Changes in the physical body itself can occur *besides*
those normally resulting from any health problems, illness, or accident that might have caused the death event.
These changes are varied and can include such things as
an unusual brightness to the eyes, a special glow around
the person, a unique sensitivity to the skin (even skin tone
changes and decreased sun tolerance), a reversal of inner
clocks such as a nocturnal person reverting to daylight and
vice versa, heightened sensations of taste-touch-texture,
increased allergies. I've heard so many survivors express
alarm about their new sensitivities, especially to drugs and
medical compounds, that they don't know what they will do
if help is needed or to whom they might turn for assistance.
"I am now allergic to any medications," one states. "This
body of mine is still my weakest link," says Dorothy Marie
Dedels, and, "Although I am fifty-two years and some, my
skin is unwrinkled and glows." Peggy Adams Raso explains,
"My eyes have become extremely light sensitive. Now I am
severely allergic to the sun;" while Betty Preston reports, "I
often see halos around people. I am often told that I glow."
And Nina Cotton says her face has changed around the eyes
and she has acquired various allergies.

My own case is the same. Almost immediately after
reviving from "death," my skin would suddenly turn bright
orange with only brief exposure to sunlight. Although this

uncomfortable sensitivity has lessened over the years, people still comment on how my skin glows and how my eyes seem to twinkle. When I first discovered how allergic I had become, I was fearful but I turned what might have been a handicap into an advantage by thoroughly schooling myself in medical alternatives and non-chemical, more natural remedies. By emphasizing wellness and illness prevention, I was able to take charge of my own situation and insure proper care whenever needed. Today, there are many practitioners of wellness and a growing number of holistic clinics where people of limited tolerance levels may go for more reasonable non-invasive treatment.

There are cases of survivors who report a physical force field or energy shield that seems to surround them. One man was attacked twice by men wielding knives, once on the street and once at his job as a counselor. In each instance, the knives suddenly deflected or broke within one foot of his body as if they had struck an invisible wall. Both attackers were so shocked they screamed and ran, leaving the man just as surprised and without any explanation as to what could have caused the phenomenon. He did say he could feel the presence of some kind of "force" protecting him at the moment each knife hit it. One woman noted structural changes in her hands, especially with her fingers. The distance between finger joints had mysteriously lengthened, and she had before and after hand-prints to prove it.

It is difficult to establish a connection between the near-death experience and any sudden, subtle, or unexplainable change in the survivor's body because of the absence of verifiable documentation; but one consistently obvious physical change everyone agrees with is that they look and feel *younger*. Years seem to roll away as a relaxed happiness comes. These people are quick to laugh, are more casual and laid back; if they get upset, and they certainly do, negative effects wear off and leave little or no imprint, just as if it were all so much water off a duck's back.

This is probably more a result of attitudinal and philosophical changes accompanying the experience than any physical causation, for the outer body can reflect the inner mind. I have noticed that those survivors who exhibit the fewest or no physical changes are usually those who had the least or no disruption in their belief system and view of reality, while those survivors who report the most physical changes are usually the ones whose experiences were more intense and impactual, profoundly shifting their worldview and thought processes.

Some become infused with boundless energy, but many others return so weakened by what happened and drained by increased allergies and sensitivities, especially to heat and cold, that they suffer relapses and more illness or become accident prone. There are those who continue to endure additional near-death scenarios or close brushes with death during additional health breakdowns. Certainly healing takes time, strength can ebb and flow, but I suspect something else may be responsible for any lingering weakness—and that is a lessening of the desire to live. It is a temptation to return to "The Other Side." Any struggle to live can appear meaningless or unnecessary. It would be so easy to go back. This temptation can linger, even for years, slowing full recovery.

What keeps us here is a sense of mission, a knowledge we have something more to learn, a job to do, or a task yet to perform, and somehow we must get on with it. Eventually the will to leave truly becomes the will to stay, and health is regained. That sense of mission is coupled with awareness of a Divine or Greater Plan and our integral part in it, no matter how insignificant or mundane such a part may be. So we drag around our bodies until confidence and strength return and we can feel reunited again within ourselves.

As time passes, the jacket we wear again feels snug and comfortable, like an old friend we almost forgot. Respect for our body returns.

Difficulty with Communication and Relationships, Finding it Hard to Say What is Meant or to Understand Language Phrasing Used by Others.
There are two main shocks the typical survivor contends with:

1. *being revived,* which means exiting a dimension of more intense involvement, and
2. *waking up to reality,* which means realizing "here" is not the same as "there."

The space-time between shock one and shock two constitutes a "honeymoon" of detached innocence, necessary, I believe, to allow the human psyche and supporting life systems a chance to readjust. This honeymoon period is like a shock absorber, a womb-like reentry phase when date, input, sensations, feelings, thoughts, insights, all toss and jump around until some kind of pattern or sense of order can be established.

During this honeymoon paradox is the only standard. The familiar is now foreign, the foreign is now familiar. It is a period of knowing but not knowing who you are and where you fit in the scheme of things. What is, isn't, and what isn't, is. Rationale of any kind is no longer rational, the world is the same, but you aren't. This honeymoon, this phase of a certain numb vagueness yet clear, insightful perception, can last hours, days, months, or even years. Until that second shock occurs, the survivor may appear mentally ill or brain-damaged when neither is the case.

Assuming mental imbalance when none actually exists can promote such imbalance.

If a survivor somehow escapes psychiatric commitment, he or she is often branded a freak or eccentric by society, which can lead to further alienation instead of integration.

This honeymoon phase can be positive or negative depending on the particular survivor's response to what happened and to treatment afterwards. Normally, the survivor who had a positive experience becomes more optimistic and relaxed later, while someone who had a negative experience tends to become pessimistic or exhibits a need to cling to life. This, however, does not always hold true. For example, negative experiencers can learn and grow so much from what happened that they emerge as positive, inspiring members of society. Conversely, a positive experiencer, even one who claimed to have seen Christ, can become so paranoid, frightened, depressed, and withdrawn, no one can tolerate his or her behavior. I have long since learned it is not so much the experience itself which is so important, regardless of what kind of experience it was, but how the survivor responds to it and the climate of adjustment afterwards. In other words, *it is not the event but the response to it which counts*!

Ramona Harris of Waynesboro, Virginia, reports "My worldview and personal philosophy are continually changing as I grow and experience more."

Christie Donovan says:

> "I feel different from other people—like I have a different goal than most. I seem to be able to understand emotions behind why people do the things they do . . . Honestly, this is one of the craziest parts—it seems like everyone depends on me emotionally. They seem to sense that I understand their inner motives. Sometimes I become very overwhelmed with other people's problems—with no one to fully understand mine."

And Colleen Anspach of Kalamazoo, Michigan, states:

> "I was fifteen when it all happened and everyone who doesn't know me thinks I look fifteen years younger than I am—no matter how old I get. I was just a child and I went through Hell. I am tough. I am a fighter. It made me strong mentally and as strong as I could be physically."

The survivor needs help, but the survivor usually doesn't know it.

Family, friends, and business associates often add additional pressure instead of giving assistance.

Survivors are not always able to differentiate between a positive or a negative situation, so they often remain involved rather than strike out on their own or express a need for change.

Near-death experiencers who were once ambitious and power-driven are now relaxed and altruistic, those who were once self-centered and temperamental are now lovingly kind and gentle, those who were once scientifically precise and detailed are now intuitive and emotional, and those who were once docile and weak-willed are now assertive and buoyantly enthusiastic. These switches of basic behavior modes are so typical they constitute the norm.

How can you resume business as usual when you are no longer the same person?

What we are discussing here is a significantly deep change in basic values and personal characteristics. The survivor changes frequencies while his or her family remain on the same wavelength as before. This can strain communications, sometimes to the breaking point. It is as if the survivor suddenly becomes fluent in Icelandic while everyone is still speaking Japanese. Language nuances fade and diplomacy is meaningless. Blunt words blurt out, events are seen for what they really are, keen ears hear what is meant rather than what is said. It is the behavior of a child, a kind of innocence which views everything as here and now and responds directly and honestly. Language skills do improve with effort and patience, but much of the conceptual framework behind language can distort. As one survivor put it, "I feel so helpless to have all this knowledge in me and not have any way to express it." And another reported "I am developing my non-verbal understandings of people and am much more in touch with feelings and non-rational forms of knowledge."

Others describe similar feelings:

Olga S. Jensen:

> "I have trouble putting my ideas into words. My mind doesn't seem as sharp as before. I have trouble remembering words, simple everyday vocabulary."

Dottie Bush:

> "I am tolerant of others, but I am no longer much interested in discussing trivial matters, and so, consequently, I talk less and listen more and this tends to 'rattle' people used to my talking a lot and they are unable to understand my changed response."

Pamela Ericson:

> "The sad part is that the older I get, the harder it is to try to explain or convince someone how it really is."

Dr. Patrick Gallagher:

> "I am enchanted by the mystery and grace of those I encounter . . . I was, of course, thrilled by the possibilities of actual, brand-new speech; and the conversation possible with total strangers in various restaurants in Berkeley transfixed me daily for hours that ended too soon . . . Communication is now simpler, easier and more pleasant for me than it ever was before."

Inner and outer environments heighten and expand. *Everything becomes more of itself*, exceeding previous norms; hence, any problem that was tolerated before now becomes unbearably exaggerated, while anything that was pleasant before now becomes incredibly meaningful and wonderful. This is especially true of marriages. Marginal ones become real problems afterwards, while successful ones become deeper and more loving. Even though many survivors go on to divorce, quit their jobs, drift, and play musical chairs with life, questioning whether or not they could ever become a marriage partner again, just as many others stay put, dig in, and discover new depths of meaning and joy right where they are. Either way, survivors discover more and the depths of more still. The near-death experience does not cause anything in and of itself except a shift in perceptions—but that shift has a ripple effect, reaching out to touch all aspects of living.

Joe Geraci:

> "I believe it is more difficult for those closest to me, my wife and children, to respond to me as I am now. They will acknowledge I have changed. I think it is frustrating for them to know I have changed, yet to witness some of my behavior which may be less than positive. I am expected to be above anger and beyond unhappiness. It took some time after my experience to accept being human again. It may take longer for them to accept my 'human' behavior."

Sharon K. Bores:

> "Relationships seem more intense, but only last a short time. I have no problem communicating but have found that others cannot accept things as they are. I

feel that everyone lives in a fantasy world, and I am the realist outcast."

Certainly, after the two main shocks are over and it is back to life as usual, old habits can be re-adopted. Cultural "shoulds" and "shouldn'ts" can return along with role playing and social "performances." Oftentimes, survivors become impatient and critical of others, feeling in some way better, and losing in that smugness the ability to understand the weakness and the fear people around them still deal with.

Some survivors label their near-death experiences a dream and seem to forget it. Many cannot or will not integrate what happened, suppressing any constructive or beneficial change it could foster. Still others successfully make the integration, immeasurably enriching their lives because of it. This latter group tend to stand out in a crowd with a kind of "glow" around them; but there are a few, called the "core group," whose near-death experience was so intense and so impactual that life "as always" is impossible. These are the ones who take the biggest risks, striking out like the babes they are, sometimes drifting, sometimes wandering aimlessly through minds and miles, bereft of former paradigms or models, willing to experiment and explore other facets of living. Their story is both inspirational and heart-rending as they form part of a new vanguard in society, and are forever changed because of it. They challenge accepted definitions of what constitutes "human" behavior.

Once you have experienced being one with the universe nothing less is of much interest. But all too often, instead of sharing this insight in practical, focused terms so others may benefit, some survivors drift into disconnected indulgences and, without realizing it, become what they claim is no longer important—selfish! They drift further and further into themselves, achieving little more than starry-eyed wonder, while their spiritual insights and uncanny psychic skills are often reduced to ramblings.

Certainly, self-awareness and self-development are necessary. How else will you ever come to understand your newness and relate again to your environment? But that quest for self-discovery too easily leads to an obsessive form of escapism and self-concern. At some point in the process, the survivor needs once more to accept and respect others, sharing and exchanging information on a more equal basis.

Just because others are drawn to you seeking counsel and wisdom does not mean you really *know* what you know or that you have anything truly worthwhile to say. Anyone can mouth "Love will solve all the world's problems," but few are those willing to get off their posteriors to do anything about it.

Change is the only constant in life and growth is the only true challenge.

Here is one fellow experiencer, Arthur E. Yensen, expressing his idea of what life's greatest goal really is:

> "HAPPINESS! Otherwise there would be no point in living. But if we look for happiness, it will elude us like a will-o-the-wisp. The hardest and most important lesson we have to learn is that cheerfulness is our greatest virtue, and that the happiest we'll ever be is while we are helping someone else. It is true that if we look after others, God will look after us—and do a lot better job of it than we can."[5]

4

Spiritual
Implications

"To stop at mere assertion of the truth that God is love is not enough. Our thought of Him and of one another must be charged with it! What profit is there in vain repetitions of the verity that God is Good, if we do not do honor to that Good in our intentions? Who of us, by simply standing on a Bible, can stretch himself to heaven? And who can fly thereto with wings he's fabricated of its pages?"

Reverend Gene Emmet Clark

After discovering death isn't, comes the discovery God is.

Most survivors fall head over heels in love with God.

During their experience they were bathed in God, immersed in God, filled to overflowing with God; and they returned convinced of God. Doubt may be a tool of science but it means nothing to a survivor. They have no doubt. They have discovered God. They *know* God is.

Previous beliefs or lack of them, devotee or atheist, make no difference whatever. The vast majority of near-death survivors come to the same conclusion: *God is real.* God is no joke, no myth, no fairy story. God is *not* a product of any religion, philosophy, superstition, politics, or ploy. God is in all, through all, beyond all. God is, was, and will always be. And it makes no difference who believes or disbelieves. That doesn't change God. God's existence is not predicated on human acknowledgment.

This discovery brings with it an exhilarating freedom to walk and talk with God without reservation or restriction.

God becomes more personal and at the same time more universal. God becomes one and at the same time all. Paradox makes perfect sense for it becomes the language of "spirit."

Reference terms change. Traditional references to God such as Father, He, Him, or Mother, She, Her can become unacceptable for each is seen as a limitation or denial of the unlimited and unfathomable immensity of God. Preferred titles are ones such as The Force, The One, Universal Mind, The Source, All, The Divine—or just plain *God*.

Religious preferences usually change as well. Of the survivors in my research, one-third continued in a traditional religious setting. Even though some of these were members of or went on to join fundamentalist or charismatic groups (even becoming evangelists), most expressed the desire to remain where they were and quietly work to uplift and enrich the ministry of their present church.

The remaining two-thirds either cast aside religious affiliations or were never involved to begin with. For these people, awareness most often shifts from standards and dogmas to what is commonly called "the spiritual quest," a need for the personal experience of God. But, interestingly enough, even these eventually come to join or support some kind of organized, structured church or philosophy, sometimes starting up churches of their own. Popular choices are metaphysical and "New Age" churches or Eastern systems. Those who prefer a more natural or simple approach usually gravitate to philosophies such as mysticism or practices such as shamanism.

Regardless of religious or spiritual preferences, the average near-death survivor is more interested in what is historically called "The Mysteries" or "The Holy of Holies." They are more in tune with gnosis, that knowing behind and at the root of all things. Superficial or restrictive teachings turn them off. Because of this, heart-breaking conflicts can arise. Consider the case of a woman survivor in Alabama who is married to a fundamentalist Christian preacher. The two have been married many years, have three children and a busy, dedicated lifestyle. Since her experience, it has become increasingly difficult for her to attend her husband's church services:

> "He's wrong. I know now deep in my heart he's wrong. What he's preaching, that's not the way it is. I feel like he's telling everyone a lie and I don't know what to do about it. I love my husband and I love our children. I don't want to upset him or anyone else. I don't want a divorce or anything like that. But I can't listen anymore. I try to pretend I'm too busy to come."

Certainly, not everyone goes through a situation as stressful as the woman in Alabama, but many do. Differences in the issues of God and religion can put survivors at variance and at odds with their family, their community, and the prevailing social view.

Another example is the story of Ricky Bradshaw. I was at a meeting in 1984 where Ricky spoke about his near-death experience. The torso of his body had been literally cut in half when he was involved in a pedestrian/automobile accident in 1975. He was clinically dead for over an hour before any pulsebeat registered, and he went on to endure twenty-four surgeries in two years. His survival is one of the most miraculous in all medical history, and he was featured on the television series, "That's Incredible." Ricky co-founded the International Association for Near-Death Studies with Dr. Kenneth Ring and has been written about in several books. While dead, he had both an out-of-body experience and a near-death scenario, which was long and complex. He was given a choice during the scenario as to whether or not he wanted to return. When he chose yes, the "Being" in charge gave him as a gift the right to view evolution and history from beginning to end. Although he recalls some of what he was shown, most has been forgotten or he refuses to discuss it.

The talk he gave that day was inspiring and filled with love, as is Ricky. When it was over, however, a medical doctor in the audience asked how anyone might gain Ricky's degree of spiritual enlightenment without dying to do it. Ricky's answer was honest and insightful: "Having a near-death experience does *not* make you enlightened. It is an introduction, perhaps more a hindrance than a help!"

He went on to clarify "hindrance" as having to live with the knowledge that "here" is not the same as "there," that now he has a basis of comparison he did not have before. It is all too easy to get so wrapped up "remembering" that ordinary life loses its luster. Ricky has remarried and with his new wife has joined the Baha'i Faith, feeling it closer than anything else he has studied or heard of in furthering what he learned while on "The Other Side." The Baha'i Faith is very important to him as is his growing appreciation of the opportunity he now has to reach out to others and spread joy and love. Although Ricky is doing fine, his relatives do not understand his point of view nor do they appreciate his choices.

The near-death experience does not make anyone anything, but it does expand everything.

It is like being on a drug high in some ways, yet no drug high can compare to the vast breadth and lasting impact of the experience. The glimpse it gives, that peek at greater and higher realities, creates a craving or hunger for more— a spiritual hunger.

We survivors have somehow raided the Cosmic Cookie Jar and had a taste of its mysteries. Like the proverbial peanut, one taste is not enough.

That spiritual hunger opens many "doors" to many discoveries. One of them is the discovery that—*people who are not near-death survivors can have the same or similar experiences followed by the same after-effects!*

These *other people* have gone through some kind of transformational event or series of events which so deeply and traumatically affected them it is as if they "died" and were reborn. Referred to many times as "symbolic death," an emotional shock or illness or an accident can trigger it. It can be caused by a religious or spiritual "conversion," an unusual vision, a fast, or a drug reaction. It can be called such names as "Baptism by The Holy Spirit" or "Kundalini Breakthrough" or "Dying Unto Oneself" or being "Born Again." It makes no difference how termed or how caused, these transformational events can be so deeply impactual that it will seem as if one way of living and thinking ended while another began. As with everything else, *response* is really what determines whether or not such an event or series of events is positive or negative. Transformations this dramatic usually instill the same spiritual hunger as near-death for, at least in the symbolic sense, the individual involved did undergo a "death."

I would like to explore this wider-reaching phenomenon further by discussing the research of a man whose investigation of spiritual enlightenment paralleled my own research of the near-death experience. He was a Canadian medical doctor and psychiatrist. His research was conducted primarily during the closing years of the last century and first published in book form in 1901. One year later he died instantly from an accidental fall on the ice. I did not learn of his pioneering accomplishment until long after I had completed my own work and published my original findings. I find it interesting that he and I were born one hundred years apart and both began a similar quest to understand after experiencing a dramatic transformational event in our personal lives. We later turned our quest into research and wrote a book about it, with each of our books disclosing the repetitious behavior patterns of people who had undergone an experience as we did. Both books focused on *after-effects and implications.*

In Search of Cosmic Consciousness

Richard Maurice Bucke, a medical professional, began a rigorous research project on the subject of enlightenment and finally narrowed his study to fifty cases he believed to be genuine. These people seemed to have another kind of consciousness. They appeared to operate on a higher, more spiritual level of mind. He called this shift of mind "cosmic consciousness."

Of the fifty original cases in his study, he ascertained that fourteen of them had attained spiritual enlightenment. The remaining thirty-six were in various stages of partial development. His book was published under the title *Cosmic Consciousness.* It was intended as a review of his research; but as time passed, it became recognized as a pioneering effort that established spiritual enlightenment as an ongoing, progressive force throughout humanity and all history, rather than a static event for the selective few. Needless to say, his work was revolutionary.

In describing the pattern of growth, illumination, and aftermath of what he feels constitutes a "cosmic" person, he also described what appeared to me to be the universal experience of the average near-death survivor. So striking, in fact, were the correlations between his research and mine that I was both surprised and intrigued. Let me show you what I mean.

First of all, this is what he calls the universal pattern of breaking through into cosmic consciousness:

1. The subjective light.
2. The moral elevation.
3. The intellectual illumination.
4. The sense of immortality.
5. The loss of the fear of death.
6. The loss of the sense of sin.
7. The suddenness, instantaneousness of the awakening.
8. The previous character of the person—intellectual, moral, and physical.
9. The age of illumination.
10. The added charm of the personality so that men and women are strongly attracted to the person.
11. The transfiguration of the subject of the change as seen by others when the cosmic sense is actually present.

Now, let us take a better look at this pattern and Dr. Bucke's explanation (not exact quotes—edited for brevity):

1. *The subjective light.* This brilliant, blinding flash was sometimes described as rose colored or as a flame but in most cases no color was given. He noted that in many cases the entire environment surrounding the individual involved would ex-

pand in size and brightness, and colors would take on unearthly hues and brilliance.

2. *The moral elevation.* Without exception once illumination had ceased, the individual involved would become extremely and unusually moral and upright, shunning forever any temptation to judge or criticize another, or be less than honest and fair, or to in any way take advantage of another. In a majority of cases, the individual refused to marry, feeling a greater duty and service to God and humanity.

3. *The intellectual illumination.* During the experience all things are made known, all knowledge is given, all secrets of the universe are revealed. The individual feels no weight, is overwhelmed by total and complete love, often encounters glowing Beings who give instructions, the "Word of God" is seen or felt, the oneness of all things is shown. The experience is compared to being reborn, a union of the soul with God.

4. *The sense of immortality.* Thinking is replaced by knowing. The individual comes to realize his or her divine identity and the fact that there is only life, life which varies by degree of vibration and ascension. This illumination brings the knowledge that salvation of any kind is not necessary, that we are all immortal and divine from "The Beginning," and that we are all gods in the making, Co-Creators with The One God.

5. *The loss of the fear of death.* Death loses all meaning and relevance. The individual now *knows* death does not end anything. Some individuals explained that death is like a birth into another plane or level of life, and that birth into this plane is like death from the other; that death itself is nothing but a change of awareness.

6. *The loss of the sense of sin.* With the experience comes an understanding of evil as simply good misused, that all things are good in God's eyes and there is no evil. Some individuals spoke of the

potential for misusing good as being present in everyone, that we are all capable of anything we choose.

7. *The suddenness, instantaneousness of the awakening.* Although some of the people involved were actively seeking enlightenment or "Baptism of the Holy Spirit," the actual moment of illumination was always unexpected and quite sudden, as if in a flash. Some remained in that state for minutes or hours, while others were transfixed overnight or for several days. Dr. Bucke was well informed about the various methods used in India for inducing this illumination, and he was not impressed. He thought the difference between induced cosmic consciousness and the naturally occurring state that happened on its own was in the aftermath with the natural version producing a more permanent, productive desire to uplift humanity on a grand scale. The only Indian guru who he felt achieved genuine illumination was Ramakrishna Paramahansa.

8. *The previous character of the person—intellectual, moral and physical.* Most experiencers were morally upright and unusually intelligent to begin with and often had strong bodies and strong wills. There were several who were more sickly and died young, but most went on after their illumination to live long, productive lives. Some of these people seemed born with genius but expanded their abilities far more afterwards, and went on to excel in many fields.

9. *The age of illumination.* In all cases the event came when the person was more mature, usually between thirty-three and forty-two years of age. Some had several breakthroughs, and all went on to experience revelation after revelation once their initial illumination was complete. The majority of cases experienced their breakthroughs in springtime, early summer, or the first few months of the calendar year.

10. *The added charm of the personality so that men and women are strongly attracted to the person.* Illuminated individuals become so magnetic that other people and animals are drawn to them. They seem to have divine protection and can walk where no other dares without danger. Their countenance affects people instantly. They do not pass unnoticed and are not forgotten. Animals are at ease in their presence.

11. *The transfiguration of the subject of the change as seen by others when the cosmic sense is actually present.* There was a marked change in appearance of each person afterwards. They would seem to glow and have a light around them. All were somehow physically changed, as if they had become another person. Their faces looked different. They seemed to be more of themselves, greater somehow.

Bucke went on to say that the vast majority of people he studied turned their backs on wealth afterwards, often adopting a plain, casual, or informal dress but always clean. These people were no longer interested in convenience, impressing anyone, or making it in business. Many took up a kind of ministry or had a compelling desire to write. Bucke makes it very clear none of these people were poor and all could have easily lived otherwise if they had so chosen, but they preferred instead the company of plain folk and simple pleasures. Yet each had grand, heroic ideas and idealism, often achieving their goals to the amazement of all.

In further describing the aftermath, Dr. Bucke states each person underwent a time of solitude and seclusion after illumination that was filled with doubt and confusion. In many cases, individuals were obviously disoriented and physically pained from what had happened and from their own inability to resume life "as always." He went on to describe perfectly *all seven major after-effects experienced by near-death survivors!*

He noted that in every case, each person wound up

leaving the organized church of their time. Some went on to initiate new religions, as with Jesus and Buddha and Mohammed, while others began to live out a more just and moral lifestyle based on personal example.

Every single person was judged insane by their peers at the time and some are *still* classified as insane on historical documents of that era even though each more than proved the worth and the value of enlightenment. *All of them experienced paranormal phenomena and psychism. Every one of them became child-like, innocent, and trusting*, even to the point of appearing somewhat stupid. Each found inner happiness and came to love solitude; their eyes twinkled and their temperament mellowed. All of them spoke in paradoxical terms. Bucke was obviously baffled, though, by the psychic abilities they displayed, and he came to feel that this was a separate development from spiritual illumination.

Dr. Bucke felt it was a mistake to study any single person exclusively or to dwell on any single accomplishment no matter how great. He cautioned that one should study from the works of as many illumined ones as possible in order to gain better insight of what spirituality is and how anyone can come closer to God. He defined *the so-called "spiritual mysteries"* as being the product of disciples or students who blurred the original messages and teachings of these illumined ones out of ignorance and misunderstanding. These disciples perpetuated for all time grave distortions from the initial revelations.

He talks at length about experiences and visions of drug users, about hallucinations caused by alcohol, and about anesthetics such as chloroform. Being a physician, Dr. Bucke had noticed the frequency of out-of-body travels with people who were anesthetized. After querying other physicians, he came to realize that *it was an established fact that people who are anesthetized usually report leaving their bodies and floating around the surgery room or go elsewhere.*

While he came to respect the out-of-body experience as accurate and valid, he labeled any scenario experienced while under the influence of drugs as "bastard." Although such scenarios were similar to illumination, Bucke considered them artificially induced, vastly inferior, and without the lasting, permanent after-effects associated with genuine enlightenment. To give you an example of a bastard experience as defined by Bucke, here is a quote from a dentist's patient who had been anesthetized:

> "I seemed at first in a state of utter blankness; then came flashes of intense light, alternating with blankness and with a keen vision of what was going on in the room round me, but no sensation of touch. I thought that I was near death, when suddenly my soul became aware of God, who was manifestly dealing with me, handling me, so to speak, in an intense personal present reality. I felt Him streaming in like light upon me and heard Him saying in no language, but as hands touch hands and communicate sensations: 'I led thee; I guided thee; YOU WILL NEVER SIN AND WEEP AND WAIL IN MADNESS ANY MORE; for now you have seen Me.' My whole consciousness seemed brought into one point of absolute conviction; the independence of my mind from my body was proved by the phenomena of this acute sensibility to spiritual facts, this utter dreadness of the senses. LIFE AND DEATH SEEMED MERE NAMES. I CANNOT DESCRIBE THE ECSTASY I FELT."

As you can plainly see, this bastard experience is similar both in content and environmental conditions to many reportings of the near-death phenomenon. Bucke also noted that this kind of vision or hallucination was *commonplace* among alcoholics, drug abusers, and anyone medically anesthetized (please note the chemical link between these types of experiencers).

Dr. Bucke concluded his research convinced the day was coming when anyone could gain spiritual enlightenment if so desired. He felt this mass awakening would herald the beginnings of a new race, a new evolution of humans:

> "So will Cosmic Consciousness become more and more universal and appear earlier in the individual life until the race at large will possess this faculty. The same race and not the same; for a Cosmic Consciousness race will not be the race which exists today, any

more than the present race of men is the same race
which existed prior to the evolution of self-conscious-
ness. The simple truth is, that there has lived on the
earth, 'appearing at intervals,' for thousands of years
among ordinary men, the first faint beginnings of another race; walking the earth and breathing the air
with us, but at the same time walking another earth
and breathing another air of which we know little or
nothing, but which is, all the same, our spiritual life,
as its absence would be our spiritual death. This new
race is in the act of being born from us, and in the near
future it will occupy and possess the earth."

There are only five points in Bucke's research that I feel are
either no longer true or perhaps never were, and are probably more a product of his time than anything else. These
points are:

1. His belief that the ability to dream in full color was
   fairly rare when today it is quite common;

2. His belief that self-awareness while dreaming was
   impossible when today this skill, classified as "lucid dreaming," is not only common but can be
   taught;

3. His belief that humanity in its evolutionary development had still not reached the ability to perceive
   all colors when today most people not only see all
   colors well, but readily perceive fine distinctions
   between various hues and shades;

4. His belief that Negroes as a race were semi-savage
   and incapable of any advanced intelligence when
   today we recognize that when given an equal
   chance, people of all races are equally intelligent;
   and

5. The fact that only three of his fifty case studies
   involved women baffled him and he was without
   explanation for it, yet history does record women
   who were illumined.

All in all, Dr. Bucke's work is remarkable and I would highly
recommend the reading of his book. He was ahead of his
time in some respects, and a mirror for it in others. Ex-
perientially, all forms of illumination *appear* genuine,

regardless of causation (whether chemical, abstract, or paranormal), but it is the *far-reaching impact and lasting permanence of the after-effects* that make the difference and are all-important.

Bucke clearly establishes that:

- it is not so much the event of illumination as it is the *result* of that event which is important.
- illuminating experiences in themselves are *common-place*.
- most illuminations constitute only a brief glimpse of higher realities and are not to be confused with actual *attainment* of "Cosmic Consciousness."

Although near-death experiences were not studied in Dr. Bucke's day, his work still applies to them for, without knowing, he perfectly described the experience, labeled its *possible* significance, and enumerated its aftermath. I suspect Dr. Bucke would classify many near-death experiences as bastard, artificial, or partial; but I equally suspect he would have been quite excited about the rest.

Another Look at the "Big Picture"

Because the issue of spirituality is so necessary in any discussion about after-effects, I want to spend some time viewing it from different angles. Scientific researchers avoid this subject altogether. A survivor cannot.

You might be interested to know that there was a time when the word "human" was divided into two parts. This expressed the connection which was believed to exist between the realm of earth and the realm of spirit. "Hu" was then thought to be the tone or sound which would evoke The Divine or God (thus helping people remember their true Source). "Man" referred to embodied existences in the earthplane that were to accomplish a specific purpose or learn a specific lesson. Hence, "Hu-Man" was literally said to mean God-Man, or Divine Beings in residence on earth.

Almost to a person near-death survivors comment on how they found their true "home" in dying, a place where they really felt they belonged. They would often identify with this "spiritual home" by referring to themselves as "Children of God" or words to that effect, realizing that they, and everyone else, are truly Divine Beings come to sojourn in the earthplane for specific reasons. They rediscover who they are and what they are doing here. Other people so transformed tell the same story.

But there is a "fly in the ointment."

Illuminating transformations are wonderful, even desirable, but just because a person has one does not mean that individual can understand or integrate what happened in a constructive manner.

Illumination carries with it no guarantees.

Sometimes it offers pitfalls instead of blessings.

People will usually react in one of the following ways when faced with a puzzling or strange phenomenon: deny it ever happened, take the course of least resistance, follow someone else's assessment, or seek out as much information as possible from every possible source and make up their own minds themselves. None of these alternatives is better or best, for the approach used depends entirely on circumstances and the individual involved.

If the illuminating transformation is admitted and accepted, then a paradox follows. Is it to be labeled a spiritual awakening or a religious conversion?

Libraries of thought have been written about this paradox and discussed ad infinitum, but as near as I can tell it is not so much a problem of identifying what happened as it is a problem of dealing with *other people's opinions about what happened.* It seems to me the only real paradox is one of semantics.

Using the near-death experience as an example, here is a list of differing semantics describing the same basic elements:

Point of View

Basic Element	Religious Conversion	Spiritual Awakening
The experience	Baptism by The Holy Spirit	Light of God

What it represented	A new covenant, born again	Enlightenment or illumination or awakening
What it was	Heaven	Home
A life force	Angel	Light Being
Words spoken	Message from God	Conversations
Words felt	A Gift from God	Telepathy
Opinion of self	Chosen of God	Children of God or Light Workers
The return	A mission to fulfill as God's Chosen Messenger	Unfinished business to complete or a job yet to do

Sometimes I think we create our own paradoxes by our refusal to be objective and flexible. We use different words because we are each different people with different belief systems. We see through different eyes and, in so doing, see what we want to see rather than what is really there. We hide just as effectively under the "umbrella" of spirituality as that of religion.

I have come to recognize that we color the meaning of our transformations either by a need for attention, a desire to satisfy others, or by making a commitment to remain true to what really happened no matter what that means. We have found "home," and we wish somehow to acknowledge that.

Michael Eldridge of Indianapolis, Indiana, a young man who underwent an illuminating transformation other than near-death commented:

> "A belief system carries with it an element of doubt, while knowing does not. The only way we can successfully do away with our belief systems is to turn them into knowing. Man does not enjoy change. Our beliefs are too easily threatened by change. The lack of change keeps the structure of our beliefs sound. Dogma is one of the few things that not only can, but must, exist in a vacuum."[7]

Transformations lead us to the discovery of other states of consciousness and stimulate a need to explore. The direction explored is eventually spiritual. In talking about the four stages of religious growth, Ken Wilber, in his book *The*

Sociable God,[8] actually describes the spiritual journey as
well. He defines the four stages as: (1) *belief*—implying the
idea of being taken care of by a God, (2) *faith*—realizing
mere belief is not enough as one must "know" there is a
Higher Spirit, (3) *experience*—where one physically experiences insight and illumination, and (4) *adaptation*—when
one is immersed in and adapted to the higher state of
consciousness.

Illuminations lead us into structured religions and
back out again, as we continue to explore and experience,
carving out our own way along "The Spiritual Path." The
need to worship can be fulfilled in countless ways, not just
one.

For myself, I have come to realize there are only two
"real" religions on this earth, *the religion of love* and *the
religion of fear*, and everyone belongs to one or the other
regardless of what they may claim. Personally, I enjoy both
religious and non-religious settings for I have come to
know there is no place where God is not. Of particular
inspiration to me since 1977 are the words of Jan van
Ruysbroeck. He says, "God in the depths of us receives God
who comes to us; it is God contemplating God."

But perhaps a word of caution might be helpful here.

The discovery of God and higher states of consciousness can become a substitute for intimacy, a subconscious
urge to experience the ultimate "orgasm." That's escapism,
in my opinion. The whole area of spiritual development and
religious conversion can indeed be escapist—a copout, an
excuse, a way to rationalize life's harsh realities and the
uncertainties of change. Since God appears as changeless
it is easy to seek haven in anything that seems of God, but
that "changeless image" is tricky.

I have noticed that although God never changes, God
always changes!

As perceptions and attitudes are never static, how we
view God always depends on our angle of view. As we shift,
"The Big Picture" shifts. As we grow or diminish, our
concept of God alters accordingly. Escapism offers little
but delay and disappointment. Neither the spiritual quest
nor religious conversions will "save us" from facing what

we have "builded" ourselves to be. Although forgiveness is very real, an old adage makes it quite clear—"God can do no more for you than *through* you."

Eastern and Western Versions

Illuminating transformational events, and in my opinion that also includes near-death experiences, revolve around the issue of an awakening. Somehow the individual's level of consciousness changes and, eventually, this can lead to an interest in spiritual matters with the possibility of later enlightenment.

There are few if any experts in this field (regardless of what may be claimed), and I do not presume to set myself up as one. Long before 1977, however, I was bent on learning all I could about the spiritual path and how the desire for it could be awakened. My impetus for this was several life-changing illuminations I had undergone previously. Because of this, I studied everything I could get my hands on, then put what I learned to work in daily life. This led me to group work and the role of teacher/student. There was little I didn't try. My dedication to this pursuit was intense, disciplined, and constant. I learned a few things from such activity, about what works and what doesn't. Then I died. Everything I once knew had to be relearned in coming back, it had to be reshuffled and turned around. From this process, I have come to view things more simply and with much laughter. What "drove" me before, amuses me now and, as each year grows into another, I find myself becoming more and more practical. To me, if you can't "scrub floors" with what you know, then it isn't worth knowing. From this vantage point, I would like to share some observations that have bearing not only on the near-death experience, but on the entire issue of transformation and illumination.

To begin with, I want to take a broader view of the spiritual quest by acknowledging that throughout all known history, there has always been a steady procession of revelators and avatars (great teachers or messiahs) who have claimed divine authority to reveal Higher Truth. These great ones often exhibited unusual powers. They healed, taught, preached, and performed "miracles" for the benefit of those in need. They claimed others could do as they did and offered to teach them how. What they offered was invariably a course in self-development that involved discipline, sacrifice, virtue, and a lifetime commitment of service to humanity. *None taught short cuts!* Although all were a product of their prevailing cultures, their messages and methods were similar in principle and can be condensed into two basic themes—Eastern and Western.

Although Eastern and Western versions of awakening are similar in many ways, they are opposite in application, representing mirror reflections of the same goal—the transformation of ordinary consciousness into higher or spiritual consciousness. Here is what I believe to be their essence:

> *The Eastern version emphasizes ascending energy*, originating from within a person's body (usually from the base of the spine), rising up until it bursts through the top of a person's head. It is an inner process that seeks inner guidance and looks for God within. It projects energy from inside out. The most familiar teaching of this version is Kundalini (Ascension into the Godhead).
>
> *The Western version emphasizes descending energy*, originating from outside a person's body, passing down through the top of the head (or through the chest area) and spreading throughout the body. It is an outward-directed process that seeks outside guidance and looks for God On High. It receives outside energy in. The most familiar teaching of this version is Christos (Descent of the Logos).

Kundalini is a Sanskrit word that means "coiled serpent." It symbolically refers to the spiritual energy that is said to be coiled into a ball at the base of a person's spine. When activated, it is said to uncoil and rise up the spine and brainstem, like a serpent stretching full length, until it bursts through the top of the person's head. While rising, it supposedly ignites or expands seven whirling vortices of energy that are located in or near certain areas of the body trunk, neck and head. These whirling vortices, called *Chakras* in Sanskrit (that means wheels) are like spinning energy generators and they relate to each of the seven major glandular centers (endocrine glands). Thus, people are said to have a channel within for spiritual energy to travel (the spine) and power generators to speed it along its way (the endocrine glands). Details of how all this works and which Chakra represents which gland depends entirely on what interpretation of which tradition you study. The various versions seldom agree except in principle.

It is claimed that once Kundalini rises full length, after activating and fully developing each of the seven major Chakras and bursting out the head, enlightenment occurs and reunion with God is possible. In actuality, however, this bursting is a signal of a shift from one mode of awareness to another: a shift, if you will, to the spiritual path. Just as the mundane life goes through various phases of development in order to spiritualize, the spiritualized life goes through various phases of development before *attainment* is reached. A Kundalini breakthrough does *not* guarantee complete or lasting enlightenment.

Christos (Kristos) is a Greek word from which "Christ" was derived, and comes as close as possible to translating "Messiah" from the ancient phrase that meant "The Anointed One." As near as anyone can tell, Jesus rarely if ever accepted "Messiah" as applicable to him during his lifetime, preferring instead the title, "Son of Man." Long after his crucifixion, it was the Western mind which named Jesus "The Christ" and established his identity as the Son of God. Since then, "Christ" has also come to symbolize Christ Consciousness or Christ Mind, which, it is said, anyone can possess. Jesus himself said, "All these things I have done, you can do, and more also," thus indicating a state of consciousness others can achieve.

The entrance of Christ Consciousness is sometimes called Baptism of the Holy Spirit, and is characterized by descriptions such as: being struck as if by lightning or a blinding flash, being consumed as if by fire or great heat, being torn as if by explosion or wind, being immersed as if by rain or flood swells. This spiritual energy seems to enter the individual's body from outself the self, from "heaven," God On High, or some saintly emissary or angel. This sudden descent or passage of energy is said to come only when the recipient is ready and worthy, usually entering through the top of the head or through the heart center and filling the entire body. This possession, this entry of divine spirit, energizes and illumines, thus transforming the individual from mundane concerns to spiritual ones. These same traditions also indicate that this event is *not* the culminating union with God but rather a beginning, a step toward that goal, as various stages or initiations are necessary after illumination before true divinity can be attained.

Both versions of awakening, Kundalini and Christos, share many commonalities. Both emphasize methodical preparation, techniques for experiencing (breakthrough), after-effects, and continued stages of spiritual growth after the awakening is achieved. Kundalini traditions insist a teacher is necessary to insure safe, steady progress and proper guidance en route but, once enlightenment is reached, the teacher's job is done and the student must continue on alone. Conversely, Christos traditions advise the probationer to seek silence and solitude alone for purifying the self but, after illumination is gained, wisdom and guidance from others are recommended. Both systems caution that beginners must be free of negative thoughts and ego desires or else the process could be dangerous or harmful, or it could backfire.

And it is no different with "pagan" or native societies that utilize hallucinogens or special "brews" (by the way, the word "pagan" simply means "country dweller" in Latin). Their ritualistic and involved processes mimic those of Kundalini and/or Christos versions with similar and sometimes identical results. I would not consider the current vogue of drug abuse on par with these native societies, for theirs was and still is an emphasis on spiritual awakenings. Drug abusers seem only interested in quick highs and great escapes, the pleasure of the moment, if you will, without any regard for what might come next or the fact that after-effects *will happen!* Any awakenings from drug abuse seldom stabilize, usually cause devastating consequences and, as time passes, result in after-effects that debilitate instead of enhance.

Kundalini and Christos mirror each other. Neither is better or best. They are opposite approaches to the same goal—a spiritual awakening that can lead to the possibility of illuminating enlightenment.

Now that I have expressed my idea of the essence of spirituality's two basic themes, I want to give some attention to recent near-death research. Several professionals have postulated that near-death is in all probability a Kundalini breakthrough, that the phenomenon would be a perfect opportunity to release pent-up Kundalini energies and propel one into higher states of consciousness without benefit of the time-honored process of gradual development. They postulate that the suddenness of breakthrough is what causes difficulty with after-effects.

This idea seems reasonable and may well be true for many.

But I would like to challenge it, for I do not think it is true as a general statement in all cases.

The Light of Enlightenment

Allow me to briefly review the real crux of Eastern and Western versions of the path to spiritual enlightenment:

Preparation. Exercises and techniques are spelled out and quite specific. Most call for rigid austerity and self-denial, divorcing oneself from pleasures and temptations of worldly involvement. Seclusion and as much silence as possible is recommended. Preparations can take a lifetime, be done in stages, or happen quickly. It depends entirely on the one involved.

Breakthrough. The actual moment when spiritual energy "*enters-in*" or "*bursts-out*" is physical in the sense that bodily sensations are felt. Invariably, these will involve physical movement such as swaying, jerking, swinging, spinning, whirling, or rocking. That moment of breakthrough can be positive, negative, or both, as exemplified by the effects which follow. Some positive ones: a sense of total freedom, the ability to "fly," ecstacy, euphoria, loss of body weight, floating, screaming for joy, dancing, laughter spasms, heightened sensations of every possible kind, feeling engulfed by love-warmth-peace-happiness. Some negative ones: a feeling of pain, nausea, fainting, headache or coma, temporary blindness or deafness, sobbing, temporary paralysis, sweating, high fever, inability to eat, drink, or remember. Usually, such a breakthrough will be accompanied by sounds such as popping, snapping, cracking, exploding, a wind rushing by, singing or music of some kind. The actual illumination that happens is as symbolic in content as the breakthrough itself was physically literal. This illumination usually takes on the form of a scenario (similar to near-death scenarios) that may or may not be preceded by geometric, color, or light abstractions. History abounds with records of such occurrences.

After-effects. The degree to which these are present depend on the impact the breakthrough experience had on the individual involved. After-effects can be immediate but several years usually pass before all are noticed. The most common are: simple/direct mannerisms which appear childlike, a glow to the skin and a twinkle to the eyes, a charm that attracts, a sense of confidence and control, detached yet loving behavior, the presence of "knowing" or gnosis, increased psychic abilities (often referred to as "Gifts of the Spirit"), loss of relevance for time or space, senses heighten and expand, needs and wants usually lessen while a joyful attitude of service to others increases. These people invariably become more moral and energetic. At first, there is usually much doubt, which can be accompanied by long periods of depression and soul-searching as the individual sorts out what happened. Understanding and a sense of meaning become paramount. These people are usually labeled insane by culturally advanced societies but revered by underdeveloped ones.

Continued growth. All sacred traditions make it clear illumination is only a beginning, an initial breakthrough to higher states of consciousness. Other breakthroughs are expected, though seldom are they as dramatic as the first. Growth continues in levels or stages, sometimes referred to as "initiations," until full spiritual attainment is reached. Many traditions teach that full attainment takes numerous lifetimes, not just one.

Now, study this summary you have just read. Doesn't it remind you of a formula for exposure to strong doses of high energy?

It seems to me that this whole issue of spiritual development is really a process of learning how to access and control high voltages. The path to God may well revolve around the unasked question—how does one handle intense power, how does one deal with "The Force"?

As far as I'm concerned, the only real difference between Eastern and Western versions of spirituality is the directional path of energy currents. That's all! What we are really talking about, then, is energy itself, differing by degree and type of voltage, and how this energy can be accessed and utilized.

We human beings are electromagnetic by nature, stuffed full of water and chemicals with a few added minerals. Any change of flux in electrical or magnetic force fields, which either surround us or exist within us, subtly or significantly alters our behavior, emotions, body coordination, and our ability to think and reason coherently. We are easily "displaced" when environmental impulses do not match those we are used to, and this includes the chemical factor of anything we ingest or absorb. We are like self-contained universes symbiotically connected to and dependent upon the universe at large, yet we are living, breathing transmitter/receivers, multidimensional by nature. We operate more as "nerve cells" than Children Of The Most High until we "wake up" and take charge of our life and our environment.

In all the people I researched concerning the aftermath of near-death, I was seldom able to isolate anything that would show me a singular path of energy was involved. Rarely did I find what I recognize as either Kundalini or Christos directional currents, but I did notice something else which caught my attention. I noticed what I recognize to be the presence of *both* power flows converging together and causing an implosion. In a way it reminded me of lightning.

Science tells us that the lightning stroke is a huge spark. It equalizes the potential difference between clouds in a thunderstorm and the polarity of soil in the ground. It is, in effect, the culminative result of ascending and descending forces, which in meeting release pressure through a visible charge. Lightning, then, is not some "heaven-borne" bolt of electricity hurled to the ground as most believe. Nor is it only a release valve. Lightning itself helps to produce nitrogen compounds that are essential for healthy plant growth.

Compare now what happens with lightning and what happens in major transformational events such as the near-death experience:

> *Lightning*, an explosion in our external environment that by releasing built-up pressure through a sudden visible charge equalizes energy differences while stimulating physical plant growth.

> *Near-death*, an implosion within our internal environment that by releasing built-up pressure through a sudden burst of light equalizes energy differences while stimulating the expansion of consciousness for human growth.

To my way of thinking each event performs the same basic functions as the other (the macrocosm always reflects the microcosm, and vice versa). But there is more which can be said on this subject. Consider this:

- A Polish physicist named Janusz Slawinski, a member of the faculty of the Agricultural University at Wojska Polskiego in Poznan, is convinced that a "*deathflash*" takes place whenever any organism dies, humans included. He explains that this flash is an emission of radiation ten to one thousand times stronger than normal, and contains within it information about the organism that just released it.

- Most scientists who have researched The Holy Shroud of Turin, Italy, a burial cloth believed to have covered Jesus after his crucifixion, and exhibiting an *exact* imprint of the man's body it once wrapped in *both* positive/negative formats containing detailed information, concluded that the only way such an unusual imprint could have been formed was through a flash photolysis (the breakdown of materials under the influence of light). This would have enabled features to have been scorched or seared into the cloth by an intense emission of radiation.

Whether external or internal, explosion or implosion, a "lightflash" seems to occur whenever opposite energy currents converge to release pressure or radiation.

A lightflash!

Enlightenment by its very definition means an experience of light whereby knowledge and information is imparted for the growth and expansion of human consciousness.

What makes us think that this experience is only symbolic? Or just an exercise? Or merely an attitudinal shift in consciousness? Or the product of wishful thinking?

What if it is literal?

Literal!!!

What if true enlightenment is that event whereby one is engulfed in a lightflash—that by its own nature contains information that facilitates spiritual growth?

What if all religious and spiritual traditions are *really* umbrellas to offer us protection and guidance as we "wake up" to who we really are, as we prepare to meet and endure

and grow through higher and higher frequencies of energy
and power on our way back to God?

What if?

Although much remains to be proved, and perhaps
never can be, an inescapable hypothesis emerges:

Deathflash	*Lightflash*
Central to life's end	Central to life's transformation
External explosion of energy	Internal implosion of energy
Outward release	Inward projection
A finality	A new beginning, "born again"

*Spirituality is a physically tangible process. True enlight-
enment is a vibrational shift of frequencies. Proof lies in
the after-effects, which clearly demonstrate the degree to
which an individual has been able to stabilize and maintain the shift that has occurred.*

But . . .

Thanks to modern electronics and high technology it is
now possible to induce transcendental experiences by
"caressing" the brain with magnetic waves. This increases
neural (nerve) firings along the base and sides of the brain.
Neuroscientist Michael Persinger at Laurentian University
in Sudbury, Ontario, Canada, has developed a helmet a
person can wear that will do just that. Persinger believes
that ecstatic states are commonplace during times of
stress, for this is when neural firings are more intense
because of the effect of stress upon the brain's chemistry.
He feels this probably explains why so many mystics go
through self-induced stressful rituals as part of their
practices.

Other hi-tech methods also exist today whereby a person can be "wired up and plugged in" to receive a whole
range of stimuli via music, pulses, beeps, tones, charges,
and currents. All these methods can and do induce trans-
condent states, visions, and all the trappings of the enlightenment experience by stimulating the brain and neural
processes in much the same manner as Persinger's helmet.
Or, at least they seem to. Epileptic seizures are known to
cause the same thing.

Does this deny what has been previously said?

No!

You can short cut the process but you cannot short cut the aftermath.

So far, no hi-tech marvel or clever invention has come anywhere close to stabilizing and maintaining conditions so created. Neither can any of these methods produce *attainment*, that spiritual permanence possible from enlightenment. Nor can they impart *genuine* information that was not previously known to the individual.

You can stimulate the brain and you can drug it. You can caress, tickle, prod, and zap it. You can play with it and you can experiment with it. But you cannot replicate the rich variety and panoramic sweep of naturally occurring enlightenment and its long-term after-effects.

The "orgasm" of the event constitutes only a small part of the enlightenment process, and that's all anyone can induce—the "orgasm." As sex is far more than a moment's ecstasy, enlightenment is far more than a lightflash experience. Partial enlightenment is very similar to what can be artificially induced, either by gadgets or chemicals, but full enlightenment and the possibility of being able to maintain it is another matter entirely.

Look at the information imparted.

Is it somehow familiar to the person, representative of him or her in some manner, either as a literal or symbolic rendering of memories they already possess in the life lived? Does it dovetail or match their belief system? Or is it more? Is it different, unique, startling? Is it impossible but accurate? Does it involve other sources outside and beyond the self? And what are the effects of the information gained? To the self and to others?

Most enlightening experiences are partial. But those that are more involved, in-depth, and impactual (and there are more of those than you might think), are making such a difference, not only in the individual's life but in the community at large, that nothing short of what we call God could be at work. Where else could such impossibly accurate and impossibly wonderful information come from? And why do we doubt? Is it because we have a limited and finite concept of what God might be?

Maybe it's not what we think of enlightenment that should be questioned. But what we think of God.

If we could move past taboos and tenets, myths and mysteries of both religious and spiritual systems, scientific and technological hierarchies, we might recognize that something very basic, very physical, and very real is at the core of enlightenment.

As you cannot "chisel in stone" what can only be experienced, you cannot replicate what is beyond human understanding.

In case you may have forgotten basic grade school science, allow me to remind you that when a light bulb is turned off the light still remains—moving ever outward and beyond. Only the bulb was turned off—not the light. But when the light bulb is left on, it illumines great distances from its own interaction with its source. Its light will remain steady as long as its connection remains true. This light, which also moves ever outward and beyond, is stronger and brighter and longer lasting—because there is more of it.

Can the light of enlightenment be so different?

The Lure of Psychism

Not only do near-death survivors and others so transformed become more interested in things spiritual, they also become more psychic. And that's a fact! Yet no one wants to talk about it, at least not in public. And that goes double for credentialed professionals.

What's more, there are few of scientific ilk who will even admit that the majority of near-death survivors eventually begin to dabble in the psychic arts; many go on to become practitioners and full-time professionals. The linear gives way to the abstract. The psychic world comes to make perfect sense.

But the psychic is a double-edge sword. What comes to make "perfect" sense isn't always sensible nor is it even desirable. With marketing glitz and obscure cults being what they are, it is often difficult if not almost impossible to separate that which helps from that which doesn't.

Really good material is now readily available—but so is a lot of trash. Too many dabblers wind up getting hurt or misled.

Since this issue is so important and so avoided, I would like to examine it from several different angles. Recommended sources are included in the resource section at the back of this book for those who want additional assistance.

Long before my near-death experiences occurred, I had reached professional status in the field of psychism and the pursuit of metaphysical knowledge. My particular expertise at that time centered around the areas of: meditation, hypnotherapy, astrology, numerology, colorology, trance mediumship, dehaunting houses, out-of-body traveling, and sensitivity training. Although I worked on an appointment basis only, this kind of activity virtually became a second job while I maintained full employment in the business mainstream.

For many years, I worked with countless people, initiating in the process Idaho's first nonprofit metaphysical corporation, Inner Forum. My goal was to make public the best and most reliable of what was then known about the vast field of parapsychology and altered states of consciousness. I wanted people to be able to decide for themselves what might be valid instead of allowing sensational claims and fancy book covers to sway their opinions. I even visited several local churches, personally, to explain Inner Forum and the intent behind it so there would be no misunderstandings. Popular support continued the organization for seven years.

Although I honor all the steps I took during that phase in my life, little of it has current relevance except as a basis for precedent. I still practice some of the skills I once had but not in the same manner; skills such as astrology, numerology, and rune casting. I continue to use them because they are helpful tools for probing the depths of the human psyche and for better understanding natural cycles. Each is a tool. No more. Sometimes I still see clients but I no longer consider myself a practitioner in the general sense of the word. Since my goal is to challenge the client to take personal responsibility for his or her life and to come to terms with habits which may deny health and fulfillment, I use whatever offering seems appropriate at the moment. Often that is meditation and prayer, and the kind of reflection possible when an objective listener responds. Most of my time, however, is carrying that goal of mine into workshops, talks, seminars, and the books I write. I now call myself a practical visionary because that is what I am.

On the basis of this past experience, I can say without any hestitation that *everyone* is psychic to one degree or another whether they admit it or not—for psychic ability is an integral part of our birthright as humans, a natural extension of sensing faculties, intuition, and nature's arsenal of survival instincts. Once a person's consciousness alters, whatever existed before becomes more; it is enlarged and enhanced, and that includes either latent or manifested psychic abilities. How long this lasts depends on how extreme the change. It is possible for those more impacted by whatever happened to them to continue expanding in awareness and abilities with each year that passes. It can seem as if a "door" has opened that will not close.

Interestingly, even though The Holy Bible is filled to overflowing with reports of psychic feats and psychic phenomena, even though the very existence of the Judaeo-Christian tradition is based on the paranormal, Western society still brands anything psychic as either "the devil's work" or nonsense. Eastern society is no different, although they admonish with different terms such as maya (illusion) and siddhis (supernormal powers easily abused or misled). Yet the psychic is everywhere present, and always has been.

Usually "the psychic" is referred to by how it manifests. Thus, mind-to-mind communication is *telepathy*, seeing without the eyes is *clairvoyance*, hearing without the ears is *clairaudience*, awareness of the future is *precognition*, mind over matter is *psychokinesis*, and being aware of ownership or what an object contains by simply touching it is *psychometry*. Every nuance of this field now has a separate label, and those labels vary from country to country and language to language.

Although labels help to identify, in this case I think they help to confuse and mislead.

It has been my experience that, although appearing as different abilities and manifestations, psychism is really differing expressions of *one* mechanism that can be controlled and trained. It is like a basic talent that can be directed into numerous channels. Call it a skill, if you will; and, just as with any other skill, it can be ignored, used as is, developed and improved with practice, or emerge seemingly full-blown from birth. Using piano playing as an example, occasionally child prodigies are born but, for the most part, people do not master great concertos without first pounding out "Chopsticks" and then spending years in dedicated study and practice.

Psychism is no differnt than piano playing in the sense of skill development. Yet its components are vague and subtle, its effects often too elusive and unpredictable—hinging more on superstition and ignorance than on practical results. Since the psychic world is outcast, it is wide open for anything, from the serious to the ridiculous. It often appears more negative than positive, its practitioners more as jealous "back-biters" than dependable professionals.

Perhaps we expect too much of what is called psychic. We are so conditioned by tales of magic and trickery that anything else is boring. When the expected is received from "tuning in" it is called a confirmation. When the *unex*pected is received it is called a revelation. Predictions that come true excite us; those that don't are forgotten. When an entity from The Other Side suddenly manifests before us we are shocked and surprised, forgetting that we as humans regularly attract all manner of phenomena, visible and invisible, daily. Greeting a disincarnate or a light being is not as usual as some would have us believe.

Psychism represents a vast world of mystery. Psychic abilities allow us to enter that world and look around.

The skill, the abilities of the psychic, operate like an antenna, extending the natural reach of our faculties. That's all. As with everything else in life, *use determines value.*

Now, let's get more specific. Thanks to Einstein's Theory of Relativity, we know that as velocity increases time slows down, that at the speed of light time stands still. Therefore a lot can happen all at once. For instance, our entire life can pass before our eyes, from birth to death, in a millisecond; years can parade by in the flick of an eyelash; past-present-future can jumble together in one sequence.

Think about that.

At the moment of a lightflash, space and time disappear. Both cease to exist. It can seem as if we were suddenly swallowed by a black hole only to emerge through a white hole. Einstein's Theory seems to describe *our inner world as well as our outer world.*

Actually, life right here in the earthplane offers a veritable kaleidoscope of myriad layers of interpenetrating, and interweaving energy currents and non-energy fields. Matter is really condensed light, glowing and vibrating in ratios native to its own level of density. Space is not empty. It is filled with infinite multitudes of substance and pre-substance, networks of energy webbing, dimension after dimension of form, and incredible variations of light and sound far beyond our inherent ability to recognize. Since humans are electromagnetic by nature and natural transmitter/receivers of signals, it is no wonder we are dubbed "psychic" when we become increasingly sensitive and open to higher, faster frequencies. The higher the frequency, the more pure its source of light and sound. Traditionally, this is said to be more positive and "heaven-like." The lower the frequency, the more diffused and dense its light source and the more distorted its signals. Traditionally, this is said to be more negative and "hell-like." There is nothing mysterious about the world of psychism unless in our fear and ignorance we claim it to be something it is not.

Based on my own past experience, I have found there *are* physical and mental components to psychic skill. Physically, I believe the endocrine system is most directly involved along with spinal fluid, brainstem and limbic, temporal lobes, blood pressure, nerve and skin sensitivity. Mentally, the *sub*conscious normally processes over a billion pieces of information per second on a regular basis, far surpassing what any computer can do. When expanded further during an altered state, the subconscious becomes virtually unlimited.

Look around you.

Notice how many psychics develop health problems that are endocrine-related such as diabetes, hypoglycemia, thyroidism, immune deficiencies, adrenal problems. Notice how many psychics regularly ingest stimulants and/or drugs to "increase" their abilities. Wine, salt, sugar, spices, vinegar, as well as cigarettes and alcohol, are known to "artificially" expand the psychic if used in excess. Now, notice how quickly many psychics age or begin to look somehow "drained." Notice also how early in life many of them die, or become mentally unstable.

The more sensitive the psychic the more sensitive and vulnerable the psychic's body.

Developing such abilities *out of context* from a balanced and healthy life is not wise. Perhaps the reason there are so many warnings against psychism is because the price for misuse and abuse is so high.

Psychism is easily perverted—but it is just as easily *converted* into helpful, constructive abilities which enliven and enrich life. Psychic abilities are not by nature positive or negative, destructive or constructive, spiritual or demonic. They simply are. How used and for what purpose determine worth.

I once heard Reverend Carol Parrish-Harra say: "The psychic is God's Fishhook. It is how many of us get introduced to spirituality. The trick is—don't get stuck on the Fishhook. It's just a bait to get you started on the spiritual path." Carol is a fellow near-death survivor and I agree with her wholeheartedly.

From the pen of the late Paul Brunton,[9] noted journalist, editor, philosopher and writer, comes the following statement:

> "Scientific, psychical and psychological research is changing the Western world's attitude towards matters which were once dismissed as fanciful nonsense.

> Such research is lifting the ideas of the ancients out of
> the undeserved contempt in which they have lain while
> younger notions sprang to lusty manhood . . . Our best
> scientists and foremost thinkers are joining the ranks
> of those who believe there is a psychic basis to life.
> What they think today, the masses will think tomor-
> row. We have begun—and perhaps rightly—as com-
> plete skeptics; we shall end as complete believers:
> such is my positive prediction."

Psychic ability is merely an extension of faculties native to
our existence, providing us with a healthy "extra." Direct
that extension toward the spiritual and those same abilities become "Gifts Of The Spirit," treasured components
to spiritual discipleship. By the way, the word "psychic"
literally translates "of the soul," the inference being that
psychic abilities are really soul abilities, part of our inheri-
tance as Children of God.

There is nothing wrong with psychic ability. It is neither supernatural, abnormal, or paranormal. But neither is
it a key to any kind of "Golden Door." There is no magic in its
use, only skill.

Reincarnation and Walk-Ins

Reincarnation is a favorite topic for near-death survivors
and others like them. For most, it becomes as a fact of life.

I've heard these people say over and over again that the
human soul grows and evolves as does everything else.
They speak of cycles and timing, asserting that one lifetime is hardly enough to perfect the "Self" on its journey
back to the God that made us. They discuss how the development of our soul might occur, perhaps happening quickly,
but more than likely taking many lifetimes, depending on
our determination to learn and grow. We have the choice,
they say, free will, to lengthen or shorten the process. I
have never heard any of them use reincarnation as some
kind of "lame-duck" excuse to avoid the responsibility and
the effort needed to develop the life at hand.

For six years I once practiced as a professional hypno-
therapist after dutifully putting in my three years appren-
ticeship, including "on stage" demonstrations. I spe-

cialized in past-life regressions, a particular technique where an individual, while under hypnosis, can be regressed or supposedly led "backward in time" to lives lived *before birth* in this one.

My experiences with almost every kind of person and situation imaginable would fill a book by itself. I, too, was regressed by one of my former instructors. Although I make no claim to be an authority on the subject, I have experienced a few things I'd like to share with you and, in so doing, challenge some prevailing notions on the subject.

At first, there seemed to be a connection between my expectations and what resulted during the hypnotic regression. I did everything I could to test my clients to make certain none were staging a performance just to please me, but all proved to be deeply under. Then I tested myself and this is what I found: if I expected nothing special to happen, nothing did; if I wanted something to happen to help the person I was regressing, then it did; if I didn't care what happened, surprises would occur; if I was excited and wide-open to the unusual, bizarre sessions resulted.

Somehow, some way what happened seemed to "depend" on the mood I was in; I "supplied" initial atmosphere and motivation.

During this phase of my work, regressions would follow typical patterns of trade-off lifetimes where either "heavenly justice" prevailed, or my expectations of what "might" or "could" happen would match what did. I took extraordinary measures to prevent this from happening but it did anyway. Accounts of past lives sounded like Hollywood productions: the cruel southern plantation owner who returned as a downtrodden Negro, the impassioned army general who came back as a humble healer, the spoiled brat who returned to a life of wretched poverty, a wife-beater who became the beaten wife, the tyrant who became the slave, and so forth. It seemed the proverbial "eye for an eye, tooth for a tooth" kind of thing, and that bothered me.

Yet, the content and success of each session I held changed as I changed. And I noticed this with other hypnotists, too, even when they denied it.

As I matured in my practice regression themes gave way to psychological enactments, as ingrained habits and personal issues would be "played back" through the drama of some historical motif. Sometimes clients would access "thought forms" rather than any specific life, or they would trip off into lifetimes that were *other than human.* Only twice did I ever encounter famous personages from history—one was a great general, the other an infamous madman. Most of the rest were rather ordinary and undistinguished.

One special session, however, involving a mother and a daughter who could not stand each other, resulted in a healing so profound and so dramatic it changed how I felt about hypnotism and about past life regressions. From that day on, evidence mattered no more nor did any kind of logic or reasoning. All that mattered was that each session held be dedicated to the highest good of all concerned. I traded technique for faith.

That did it!

Soon after, I encountered the human soul. It was most unusual how that happened. The soul just "popped" in and took over. Once I recovered from the initial shock, such sessions began to occur more frequently. It didn't matter who the client was or how I felt or what I did. When the soul "came on the scene" all the rules changed.

The soul, anyone's soul, was unlike an individual or a personality type or any kind of incarnation. It was unique unto itself. I came to recognize the soul as a detached and loving source of limitless knowledge and endless compassion. The room temperature would feel warmer when it came and the client would seem to glow. Advice would be given—either for the prostrate client, me, or another not present. The soul never limited itself or played favorites. Sometimes discourses would issue forth on life and its meaning; gentle, effective discourses that seemed somehow awesome and sacred. The soul's voice, no matter from what client, nearly always sounded the same or similar. It was without identity, eternal, yet personal enough to put into perspective the most mundane in life. Clearly, it was in charge.

Not long after, though, I closed my practice. Prospective clients made it quite clear they were more interested in finding something to blame their troubles on than in searching for their own soul. I referred them to other hypnotists and shut my door to the experience. My priorities had changed and me with them. Soon enough, my life took a different turn.

The near-death experiences I survived were overwhelming to me. Coming back meant relearning and reshuffling from scratch. Today, past-present-future mean little to me except as interspersed, holographic collections that blink on and off like sparks of radiant light. My comprehension of reality has also changed. I experienced time as a thick, jelly-like substance that can be molded and formed; gravity as a blanket of spirals that can be spun and rolled up in waves; patience as a dimension of consciousness rather than just a virtue or character trait; space as a reflection of solidified light; and manifestation as a series of echos from some original thought-tone.

As you can imagine, popular theories of reincarnation no longer have much interest for me. I am convinced of its existence but not of how it operates. Life after life is not as valid to me as life *within* life, for what seems to pass in progression is all too often an illusionary fragment from some larger reality. Since life is continuous and nothing wasted, I have come to realize we are forever confronted with the consequences of our own choices. Whatever we do about that is what creates our heavens and our hells. The rest is up to us, for choice is the life process—forgiveness its protection. Merely to recognize something is to participate in its existence. I found that we never left the God we thought we lost because *God is all that is*.

I now define reincarnation as the opportunity to meet our own projections reflected back to us.

As for the human soul, I have a postscript to offer you. Nine years after I gave up my hypnotherapy practice I came across an article in a professional journal describing the discovery of the Inner Self Helper (or ISH) in the treatment of people with multiple personality disorders. Using hypnosis as the method of treatment, therapists were able to isolate a peculiar "voice" in some cases that was unlike any of the other personalities manifesting through the patient. Stating it was eternal, the voice had no identity, was compassionate and loving, gave objective advice for the patient's best interests, claimed no relationship to the other personality manifestations yet understood clearly what was happening and suggested solutions. It would guide and instruct the therapist, rather than the other way around, and it seemed to be the central organizing "core" in charge.

This discovery of the ISH sounded so much like my own encounter with the soul that I called and personally met with several therapists involved in this kind of work. Off the cuff, we were in agreement with the idea that the soul is central to each person and that the ISH in all probability is the soul, but professionally they wished to remain somewhat conservative, as evidence is still preliminary. They were excited, however, about the implications and so was I. The discovery of the Inner Self Helper may indeed be a giant step toward recognizing the validity of the human soul.

The idea of walk-ins is also a controversial but important topic and I want to address it.

The term "walk-ins" was supposedly coined by the spirit guides of modern-day writer Ruth Montgomery. She is a former newspaper journalist who has done well in the metaphysical market, tempting and tantalizing her readers with abstract concepts and "higher truths." She is certainly an excellent writer and her books are thought-provoking.

Among her latest is *Threshold To Tomorrow*[10] where she describes walk-ins as "advanced souls" who are somehow "allowed" to walk in and inhabit recently vacated bodies. In order to accomplish this feat, these supposedly advanced souls agree to revitalize the recently vacated body, execute whatever remains of the former soul's obligations, then begin their own mission to help humanity. Montgomery claims that the reason for such "switches" is to allow advanced beings a short cut into earthly life. The soul formerly in residence within the body is apparently "excused" from finishing out the life and is freed to either develop elsewhere on other planes or receive another body through the process of rebirth.

She goes on to state that these switches occur during extended periods of unconsciousness or during a near-death experience. She has no idea how the switch works, but claims an agreement must be reached between the two souls involved or the switch cannot happen.

Montgomery identified a number of people, both living and dead, as walk-ins, people such as the late Anwar Sadat. A living person so identified is Reverend Carol W. Parrish-Harra, who had believed herself to be "another person" long before Montgomery ever wrote books about the subject. In response to publicity generated when she was so named, Carol wrote her own book entitled *Messengers of Hope*[11] ("messenger" being her version of Montgomery's term "walk-ins").

Carol's near-death experience happened in 1958 during childbirth and, of course, changed her life. Her story of struggles and transformation is inspiring, as is her quest to "find herself." I met Carol in 1984 and was impressed; but, to be honest with you, I found nothing in her story that would set her apart from anything a typical near-death survivor "grows" through.

Ruth Montgomery's original description of walk-ins, however, mimics the *average behavior pattern of the average near-death survivor or anyone else so transformed.*

It is *normal* for such people to believe themselves new and different.

It is *normal* for such people to even look different and act as another person.

It is *normal* for such people to be revitalized, more knowing and able, to possess skills new or expanded from before.

All this is normal!

There are tens of millions of people throughout the world who would fit this pattern. Are we all advanced souls supplanting our lesser fellows in some race to grab a quick entry back to earth? Even in light of some future cataclysm and the dawn of a new age this doesn't make sense.

I would like to take a moment to reconsider this whole idea.

There *are* historical references to Montgomery's walk-in theory in mystical and metaphysical literature, and in legends from various cultures—but the terminology differs. "Exchange" was more commonly used to describe souls who traded places in a given body, while "walk-in" was a term referring to anyone who might walk into our dimension from another, stay for whatever reason and for however long, and then walk back, seeming to appear and disappear in thin air as the individual came and went. Such reportings still occur today.

The older "exchange" stories are *no* different from modern-day renderings of near-death survivors and others like them. It would seem that, since the whole idea of enlightenment has never been readily understood or accepted by the general masses, it would be far easier to claim those so transformed as "new" rather than trying to understand how they might have "changed." No one, however, can really judge what might have been the truth of what happened in the past, for we can only do our viewing through the eyes of today.

I have met three people who do seem to fit Montgomery's *idea* of walk-ins. Two were adult women, the other a young man; one claimed that distinction, the other two weren't certain and for that reason made no such statement. All three had the strangest eyes I have ever seen, eyes that would search and roll around as if "trying to get out," then stare so intently I frankly found it disconcerting. Yet that wasn't all. These people really were "different," as was the feeling I had in their presence. They really could have been what Montgomery described. And why not? This world of ours is an incredible place of far stranger things than this. It matters more to me what an individual is doing right now with what he or she has to work with than any claims of special identity. I guess that's my Western heritage showing through.

But I seriously question the purpose of it all.

Every "walk-in" Montgomery wrote about or those I have met went through extensive and lengthy periods of confusion and depression, with little more to offer than disconnected, dreamy ideas. None had the ability to utilize what they claimed to know or to empower others until *after* they had engaged in years, and I do mean years, of study and training to learn how. This is hardly any kind of short cut. They might just as well have been born in the normal manner and matured without the additional burden of their questionable origin.

I cannot deny the plausibility of walk-ins as defined by Ruth Montgomery, but I can advise healthy doses of caution and skepticism. The whole thing makes little sense if viewed honestly. People like near-death survivors are quite vulnerable. Sometimes they are almost desperate in their desire to understand what happened to them and why. The notion of walk-ins seem a handy label that could allay gnawing fears and confusions. In all probability, however, people like this, myself included, have simply become more of themselves, an expanded version of the original model.

Being "more" of yourself isn't glamorous and it doesn't inflate the ego but it is livable and infinitely more practical. Becoming "more" compliments what enlightened leaders of all ages and throughout all cultures have taught—about free will, spiritual growth, and the evolution of the human soul. And it does make sense.

You know, each of us must have our visions and our awakenings regardless of how, otherwise there would be no inspiration, no hope, no urge to stretch and grow beyond what seems our limits. As we become more sensitive to our inner worlds and outer environments we are enriched beyond measure. All living systems interrelate and are interdependent—*and all systems are living!*

My experiences have taught me that all pathways lead to God, eventually, but some involve more detours than others.

Life is not predicated on belief or disbelief.
Neither is God.

5
Brain
Shift

*"Oh man! Admire and model thyself after the whale!
Do thou, too, remain warm among ice. Do thou too, live
in this world without being of it . . . retain, O man! in
all seasons a temperature of thine own!"*

Herman Melville

Near-death survivors are often told that they are brain
damaged solely on the basis of how long they were "gone"
and how they now appear to think and act. They are *assumed* brain damaged, especially child experiencers. I suspect this is also true of other people who underwent an
impactual, transformative event, but since my research
centered on the near-death phenomenon, I will concentrate
on its survivors.

To assume brain damage on the basis of observation
alone is misleading. Physical tests must be performed to
assess location and extent of damage. Eyesight examina-
tions are also used. In my own research, only three people
were so declared on the basis of clinical testing, and two of
those made complete recoveries. Yet well over half the
people I researched were told *without testing of any kind*
that they were brain damaged on the basis of how they
appeared to respond. I was one of them.

Just because a near-death survivor displays altered
faculties and unusual behavior does *not* mean he or she is
brain damaged.

Survivors may appear mentally ill, retarded, or some-

150

how damaged, but they seldom are. *Appearances can be deceiving. Assumptions are dangerous.* Serious setbacks can result from quick or improper diagnoses. Such a pronouncement, when it isn't true, can be devastating.

This mistaken assumption occurs so often I wish to face the issue squarely and ask a question: What if another condition is involved here, a condition similar to brain damage, yet totally different?

I call that condition *brain shift.*

Seldom is a near-death survivor brain damaged, but most of them are brain shifted. Our faculties, attitudes, and modes of thinking shift, and that shift can be slight, severe, or vary by degrees of change present. That shift allows us to operate differently, sometimes appearing as if we were another person. It can be permanent, but usually will diminish with the passing of time. In some cases, it can disappear altogether.

The term "shift" indicates "changing places," but I propose a deeper, more specific meaning. I propose that "brain shift" be a term that best describes the physical condition of a brain that alters the way and the manner it processes information, switching old channels into new ones, enlarging and expanding its abilities and awareness. This alteration or shift could have been precipitated by chemicals or electrical impulses, or perhaps something else; but, whatever the cause, the result is a recognizable, definitive shift, a change in modes of operation. The brain is not damaged—it is changed. The brain is not handicapped—it is enhanced.

Our brain is an organ and, as with other body organs, it functions according to input, utilization and outgo—much the same as a computer. But the brain is much more than that. It is an ever-changing kaleidoscope of electrical peaks and valleys which can repair, enlarge, and enhance its own ability to process, retrieve, abstract, and calculate. It is almost holographic in its ability to recreate itself from any given part. The secret of brain seems more in stimulus received than in shape, size, or make-up of its mass. Nor does chronological age make as much difference as was previously believed. The more enriched and stimulating our environment, the more the brain responds by growing in abilities to match the stimuli. An example of this is the scientific finding that brains of city dwellers and brains of country folk differ *structurally*, indicating that the human brain does indeed adapt to environmental demands. According to neuroscientist Efrain Azmitia of New York University, "You can't have a learning change without having changed the structure of the brain in some way."

During the near-death experience, environmental demands shift suddenly and radically. The brain is confronted with a new challenge. Survival is at stake. Considering the kind and the extent of after-effects from the experience, this indicates to me that the brain adapted. It changed. It shifted.

While adapting to this shift, what if the brain also adjusts to access and to receive octaves of vibration beyond what is known of the electromagnetic spectrum? What if the brain extends beyond this dimensional environment we call the earthplane and includes dimensions elsewhere? What if what the brain shift survivors go through is a precursor to the next step in our evolution as humans? What if a brain shift is where we are *all* headed?

So far, this book has concentrated on the aftermath, the after-effects of surviving death. It has also addressed the fact that many people other than near-death experiencers undergo and/or exhibit the same or similar after-effects. Spiritual implications have been covered as well, but we have yet to tackle more in the way of physiological components. Although nothing can be proved, at least not yet, much can be suspected and pondered.

Several decades ago I noticed that any change in consciousness was accompanied by visible changes in the physical make-up. The two seemed to parallel each other—a change within meant a change without. What we think, we reflect. While working with altered states and various forms of parapsychological experiments, I again noticed how faithfully our outer environment mirrors our inner environment. I came to realize our body and our mind comprise the same team working for the same goal. They are not separate but form the "bodymind." What affects one shows up in the other. That is why holistic healing, for instance, is so much more effecting and lasting than mechanistic healing. You cannot heal one part of the self without healing all parts of the self if you want the healing to last. Anything less is dealing with symptoms and not cause.

The near-death experience is no exception. Physiological changes parallel psychological changes that parallel parapsychological changes. In other words, a change in one area will beget changes in all areas. The near-death experience is not an isolated event tucked away in some scientific vacuum. Rather, it is a dynamic process of broad-ranging effects and influences.

I wish now to examine more of the possible physical ramifications of the phenomenon itself, *not* suggesting that these additional physical components cause the experience, but rather suggesting that they accompany and parallel the experience.

Who is to say what triggers what? It's like the age-old puzzle: what came first, the chicken or the egg? Perhaps the only honest answer is—neither.

It is my hope this chapter will prove challenging.

Chemical Yellow

There is something unusual about seeing yellow. Let me explain, using several different examples.

For those near-death survivors who could recall, the first color encountered during their experience was usually either yellow, or yellow-gold. Some described it as just plain gold. Others saw it as more of a yellow-white, gold-white, or radiant white. Invariably, survivors commented on how different that color or light seemed; bright, yet somehow easy on the eyes and not at all like the yellow-gold-white tones of earth. In checking through survivor files at the International Association for Near-Death Studies, I again noted the preponderance of people who first saw yellow or shades of yellow-white during the onset of their experience. Some continued to be surrounded by this color until revived. Although other colors or light came next, such as rose, blue, or green, the overwhelming majority spoke of yellow. It was also interesting to me that although yellow occurred at the onset, many times it changed; first becoming brighter and more mellow as it deepened into gold, and/or then becoming lighter and more radiant as it transformed into a glowing white.

This immediately caught my attention for I had noticed peculiarities about yellow long ago.

For over fifteen years, I had taught people both in large and small groups how to meditate, alter their state of consciousness, project their mind, and take out-of-body trips. With eyes open beginning students would often comment on how surroundings would take on a slightly yellow caste, as if viewed through a yellow filter or screen, when they were first able to alter consciousness and start separating from their bodies. This yellowish coloration would continue until they made full separation, then it would usually disappear and bright colored vision would be restored. The more proficient a student became, the less yellow was seen, until it ceased altogether. Those with eyes closed also commented on a spread of yellow across their inner vision or yellow lights, followed by a more yellow-gold or yellow-white color. Usually, this color range would cease as the student became more involved in the experience but, sometimes, it would continue as a backdrop or background hue. Again, the more experienced the student, the less if any yellow. This color phenomenon was so consistent and so accurately timed that I came to regard it as a measuring device I could use to assess whether or not a student was actually altering the physical make-up of energy within them and their speed of brain-wave activity. I came to associate yellow with some kind of triggering device in the brain.

Years later, I researched human eyesight and the evolution of colored vision in humans and I came across some interesting correlations. There is no color cone for yellow on the retina of the human eye. We have cones for red, blue, and green, but not yellow. Yellow is created by a chemical reaction in the brain. The same is true in photography. Color negatives can only imprint red, blue, and green; yellow is a chemical reaction that occurs during developing. Yellow exists as a primary color only with paints and dyes. It is *not* primary in the light spectrum. Yellow is actually more of an illusion, a non-color.

According to the books I've read and the doctors I've consulted, it is surmised that in the evolution of colored vision, the "purple" rods of the retina developed first, enabling a type of night vision where degrees of light, dark, and gray could be distinguished. As our surroundings became brighter and there was need for day vision, it is thought we next viewed the world as if through a yellow filter while our retina prepared itself for additional demands. White probably came next as a reaction to sunlight, and affords extra protection from the bright rays. As retina color cones finally developed, most authorities believe we first saw reds, followed by brown, black, and green. The ability to see blue is a fairly recent event by evolutionary standards, probably happening around two thousand years ago, although blue was unknown in biblical times. Interestingly, the widespread ability to dream in full color is one of our newest features as an evolving species. Even as late as the mid-1800s, it was considered a phenomenon. To understand this rationale, one needs to keep in mind the fact that history is devoid of its mention except in cases of the gifted few or within specific groupings of people. Today, full-color dreaming is so common, most people simply take it for granted.

Yellow, then, is thought to have signaled the crossover phase in our early evolution, that time of chemical and physical shift when we switched from a shadowy world to brightness, from perceptions of gray tones to a more vivid, distinct color range. Our vision changed when we began to decrease dependence on our reptilian-style brainstem and increase utilization of our expanding mammalian brain.

Symbolically, down through the ages, yellow has always meant "change," and its sudden preference by a wearer was considered a harbinger of newness and changing times in that person's life. It has come to represent an influx of energy and excitement, and is often associated with freedom, the ability to fly or float, lightness, new birth, cheerfulness, springtime, and youth. We get a "lift" from yellow as if it were a revitalizing tonic. It reminds us of the sun, laughter, new growth, vitality, and vigor. As the color darkens into gold, it is said to symbolize the male or father principle and the beginnings of logical, analytical thinking (reason). As it becomes lighter and more white, it is said to symbolize spiritual development, intuition, and abstract thinking. Should it take on silver characteristics, it is then said to represent the female or mother principle and the beginnings of emotion and feeling.

When training people to see auras, that halo of light emanating from and surrounding all things, most people first see a thin white or yellow band of color. Other colors may be seen later, after the ability is more developed, but the yellow-white range represents the beginning phase of readjusting vision. Artists have always painted such halos of light either yellow, gold, or white. These halos are most commonly painted around the heads of special people to signify importance or spiritual attainment. As a person starts to faint, a rush of yellow or a yellowish haze is seen before passing out. Drug users, especially those on hallucinogens, report the preponderance of yellow colors as they begin their experience, usually followed by white flashes or white sparkles in the air. I've heard of doctors who use a penlight to shine in eye pupils of patients thought dead; if the retina area is yellow then they know the soul is gone.

It seems to me that the connecting factor throughout all these situations is some kind of chemical/electrical stimulation or change. As the state of consciousness alters so does the physical brain. Yellow by itself is chemical in nature and unusual in the sense that it cannot be viewed or photographed directly but is a "*created*" color, created by the very brain that views it. Whatever chemical process produces yellow does so daily, routinely, easily. Yet, if we were able to isolate and identify that process, I believe we could then be another step closer toward isolating and identifying how consciousness alters, how soul separates from body, how near-death might begin.

The fact that the process of seeing yellow is such an ordinary one suggests to me that altered states and out-of-body experiences are ordinary, too, and not at all the "mystery" some would have us think. It also suggests to me that perhaps because of the preponderance of yellow in near-death episodes, the event itself may also be "*created*" in the sense of being used, perhaps by the soul, as an adjunct or alternate to full death.

I believe the color yellow is a clue we have overlooked.

The Limbic System and the Mind

By now just about everyone has heard about or is familiar with the scientific research of left and right brain hemispheres. It is a popular subject and the topic of seemingly endless books, seminars, and television talk shows. From this research, society is being challenged to view the brain and how it functions differently and, in turn, to reevaluate expectations of human performance.

We now know that the left hemisphere controls the right side of the body and is more concerned with analytical reasoning; the right hemisphere controls the left side of the body and is more adept in creative abstractions. Although tasks seem segregated, one hemisphere can perform tasks of the other if necessary.

But since the human brain cannot distinguish between what is real and what is imagined, as both register the same in memory, more recent research is in pursuit of "mind." Findings so far indicate that brain is not the same as mind. Brain channels mind. It amplifies and filters but does not originate. Mind is more than brain. But where in the brain is the entry point for mind? And what is mind?

Neuroscientist Jonathan Winson, who works at Rockefeller University in Manhattan, has made a bold statement that he believes the limbic is the "exact" location of the human mind or psyche. In his book, *Brain and Psyche: The Biology of the Unconscious*,[12] he goes on to postulate that the limbic operates as an "executive office" that decides what input is stored away in memory and what is forgotten, that it makes "decisions" of a type and range once only thought possible of right and left brain hemispheres. Whether Winson is on target or not, he is part of a new vanguard of researchers who have recently rediscovered the limbic system of the human brain.

So what is the limbic system? Well, let's take a quick look at this little known but important part of our brain.

Located in a semicircle in the middle of the brain and capping off the topmost extension of the brainstem is the limbic system. It is a conglomerate of various parts and sections, and is known to be the seat of our basic instincts for sex, hunger, sleep, fear, and survival. Often referred to as our "gut" or third brain, the limbic originates the wide range of emotional perceptions and awarenesses that are elaborated and refined in left and right hemispheres. It has a direct neural connection with the heart. Evolution wise, this small but extremely efficient system has been around for some thirty thousand years or more—yet only recently has it been recognized as *the most complicated structure on earth*! Many professionals now believe if it does not originate mind, it is certainly the gateway to it.

In coming to recognize the importance of the limbic in any discussion of near-death after-effects, allow me to make a short detour and bring into focus some neurological testing in the area of distorted sensing.

Omni magazine was the first to my knowledge to give any public attention to the work of Dr. Richard Cytowic of Capitol Neurology Lab in Washington, D.C.[13] Mostly on his own time and because he was interested, Dr. Cytowic has been investigating a physical condition labeled *synesthesia*—receiving more than one sense response at the same time from the same stimulus. One of the cases he talks about is that of a young woman who could see images in the air as words were spoken, such as the time when she went to buy an ice cream cone and asked what flavors were available. When the vendor gruffly answered "only tutti frutti," the woman saw "black cinders and coal" spew from his mouth as he spoke. This image to her meant he was lying, and indeed he was. Cytowic discovered this kind of multiple sense impression is a product of the limbic system and is present, by his estimation, in about one percent of the population.

People may have various types of unusual or intermingled sensing abilities. The French poet, Arthur Rimbaud, for example, recorded the precise musical notes he heard when each color "sound," and was said to have had *chromesthesia*, or the ability to hear a distinct note when a color is seen. Historically, people like Rimbaud were thought psychic or insane but, thanks to scientists like Dr. Cytowic, we now know such sensing deviations are entirely real and valid, and involve the limbic system.

Near-death survivors report so many cases of intermingled sensing abilities that I have come to consider the condition a *normal* part of the after-effects. Naturally, some people are more affected than others but, in time, the puzzling phenomenon generally lessens or sometimes fades. In the meantime, however, any survivor who tries to describe what is happening is thought to be lying. For example, one woman beleaguered by such sensing distortions, which for her were also accompanied by psychic phenomena, sought help from her family and health-care professionals, only to be accused of witchcraft and labeled "possessed." She vehemently denied the charge, but was too confused to offer any reasonable defense. She finally moved away to avoid the stigma. In my own case, though, the presence of multiple sensing faculties has steadily increased instead of decreased.

In the first grade, I was the only child in school who could see music, hear numbers, and smell color. Since it never occurred to me that I might be different from anyone else, I held nothing back. This resulted in a steady stream of punishment, sometimes corporal, but most of the time I was required to sit in front of the class on a tall stool wearing a conical cap with the letters "Dunce" printed on it. I was on display as an example of an "over-imaginative child who told lies." The only way I finally learned to avoid such episodes was to invent fictitious responses. This situation, along with an unsettled family life, created a peculiar dilemma for me regarding authority figures: whenever I told the truth I would be punished, whenever I told a lie I would be praised. After years of telling "whoppers" and trusting only the kingdoms of nature, I rebelled, developing instead an obsessive need to seek out my own truth independently, to question everything and to arrive at my own decisions. This childhood-dilemma-turned-adult-fixation became a major issue during my struggle to regain my health after surviving near-death thrice over.

Although I have never been tested for synesthesia, it is apparent I was born with something akin to that condition. However, as I reached the teen years, these "extra" sensing modes began to diminish, with the ability to smell color fading entirely. It wasn't until after the birth of my third child, while still in the hospital, that the multiple sensing abilities returned (except color smell), albeit in a state of disarray and confusion. Upon recovering from a nervous breakdown three years later, these sensing differences straightened out and became more dependable. At that time I interpreted this to mean I was psychic so I launched a rigorous training program to develop this potential. These "extras," along with all my other faculties, were heightened after the near-death experience, and remain part of my life today.

With this kind of background, it is understandable that I asked fellow survivors so many off-beat questions and why I studied them so intently whenever possible. I kept noticing something that seemed incongruous to me. I could understand why I was the way I was, but I could not understand why these people, these *other* survivors, also had multiple sensing abilities. How did that happen? I did find a few who had had problems similar to mine in their childhood, but most had not. Why, then, were these people describing in detail intermingled and multiple sense impressions that were *the same as mine*? Had the deviations been different than mine, that would have been another matter but they were the same. I began to suspect that the near-death experience had somehow caused it, and that whatever was involved had also caused the capacities I was born with.

During the same time in my life when I was experimenting with psychism and altered states, it was established in laboratories that almost anyone could be trained to see beyond the range of seeing, hear beyond the range of hearing, feel beyond the range of feeling—and also to intermingle and multiply sense impressions. We found people could be trained to do incredible things, naturally and easily. When I compared these older findings with what I was currently noticing, and added to that new discoveries concerning the brain and the limbic, I began to make some exciting correlations.

Take a good look at after-effects thus described in this book and reconsider them, including: heightened and unusual sensitivities, psychism that parallels survival abilities, visually seeing images in the air, dissolution of time/space, unusual response to light and to sound, seeing layers of energy webbing in nature. Why would enhancements such as these exist if the limbic was not somehow directly involved? And what is the limbic connection?

Science now tells us that the brain and especially the limbic are saturated with melanin molecules—melanin, which transforms energy from one form into another, especially of light into sound and back again; the dark pigment readily seen on human skin, which is being vastly reevaluated as to its probable purpose in the scheme of things. The brain cannot see light from outside itself but it can see "light" produced by the melanin molecule, which in turn is believed to give "light" to all other input the brain receives. So important is melanin that it is now being proposed as the molecule of consciousness.

Isn't it interesting that the proposed molecule of consciousness coats the possible gateway to the mind?

Isn't it interesting that the limbic system has a direct neural connection to the heart, which is equally saturated with melanin molecules?

Could that possibly explain the floods of universal love and brilliant light that overwhelm experiencers, at least to some degree?

Could such a floodtide of light and love be the result of a lightflash?

Could the limbic be that part of the human body which signals a brain shift? *And then leaves its tell-tale "prints" in the form of sensing deviations?*

It may well be that the near-death experience is *a separate event*, related to but not dependent upon the outward appearance of impending death. We have missed a few "puzzle pieces" in researching this phenomenon, in my opinion, puzzle pieces such as how similar near-death is to "symbolic death" (that transformation possible from any traumatic event), and how the incredible power of mind can literally override existing barriers and turn things around—shifting the brain and bypassing the expected.

Another Look at Near-Death Symbols

A practical way to view the mind is to divide it into the three main levels of attention it seems to follow most often. Not that there are any real divisions in actuality, for mind is mind, but rather because symbolic representations are easier to remember and to understand. Traditionally, it is said that the mind consists of conscious, subconscious, and superconscious levels. Here is how I define them:

Conscious. Appears more wide-awake and alert, collects and interprets facts and details from objective reality. Associated with left brain hemisphere.

Subconscious. Appears more dreamy and detached, sifts and intuits creative possibilities from subjective reality. Associated with right brain hemisphere.

Superconscious. Appears more wise and knowing as if connected to larger expanses of mind such as group, race, or universal mind, infuses guidance from collective reality. Associated with limbic system.

Thus, we are said to possess *both a triune brain and a triune mind.*

Notice before we go on that the term is *subconscious*, not unconscious. "Unconscious" implies a state of sleep or lack of awareness, being without mental faculties; yet, current research has shown that the mind never sleeps, that it is always very much aware and fully functional. Anesthetized patients, for example, can still hear, see, and think. Under hypnosis, or even fully awake, such people can often recall surgical details accurately.

There are many different techniques that can be used to reach and explore levels of mind. For instance, by altering the speed at which brain operates (frequency of cycles per second), the various levels can be more readily accessed. This is not difficult and can be done *without* potentially harmful crutches such as drugs, gas, alcohol, electric shocks, or fasting. Just going to sleep every night takes one through the various speeds of brain rhythm and allows entry to all levels of mind. We can even share in each other's "mind pictures" while they are happening, as when more than one dreamer inhabits the same dreamscape as the central dreamer.

There is nothing mystical, religious, or even fearsome, in my opinion, about altering consciousness. We do it all the time, whether we realize it or not. *Altering consciousness is a natural process.*

I came to recognize the death I met in dying. It was quite similar to other levels of higher consciousness I had previously reached. In fact, death was so much like those other states, I felt a sense of ease about it. Although death was familiar to me, it was at the same time very different, different in the sense that it was more intense, more involved, deeper, and more powerful than anything I had experienced before. Even with all my training and experience with altered states, I was *not* fully prepared for what happened. Certainly, my previous training was helpful in that it enabled me to exist in strange surroundings without fear, and it dissolved any need I had for an ego identity, but as things turned out my training was not enough. I wound up being just as surprised and unprepared as anyone else. Death was indeed a paradox, familiar yet unfamiliar, like an old friend who had suddenly become a complete stranger.

Maybe the death I met in dying is something similar to but different from the death I thought it was. Maybe the death I met was *a separate but parallel event* to the act of dying.

To explore this idea further, I want to take another look at the near-death scenario, only this time I want to be more objective with the symbols it projects, especially in view of all the information thus far discussed:

Disconnection. We are somehow jiggled, hit, shook up, or broken loose from some connections inside our physical body. Conscious mind ceases to function. There is momentary silence, darkness. Nothing moves. Survival systems are on extreme alert, waiting.

Cross-Over. All disconnections are not made, allowing additional chemicals to further activate and empower the upper brainstem and the limbic. To insure survival, a brain shift takes place, diverting mind to a separate but parallel condition to full death. Possible futures switch. There is a jerk, sound, sudden movement, snap, or perhaps something like a wind. Lights can flood by or flash. Our field of vision can be light or dark. There is a feeling of great activity.

Journey—Possibility Number One (External Experience). Speed accelerates, there is a sense of forward and *out*, of changing places and moving rapidly. We are now out of our body but still within our familiar world of conscious reality. We have no weight and no restrictions; we can float, hover, or fly anywhere. The body and death scene are viewed dispassionately. Exploration begins with the desire to contact others present. Contact attempts cease when it is discovered we cannot be seen, heard, or felt by those present. There are feelings of peace, ecstasy, and joy, of being free and unhampered, of understanding life and its meaning. At this point, the individual usually returns to his or her body, reconnects, and is revived. Many of the external experiences are later verified as accurate.

Journey—Possibility Number Two (Internal Experience). Speed accelerates, there is a sense of forward and *up*, of changing places and moving rapidly. Dark or light fields of vision still prevail.

Movement is very much akin to moving up the brainstem and the limbic and spreading out through various parts of brain as we traverse a tunnel, enter through a doorway, or pass through a corridor by flying, floating, or somehow rushing along. This in-between space, this journey, functions very much like a preparatory compartment or a pressure chamber where one can readjust and prepare for another environment. While we are in this preparatory space there is a marked change in our structure or mass and frequency of vibration (either higher or lower). This space is quite literally a safety zone. Beings or animals can appear, lights can flash, telepathic communication can take place. A brilliant flood of yellow, yellow-gold, yellow-white, or white begins, and it intensifies as we near the end of this zone. There is a veil or a curtain, like a force-field, we must pass through to reach our destination.

Destination. It is possible to first encounter a guardian or keeper at this entryway or gate. When we pass or break through, we enter a world very similar to subconscious dreamscapes, magic fairylands (fey), or spiritual visions. Everything is unusually bright, clear, and quite possibly musical. All our faculties are heightened. We suddenly know all things. There is a sense that we have found "home." Love, peace, and joy are intensely felt and euphoria reigns. At first there is no thought of loves ones "back on earth."

Involvement. Not everyone who enters gets involved, but for those who do the action is more intensely experienced than anything else that ever happened during previous living. This intensity seems to shift the world we have reached into yet another, more advanced octave of sight and sound. It is as if this new world becomes even more of itself. Loved ones previously dead can be met and conversed with (they usually appear "youthful" but not necessarily younger than when last seen). Various interactions can occur with any inhabitants present, including instructions, explanations, and the giving of messages. Any religious leaders and religious symbols encountered will always match the deep beliefs of the experiencer, yet the experience itself reflects all beliefs. We become as if gods and realize that our true identity is divine. Interactions either shatter or confirm previous knowledge, with the experience becoming like a giant "washing machine" as it cleans out our inner chambers and all we've shoved inside. This area likens to a "halfway house" arrangement, where we realize or are told we must get our act together. A past life review can occur followed by evaluation or judgment. It seems that before we lose all ties with our past, we must first understand who and what we have been and the consequences of our choices.

Leaving. There is a feeling of restriction or line of demarcation separating or preventing us from further passage or longer stay. We have experienced the depths of our own inner being and glimpsed the universal collective, but further entry is not allowed. We must return. We are told or have a feeling of mission, a job yet to do, and more to learn. Movement begins, usually back and downward, to retrace our journey here. There can be a jerk, snap, or pop as we return like an overstretched rubber band back into our body.

Reconnection. For those who can remember, there is a feeling of returning larger and bigger than the body size, thus necessitating a need to shrink or diminish somewhat in order to fit back in. There is a marked contrast between our lack of weight and the body's heavy weight. Dizziness and disorientation are usually our first reaction when consciousness is regained because of the speed of leaving and re-entry and the various chemical we were "bathed" in. Speech may or may not be possible at first. Inner systems switch again as our

> brain begins to shift back to a more normal state. Being revived is not always pleasant. Reactions vary.

Only seconds or minutes may have lapsed, but for the survivor it seems more like hours or days. Once begun, *the near-death experience is no longer dependent on the condition of the physical body nor its close proximity*. Once begun, it will "play" itself out until its conclusion. Scenarios experienced are *both* personal and universal; personal in the sense we face and purge our own belief systems; universal in the sense all human beings are very much alike and have similar motives, needs and drives.

The near-death experience is, in my opinion, *both* a movement through brain and a movement through mind. It is *both* symbolic and literal. *All phenomena thought unique to it by researchers are by no means unique.*

Through altering one's state of consciousness, or in the dream state, people have always been able to see and greet loved ones newly dead (even without foreknowledge of that death), speed to the site of others in trouble to help out or absorb another's pain (without taking their body along), access knowledge or information previously unknown to them, travel without their bodies and accurately report whatever was experienced, know or remember the future. Even glimpsing or contacting higher mind or God-mind can be done through an altered state. None of this is unique to the condition of near-death.

To my way of thinking, the elements that make the near-death phenomenon unique are:

- the drama of impending death
- the sudden unexpectedness of everything
- the complete lack of any desire for such an event
- the intensity of the experience
- cases that happen in a hospital that can be clinically verified

I do *not* think the individual involved was meant to die or in fact could die because all connections to the body and its

life systems were not broken. Even if a person is pronounced dead, unless *all* connections have been severed,
that person is not dead. And *not* all body connections are
readily visible or apparent.

I have noticed that there is more involved in the death
process than just dying. Part of the death process seems to
be the extraction of various sensations and memories
stored throughout the body in various muscles, bones,
organs, viscera, and connecting tissues.

Old mystical and spiritual texts warn that three days
should lapse before a corpse can be burned or tampered
with. The warning explains that the departing soul (that
regulating force that directs mind) needs time to remove
all its history from body parts, and is somehow energized
by early stages of decay from the vacated corpse. The
warning further explains that during these three days, it is
possible for the departing soul to change its mind about
leaving; and, in case this should happen, the body should
still be intact and available for rehabitation. After the full
three days have passed, it seems not to matter what becomes of the corpse. If three days could not be respected,
then natural, at-home burials were preferred to burning or
any method that would violate the body. It was cautioned
that premature destruction of the body (on purpose or
accidental) meant premature return to another life before
the soul could be fully readied.

No one knows, of course, whether or not these ancient
warnings are true, but it seems to me there must be some
grain of truth in them, for all legends and tales are based on
some core of fact. It is very interesting to me that the movie
Brainstorm (the last film of the late Natalie Wood) has
several scenes showing a force, like the soul, searching
through its own inner body parts before it leaves after dying
and fully disconnecting from its body. The scene revolved
around the woman scientist who had just suffered a heart
attack and managed to hook herself up to the recording
equipment in time to "film" her entire demise. That search
her soul made through her body's inner tissues looked to
me like an attempt to drain or somehow remove stored
energy or some kind of informational memory. Whoever

wrote *Brainstorm* must have had some knowledge or intuitive feeling about what might happen to the human body after death and what activities the soul might initiate after being released.

It is of importance to me that no near-death survivor has ever described a *total* release or disconnection from his or her body, or a memory retrieval. Yet I have heard such things mentioned from the deathbed of those about to experience full death. Although I have never seen the legendary "silver cord" (that etheric umbilical that is said to connect each individual soul to its body), I have been told it must break before full death can happen. Until it does, the person is not completely dead, even if it means the physical body must linger on for years or vegetate until the final break occurs.

No survivor has ever mentioned anything about a connecting cord or its breaking, at least none of record. But there are recorded statements from the deathbed which describe this cord, including the moment it severs. Statements are also made that suggest the beginning of memory retrieval.

Much of this can probably never be proved scientifically, even though research is proceeding in that direction. By considering the near-death experience in context with the life of the one who produced it, we can gain a more objective view of the subject. Then, too, by broadening our field of inquiry to include other disciplines of research, we can improve the questions we ask.

A Growth Event

When you keep everything in context, that is to say, the development of the individual's life with the development of the individual's near-death, you see all kinds of fascinating correlations.

For instance, during my own research of the phenomenon, I discovered a pattern to the way death visited most people and it went like this: a little over half the men I contacted died because of heart-related ailments while another twenty-five percent were involved in violence or accidents. A whopping seventy percent of women experienced their episode during childbirth or miscarriage.

When viewed symbolically, I take these figures to be indicative of the fact that in our society men are not encouraged to express their "heart" or emotions openly. Aggressive, athletic behavior is promoted but not gentleness or loving kindness. Men are expected to perform as stalwart paragons of strength and success. Weakness is not tolerated. It should come as no surprise, then, that so many men suffer heart stress, commit acts of violence, or are involved in accidents. By repressing or holding in their emotions, they build up pressure that must be either externally or internally released.

The process of pregnancy and childbirth has always symbolized a time when a woman is completely transformed through the high drama of co-creation, which carries with it the ever-present possibility of death, either for herself or her child. Although women died more often in the past from childbirth and related conditions, women today still "die" in the sense that the birth of a child demands both the surrender and the rebirth of the mother. Death, whether literal or symbolic, is an integral component to birth.

Birth and death are so intermingled historically that it is difficult to separate one from the other. Any birth indicates some kind of death, and any death indicates some kind of birth. Even elements of the near-death experience itself are symbolic of birth—the dark tunnel, movement toward a light, emergence into a bright new world.

Symbolically speaking, then, my research suggests that the manner of a survivor's "death" seems connected somehow to the near-death experience that follows.

Length of near-death scenarios followed a "design" as well. Most of those I researched whose experiences were very short and consisted of few elements or symbols were usually the people who seemed in need of a little "nudge" of some kind toward making life changes. Conversely, most of those whose experience was long, complex, and quite involved seemed in need of more far-reaching, major changes in basic attitudes and lifestyle. Length of experience, then, seemed to depend more on the strength of changes that would be most beneficial to the individual than on happenstance or chance. It's almost as if the soul must be involved on some level, or perhaps the individual's own subconscious self, for the death event is invariably timely—no matter what causes it.

There were general personality patterns, too. My research indicated that people who had more fixed belief systems and inflexible attitudes about life often returned thinking their experience was a religious conversion, or feeling a need to somehow evangelize about what they learned from it. It is almost as if they traded one belief system for another, no matter how changed or different that new system might be. But those who were more flexible and curious, more open and willing to begin with, often returned so bewildered and confused they seemed bereft of any belief system at all. This latter group usually had the most work to do redefining life and its meaning, but they were the least likely to evangelize. They seemed to spend more time remaking themselves than trying to remake everyone else.

There was one pattern and only one I found present in every single case I contacted or came across and that was: *During the near-death "scenario," experiencers had the opportunity to come face to face with whatever they had fully integrated into their deepest "self" while alive.* Regardless of any extra or unrelated features, this was the one, overall, consistent theme.

If you are honest about near-death scenarios and keep them in context with the life of each experiencer, you will discover each scenario complements on some level the *inner* reality of the one who experienced it. *Always! Including children!* For a child brings forward into his or her birth the sum total of whatever had existed before as well as whatever was absorbed during gestation in the mother's womb. As a birthright, each child possesses both a triune brain and a triune mind. The only difference I found between child and adult experiences is that children's symbols were more pure in universal content while adult's were "colored" by personal overtones from years of living.

As adults, we color our life experiences with our deep beliefs, hence our near-death scenarios will complement those beliefs. A Christian is apt to be greeted by Jesus, a Buddhist by Buddha, a Jew by Father Abraham, a Moslem by Mohammed, and an atheist by his or her next-door neighbor. Those who were more open to begin with are apt to ride a light wave or tour the universe, while those who were more fixed in thinking to begin with are apt to enter a walled room in some kind of structure. The more open seldom see themselves wearing any kind of body; the more fixed almost always do. If we know deep down within our heart of hearts that we have done our best in life and could do no more, we seem more apt to encounter "heaven." Conversely, if we know deep within that we could have done better and have few excuses to offer, then we seem more apt to enter a "hell" or have a negative experience. The pattern of near-death will complement on some level the pattern of our deeply recessed inner life.

But what we say we believe and what we actually believe are usually two different things.

Very few of us are in touch with our deep beliefs. St. Teresa of Avila said, "After you die you wear what you are." That indicates to me that integration is the real secret, not what is consciously believed but what is viscerally absorbed. To my way of thinking, whatever we meet in death has a relationship to whatever we have integrated within the depths of our being while alive. We meet "the real us" and that is what we "wear." Since most near-death scenarios are positive and uplifting, that says to me that people are far more loving and worthy inside and out than they think they are.

And I suspect that whatever we meet in death does not remain "as is" but changes and evolves into something more. I also suspect there are stages or phases to the "more" that life on-the-other-side-of-death becomes. I base these suspicions on years of research plus what I experienced during and after my own deaths. I came to recognize that we are unlimited in our potential for growth and change, and in our ability to evolve beyond the limits we set for ourselves. I have not recognized in death any kind of finality worth mentioning and I fail to see how anyone could become "trapped" at any stage of what they meet. I regard the indication that we have the opportunity to face our own belief systems in dying as merely "*Step One,*" and I am convinced there is much more—*after that.* The scope of some near-death experiences convince me of that.

Life insists on growth and change. If we block those urges, something will happen to unblock them. If we forget common sense and balance, something will happen to help us remember. You can count on it. That "something" I call *a growth event.*

Growth events come in all shapes and sizes. They can be negative or positive or both. We can have repeats if we miss one, or we can receive a whole series of them, one right after another. Some examples of growth events are: losing when we were certain we would win, or winning when we were certain we would lose; being forced to slow down in life when we wanted to go faster, or being speeded up when we wanted to go slow; suffering when we wanted to prosper, or prospering when we were unprepared or even unwilling.

A growth event is any kind of sudden, unexpected twist in life that twirls you around and changes your attitudes and stretches your mind. *I think the near-death experience is a growth event,* perhaps even one of those "reserved" for people who need a good "shove."

With children, I think the growth event is for their parents and loved ones and provides a long-term learning experience for the child. For look at what happens when a child dies or suffers a trauma. The parent and *any others so involved* are invariably stretched beyond what they felt was their capacity, and are challenged in ways they never thought they could be. And the child, *even a tiny infant,* never forgets! At some point, as the child matures, the event will eventually become a part of his or her growth.

Growth events, all of them, give us an opportunity to face our inner selves and "clean house," to glimpse the collective mind and higher realities, to expand beyond limiting ideas, to discover the impossible and experience the "paranormal," to become in some way transformed. As lightning fertilizes plant growth, enlightenment "fertilizes" human growth.

Many near-death scenarios contain *extra* features of a

transcendent quality above and beyond symbols from personal belief systems. Often, information is given which later proves accurate. This tells me the near-death event *not only* allows us to encounter our deepest self, but it stretches us even further. It pushes us beyond ourselves and whatever we have made ourselves to be.

The near-death experience is a teaser, an introduction to what lies "beyond" and a second chance at life. It is not a miracle. *It is an opportunity!*

I no longer regard the near-death experience as an isolated event but rather as an integral part of a *process* of growth and unfoldment unique to the individual *yet* universally relevant. Since it is so accelerated and impactual, perhaps some of us need to play "catch-up" and grow a little faster than others. Symbols encountered in each scenario are both personal and universal simply because *all* symbols are both personal and universal—differing only in how you interpret and use them. We humans are more similar than different. There is actually nothing so personal or private that another could not learn from it.

There is a difference, though, between the coming of near-death and the coming of full death. I have some observations about this I would like to share with you.

The Coming of Full Death

Some near-death survivors had an "inkling" something was about to happen but, for most, there was no hint at all. Even for those who sensed something, the near-death experience was still a surprise. It was unexpected. I have noticed that *near-death is recognizable by the lack of foreknowledge that it is about to occur.*

There is not so much a feeling of "fated" attached to the experience as a feeling of "needed."

George A. Roberts of Hamilton Square, New Jersey, a survivor of death who experienced a scenario, wrote a long account of his experience explaining how he came to believe that he could not possibly have died because of the "strange" way events arranged themselves. In brief:

- He had an opportunity the day before to buy a burial plot and refused.

- Because of unexpected car trouble, his wife made a quick trip home and found George perplexed by a seemingly simple pain.

- The pain was not unusual but for "some reason" George insisted he be taken straight to the hospital, a reaction out of character for him.

- He had his heart attack with a doctor at his side in the cardiac care unit.

- While "out," he heard his wife telepathically calling for him through the voice of another, and he followed her voice back.

- Afterwards, he clearly saw his brother physically standing at the foot of his bed when his brother was *not* in the room at all—verifying for George the reality and importance of the entire episode.

George readily admits how needed the experience was, that it demonstrated for him how much better and more wonderful life could be.

Another survivor of death who was *not* conscious of a near-death experience, yet behaved as if he had had one was also named George—George Lucas, the creator of *Star Wars*. As a youngster, George Lucas was considered a punk. He was a non-achiever, non-athletic, non-assertive, non-studious, and non-romantic. According to his father, he was only good at two things—cruising and hanging out. He wanted to race cars and that seemed to be his only ambition. Three days before George was to graduate from high school, without warning or advance behavior clues, he was involved in a spectacular car crash, hung between life and death for three days, and was hospitalized for two weeks more. Today, his father refers to this time as the dramatic turnaround for George. It was almost as if he became another person, so total was his change. He became very philosophical, believing he was saved for some special mission he had yet to fulfill in life, and went on to display after-effects typical of a near-death survivor even though he did not have either a scenario or an out-of-body experience. He seemed imbued with a mysterious "force" after the crash and became intensely goal-oriented, went to college, and later enrolled at the University of Southern

California's Film School. The rest is history. George Lucas used his experience and what he learned from it to give the world another way to view God, spirituality, virtue, and inner strength. He gave us all "The Force." As I am certain most would agree, that accident was probably more "needed" than fated. It was an introduction to what George later enlarged upon and developed in his films.

Brushing death, either as a near-death experiencer or not, is unexpected, sudden, a surprise. It is "unannounced." This is not usually the case with the coming of full death. Full death is different.

Because of my background, I have often been at the heels of death, first as a policeman's daughter, later when my former husband became a crop duster pilot, and finally when I served as a healing channel for those ill or about to die. I have either been at the scene or been privy to the conditions of many deaths and I noticed something. For a while, my former husband and I became a team interviewing and speaking at length with surviving family members and friends of those who suddenly died, especially by accident, and particularly in cases involving multiple deaths. We started out with farm accidents, then branched out to include automobile pile-ups and airplane crashes. Our interviews confirmed the pattern I originally noticed, and that pattern is this: *Accidental or sudden death is "known" about in advance by the one about to die, and that knowing is displayed in subconscious behavior clues.*

Just as with animals who "know" when their time has come, humans "know" too! If there is an exception to this, and there may well be, I have yet to find it. I have come to suspect that accidental death is not all that accidental.

I discovered that people who sense their coming demise usually express this "knowing" in a particular behavior pattern similar to the following:

- Usually, about three months to three weeks before the death event, individuals begin to change their normal behavior.
- Subtle at first, this behavior change begins as a need to reassess affairs and life goals and, at the same time, become more philosophical.

- This is followed by a need to see everyone who means anything special to them. If visits are not possible, they begin writing letters or calling on the phone.

- As time draws near, the people become more serious about straightening out their affairs and/or training or instructing a loved one or a friend to take over in their stead. This instruction can be most specific, sometimes involving details such as what is owed and what is not, what insurance policies exist and how to handle them, how possessions should be dispersed, what goals, programs, or projects are yet undone and how to finish them. Financial matters seem quite important, as is the management of personal and private affairs.

- There is a need, almost a compulsion, to reveal secret feelings and deeper thoughts, to say what has not been said, especially to loved ones. There is usually also a need for one last "fling" or to visit special places and do what is most enjoyed.

- The need to settle affairs and wind up life's details can become so obsessive as to appear "spooky" or weird to others. Many times there is a need to talk over the possibility of "what if I die," as if the individual had a dream or premonition. The person may on occasion seem morbid or unusually serious.

- Usually, about twenty-four to thirty-six hours before the death event, the individuals relax and are at peace. They often appear "high" on something because of their unusual alertness, confidence, and sense of joy. They exude a peculiar strength and positive demeanor as if they were now ready for something important to happen.

This pattern has held true in people from the age of four on up, regardless of intelligence level. I have also observed it in some people who were later murdered. It is somewhat similar to the behavior pattern exhibited by people who have been verbally told that they are about to die, such as cancer patients.

One example of an "accidental death" that follows the advance behavior pattern is the case of Donna Surratt of Staunton, Virginia. Donna was in her late teens, a student at nearby Blue Ridge Community College still living with her parents and siblings. She was killed December 19, 1979, in an auto/truck collision near Churchville, Virginia. For several months before her death, she had exhibited the typical pattern and had also been secretly constructing a poster. The poster seemed to be very important to her. She propped up the finished creation in plain sight on her bed before she left that day; a half hour later she was dead. After the initial shock was over, her parents went to her room and opened the door. Before them was the poster, a montage of colored paper made to look like a stained-glass window with large black lettering. It read:

> DEAR LORD
> YOUR WILL
> NOTHING MORE
> NOTHING LESS
> NOTHING ELSE

Although Donna may seem like an angel unawares, and undoubtedly her deep faith and sense of knowing inspired many, her case is really not that unusual. Certainly, some people demonstrate more obvious behavior changes than others, even openly talking about their coming death a year or so in advance. There are even some who know exactly when and how they will die. Most people, though, do not discuss any such anticipation for fear of troubling others or being labeled "crazy."

Regardless of the degree of knowing and whether or not that fact is communicated to others or even admitted, I have come to realize people still know when their time has come, and you can tell they know by being alert to any behavior clues. Of course no one can really say whether or not the manner and the timing of full death is fated, chosen, or perhaps pre-arranged before birth; but, as far as I'm concerned, when the time comes to leave, the "message" gets through and the one about to die *KNOWS!*

Even though I spoke of dying two years before my experience and must have subsconsciously known what could happen if I didn't make some changes in my life, I did *not* display the characteristics of one about to fully die, and neither did any other near-death survivor I know of.

The vast majority of survivors readily admit to believing they were not meant to die, that the purpose of their "near-miss" was to shake them up, and inspire them to make significant life changes. For instance, I had instinctively labeled my own experience "The Heavenly Sledge-Hammer Effect," for it "woke me up" to how stubbornly I was clinging to self-defeating habits and attitudes.

Not everyone "catches on." Some survivors fail to see any possible purpose for what happened to them, and they reject any attempt to suggest that any good could come from it. These people, however, are a small minority.

My research has shown me that:

Near-death. Is a second chance at life, an unexpected opportunity to turn around and learn anew, one of life's more accelerated growth events.

Full death. Is an exit point, a "graduation" if you will, enabling us to pivot from one vibrational frequency to another—it is familiar, and its coming is known.

6

How to Help
Near-Death
Survivors

"Only that day dawns to which we are awake."

Henry David Thoreau

The moment of being revived from a near-death experience is a moment of overwhelming conflict, not only for the survivor but for *all* concerned.

To understand this, try to imagine what it would be like to feel yourself suddenly jerked away from what could have been the most exciting experience of your life or from a place of such incredible beauty you think it heaven, only to be forced back into a confining body with an equally restricting lifestyle you had thought were both finished? Now, be honest. Would you be pleased or angry?

Regardless of how you answer that question, how do you think your reaction would be received by those professionals working hard to save your life—or by your worried and frightened family?

Suddenly, all involved are at cross-purposes. Emotions and feelings collide. No one really hears or listens to the others, much less makes any attempt to understand what might be happening. Those first few moments, hours, or days immediately after the experience set the tone for all that comes next. After being revived—

The Most Common Negative Reactions From Survivors Are:

Anger, for having been revived and forced to leave wherever they were.

Guilt, for not missing or even being concerned about loved ones.

Disappointment, at discovering they are once again encased in a physical body and have to breathe, eat, and use the toilet.

Horror, if their experience was frightening or any type of hell.

Dumbfounded, if they want to talk but can't or are afraid to.

Depressed, at realizing they must now resume their former lives, that they couldn't stay where they were.

The Most Common Positive Reactions From Survivors Are:

Ecstatic, at the wonder and beauty and glory of it all.

Thrilled, because they feel so privileged to have experienced such a miracle.

Grateful, that anything so incredible could have happened to them.

In Awe, possibly even beyond words or the ability to speak.

Evangelistic, and immediately desirous of telling others the good news about death and God and the power of love.

Humbled, by the magnitude of what happened.

Regardless of initial reactions, and there may be *several different* ones, the next response is usually puzzlement. What does it all mean? Why did it happen to me? What do I do next? Was it real? Will anyone believe me if I tell them?

There come a million questions and no answers. No one can help a survivor for a while—except to just be there and listen. Often there are many tears. It was a miracle. Or was it?

But what if the survivor was a small child? An adult, most adults, can somehow stumble along, learning by trial and error, reaching out for help, pounding on doors until someone empathetic and caring answers. In short, if they have any gumption at all, they can pick up the pieces of their life and start over again. But with little ones, problems and needs can be much more difficult to identify or address. Mrs. Diana Johnson of Desert Hot Springs, California, tells about her son, Jeremiah:

"He has these dreams. Sometimes he says he dreams about castles in the sky. Some are bad. He just says he sees things in the sky. Then he gets a faraway look. The day after one of the bad dreams, he'll be just awful. When he's had a good one, he's a sweetheart. When he started school (first grade), it was a disaster. He got real moody after the drowning. At school, he seemed to be real defensive and arguing. The teacher said he was a little monster. Totally not what he's like at home. I just don't know what happened. He was fighting and aggressive. They even said they might kick him out of school. We took him to a psychologist. I'm thinking of taking him out again. I'm just not sure about her attitude. I told her about the drowning and his experience, and she won't talk about it. She says, 'You know children and their imagination.' She said we shouldn't make much of it. I think he really needs help sorting it out. It's a real turmoil for him. He wants to express it so much, and he gets so upset because he just can't find the words for it. When he gets moody, I'll ask him why. 'I think I'll keep that my business for a while,' he says. It's like a grownup person in a little body. He seems to have no sense of fear, and that scares me. Pain doesn't seem to bother him, either. It just doesn't bother him. He gets this faraway look, and if I ask, he says it's so nice there. Is he going to try to do something to get back there? I think there's something there too that he doesn't want to talk to Mom about. Something is bothering him that he can't tell me. What do I do? I mean, I'm saying, 'Come back, Jeremiah,' and God's up there, and what do I do now? I said, 'Would you like to talk to somebody who knows about all this?' He said, 'Oh boy!' I think there's something there he really wants to get out and he just can't with me."

Children have the same basic kind of experiences as do adults and a similar aftermath, but there are differences. Children too often lack words to describe what they went through, nor can they adequately explain their confusion or pain or anger. An adult is more likely to be given some degree of respect and attention but a child is more likely to be brushed aside as over-imaginative or lying. Children are not taken seriously, nor are they believed.

But what if that child recalls a time *in early infancy* when he or she died or nearly so? And what if that child also recalls having been with God during that time or with light beings or angels, or having traveled around the room out-of-body?

Recent findings from professional researchers are just that startling, that apparently babies *can* have such an experience, remember it, and attempt to communicate what happened when they are old enough to be more proficient with language. Even babies! If this continues to be verified, then what does such a finding indicate about medical surgeons and their penchant for operating on tiny ones without benefit of anesthetics? Do these babies know what is happening to them? Will they remember it? If infants are capable of remembering a near-death experience, why wouldn't they also be capable of remembering something as traumatic as surgery without benefit of anesthesia?

Implications surrounding infant near-death experiences force all of us to not only reconsider what children have to say, but how we as a people treat human life.

A word of caution here, though, for anyone involved with a survivor: *they may not want any help.*

Regardless of how much it is needed, help may be turned down. I have yet to meet a survivor who could adequately perceive his or her condition during *the first three years* after being revived, me included.

You cannot help someone who is convinced nothing is amiss.

Sometimes patience is the greatest gift you can give. Sometimes only the passage of time makes any difference. Survivors need help, all of them, at one time or another; but, help is not always accepted, neither is it necessarily welcomed.

Let me give you a personal example. Charles Wise was the second proofreader who worked on this book. He is a retired lawyer and author of many fascinating books, especially on Jesus, spirituality, and psychic development[14] After Charles finished checking the manuscript, he recalled the time of our first meeting and admitted his impressions. "You appeared confused and mixed-up to me. Not at all the type of person I would like to know or call friend." The time of our first meeting was during May of 1979, two years after my near-death experiences. It was a time when I felt myself to be "guided" and filled with joy and confidence. I saw myself as wise and knowing but Charles saw me as a perfect mess. Today, Charles and I are the best of friends, but his admission about our first meeting struck me. I wonder how many other people, of the nearly two thousand I met and spoke with, saw the "me" Charles saw. It is a sobering thought.

But, even when we think we've "made it" and life again seems grounded and practical, we can misjudge and behave in a manner that seems to deny what we claim to have learned. Again, let me give you another personal example.

When traveling through Connecticut in September 1986, I was asked to give a presentation of the after-effects material to a local chapter of IANDS. It was a last-minute invitation and I accepted. Before I went, three or four different people advised that this particular group had been meeting for several years and never seemed to progress any further than swapping stories. This concerned them. Although I had presented this particular material to the public before, several times in fact, I had never presented the final version of it to any IANDS chapter. These people were my peers. But, if a bold delivery was in order, I would comply. Nonetheless, the idea made me uneasy.

During my talk you could have cut the negativity with a knife, it was that thick. Those in attendance were obviously disturbed about what they heard. When I later queried a psychiatrist who was there, he answered by saying I had been "awesome" and had done a great job. He thanked me for coming. Another individual in a position to make meaningful remarks suddenly disappeared when the talk was over. Nothing else was said.

The following spring I was again in the area but discovered unkind things being said about me in several towns. By making a few phone calls I was able to meet with two people who had attended the talk I had given the year before. I asked what was wrong. This is what I was told. Contrary to the advice I had been given, the local chapter was rather a collection of people still in shock from their experience, some even dealing with serious family problems. Not only was my talk too confrontive, people were enraged by it. They played a tape recording of the talk over and over again as they searched for every flaw they could find in my delivery. I was stunned. I asked why I had been told to be firm when in fact people in attendance were yet quite vulnerable. It was obvious my question rankled. Apparently, there were "differing" opinions.

It was admitted, however, that because so many "feathers were ruffled" many people were able to use that night as a catalyst to help them face issues previously avoided and make significant changes in their lives. All was certainly not lost. I apologized, nonetheless. Whatever was or wasn't the truth of that fiasco, it seemed to me that another equally important issue had emerged from that evening. And that issue is that invariably near-death self-help groups attract more "outsiders" than survivors. Naturally, these curious non-experiencers want to progress and move forward faster than survivors and tend to lose patience and interest after a while. Yet, the survivor needs time, and lots of it. These non-experiencers often wind up controlling topics discussed and meeting formats simply because they represent the larger number in attendance. Survivors get the back seat even in groups created especially for them.

In this particular case, the non-experiencers were right about the need for progress, but the survivors were right, too. The material could have been presented differently, perhaps as a dialogue or in question/answer format. I had known better, but I just plain goofed. It is interesting to me that my sternest critics, those who "jumped" the chance to complain and find fault, were fellow near-death survivors. Those who were more understanding and open were the non-experiencers. What I had meant as helpful assistance was felt to be an assault on my own kind. As those who came that night eventually benefitted because I had been there, I, too, was able to change my speaking style because of what happened.

I think we need to remember something here. Near-death survivors do not lose their individuality just because they have expanded into a more universal awareness. If anything, each of their given characteristics becomes more pronounced. Whatever existed before becomes more noticeable after. This means weaknesses as well as strengths. Because of this, survivors can be difficult to deal with, and their lack of clarity can be frustrating.

It takes time and it takes patience.

I would recommend the following five-point plan as the best way to help near-death survivors:

1. *Active participation* of empathetic listeners who exhibit interest instead of scorn. Give the survivor plenty of time to talk. If he or she is a child, encourage drawing or play acting.

2. *Absence of pressure* to resume everyday life routines. Let them ease back. For a while, don't expect them to be the same person they once were, and don't be too surprised if they want to make sudden or unusual changes in their life.

3. *Freedom to explore* ideas and ask questions without shame, ridicule, or guilt.

4. *Supportive therapy* of some kind, even if it is just a family rap session conducted in a non-judgmental manner. Group therapy with fellow survivors is ideal, but ONLY if professionals or caring strangers are also present to give clear feedback. Survivors need *other* viewpoints and opinions besides their own, but not to the point of being overwhelmed.

5. *Exposure* to as much information about the near-death experience and its after-effects as possible, including scientific findings, books, and articles.

Once survivors realize how normal and natural their problems are for what they went through, the faster they will stabilize the after-effects and the easier they will reintegrate back into society.

Of the survivors I researched, twenty-five percent returned to life as usual, sixty-five percent made significant changes in their life to some degree, and ten percent radically altered behavior normal for them. Most of those in the ten percent bracket experienced long, complex scenarios and are considered to be the "core" group.

Sometime during the early stages of recovery, each survivor needs to confront the most important question of all: *will you accept or reject your experience*?

Until the survivor reaches a decision on this important question, I do not believe any real or lasting recovery can occur. In my opinion, it does *not* matter which choice is made just as long as a decision is reached. Neither choice guarantees a positive or negative outcome, for this depends entirely on individual responses. Vacillation only delays the process. A refusal to decide *is* a decision to reject.

I have already covered discoveries made about acceptance versus rejection in the second chapter of this book, but, to jog your memory, I will review briefly:

Acceptance means risk. It means facing the possible specter of insanity by believing what you cannot prove *even* if you have clinical verification of your death. It means being different from your fellows and possibly alienating your own family, but it also means the satisfaction of remaining true to your experience, whatever that implies.

Rejection means denial. It means forgetting, denying, or casting aside what you had once thought true and wanted to believe. There is little risk here and little chance of threatening anyone. It means life as always, but the possibility of later restlessness and discontent, perhaps being haunted by your experience.

Acceptance is no panacea and rejection is no escape.

It is a no-win/no-lose situation where successful integration can be made either way. Life resumes. Nothing stops or
waits on survivors. At least having made a choice directs
individuals toward a path of recovery and, for the most
part, ends the gnawing struggle of belief versus disbelief.

Not everyone who accepts their experience becomes a
positive member of society again, and not everyone who
denies their experience has actually opted for the easier
path. Denying can mean the beginnings of self-distrust and
a weakening of self-confidence and creative potential. Acceptance can mean the beginning of radical, aberrant behavior that is excessively threatening to others and un-
productive. Neither way is easier or harder. I chose to
accept my experience because I wanted to believe it was
true; I wanted to believe in myself and I wanted to believe in
my ability to accurately perceive alternative realities. But
just because I accepted my experience does not make my
decision necessarily positive *nor* does it validate anything.
My decision simply means I did what I thought best for me
and the way I wanted to live my life.

The average near-death survivor is for all intents and
purposes a child again. They are reborn and, as with all
children, they need time to learn or relearn their ABC's.
Some learn faster than others. Ignorance and indifference
delay the recovery process.

Some survivors, however, wind up arrogant know-it-
alls, overly critical and demanding of their fellows, feeling
others to be lesser and not as "evolved." Although their
view may have broadened, they often lack the very patience
they claim to possess in such abundance. Being in awe of
survivors or treating them like saints is just as detrimental
to their recovery, in my opinion, as ignoring or punishing
them. Just because they seemed to have felt the presence of
God does not make them godly. Just because they may have
been given a message from a being of light does not make
them in any way "chosen."

*Help for the survivor must include help for his or her
family.*

In many cases, the survivor's family suffers more grief

and hardship than does the survivor, especially if there are young children yet at home. These people didn't have the experience, and they don't understand what is going on *or* why their beloved has suddenly become a stranger. Family members could learn as much dealing with the survivor as the survivor could learn dealing with the experience.

The near-death event and its aftermath can be shared with all those touched, so that each person can have an equal opportunity to benefit from the challenge it presents.

And there are cycles to recovery!

I found that it takes the average survivor SEVEN YEARS to stop "floating around" and come back down to earth.

Even if survivors seem completely recovered during this time period, they seldom are. They are still detached from the rest of society. No matter what they claim or how they act, that first seven years is disconnected. Family and friends can see it, but survivors usually do not.

Of these seven years, the first three are usually the most difficult for all concerned, for it is during this early phase that the average survivor is the most disoriented and significant others are the most confused as to why. The survivor during this time is interested primarily in self and the newness of everything, even though they seem more loving and courteous. They can become so absorbed in whatever they are doing or thinking that the rest of the world ceases to exist for them, and other people are ignored. Schedules are unimportant. For this reason, they appear selfish and unreasonable. Former goals and interests diminish or fade. All that matters is *experiencing newness* and learning everything they possibly can, even if their actions offend or insult others.

At about the fourth year, the average survivor's behavior begins to alter. They become easier to deal with. It's as if the survivor has finally discovered other people and the wisdom of addressing the needs of others. They reach out more during this time period and become keenly aware of society and the pressure of work and lifestyle. Former goals and interests can resurface but each will have a different significance than before. The survivor is still detached but, by now, he or she is much more involved in life and more sensitive to other people.

It takes at least seven full years before the average survivor regains true comprehension skills and finds comfort in being back "on earth." Using the seventh year as a marker, before and after differences are remarkable. Even survivors usually recognize the difference and are amazed at how disconnected they had been. Although few are those who ever "fully" recover (and some never make the adjustment), the majority are surprised and even amused at how much more "normal" they and life become after the seventh year.

I doubt if all after-effects ever fade, but they do alter and change as time passes. The biggest difference I noticed in myself and others like me after that seventh year, was the ability to be more clear and discriminating. I have come to realize that both clarity and discernment are invaluable assets.

It takes time to recover. No matter how hard the survivor tries to hurry up recovery or pretend everything is fine, he or she is still visibly affected and not "all there." There seems no way to short cut this first seven years, even with the most understanding and supportive of environments. *It takes time.*

Struggles of the first seven years, however, have an interesting side-effect. When these years have passed, and depending upon how successful the individual was in adjusting, life gets easier. It is as if the survivor has come "in phase" with the natural rhythm of life itself.

Science tells us that it takes about seven years for all human body cells to replace themselves. Cells die and new ones are born at differing rates of speed depending on where in our bodies they are located, but after about seven year's time, all have been replaced and we are renewed for another full cycle of existence. Seven-year cycles are the most common and the most repetitive of all natural cycles. The near-death experience, if successfully integrated, seems to put the individual in phase with nature and on track with the natural ebb and flow of life's energies. We feel better, are more at ease and invigorated; our place in the scheme of things seems more assured, and life itself is more understandable.

After I delivered a talk on the major after-effects of near-death at Fairfield, New Jersey, in October of 1983, a man by the name of Jerome Kirby came up to me. He talked non-stop, almost crying with relief to discover how normal he was, how like most other survivors he was. At the age of seven he had died and been revived, but his life was forever changed by what he witnessed while "dead" and he was unable to fit back into either family, school, or society in any fulfilling way. His experience haunted him throughout his life and affected the development of normal relationships with his peers. Although he was now a successful bookkeeper, he still felt lost and strangely alone. My talk had explained to him why he felt that way and how he could best deal with it. While he was telling me his story and how excited he was to hear me, he transformed in front of my eyes from a tense, suspicious, and withdrawn individual to a man at least ten years younger, relaxed, and at ease. confusion and pain from nearly three decades evaporated. He had finally discovered he was okay!

There are countless Jerome Kirbys in this world struggling to understand what happened to them. Just knowing how normal they are could make all the difference. They need to know they are okay, that their new kind of humanness has a place in this world, that they will not always be as confused as they are now, that in time the puzzle pieces of their life will fit together and make sense. They need our willingness to let them change and grow. They need our patience.

The near-death experience can and should be a springboard to a far more enriching and meaningful life for all concerned. It need not be a heartache or a forgotten dream.

Any major life trauma is a "death" and, because of that fact, there are many different kinds of survivors struggling to begin again, and to understand. After-effects and recovery patterns true for near-death experiencers are also true for many other people. Any sudden, dramatic change can end life as we know it, but it doesn't end us.

We are all survivors!

Repeated most often from "The Other Side" is the message: "*Love one another.*"

I hope the world is listening.

7

From the Author

Longevity is meaningless!

It is the quality of life, not the number of years lived, that determines the worth of life. Those who have shifted consciousness know this.

The new life found after shifting eventually becomes more sensible, more honest, more open, and infinitely more enjoyable and loving. Although we often seem unable to "fit" back into society, we actually fit better than ever for we have more to share. We become assets, not liabilities. We enrich and enhance, not detract. It is sometimes difficult to remember that when times are rough and life makes little sense. It really takes until after our seventh birthday before any of us can even begin to claim the kind of objectivity and discernment which characterize integration, a sign "we made it."

There are no differences between those who were clinically dead and those who were not, except in the eyes of some clinicians. Experiences are the same. Results are the same. After-effects are the same. Patterns are the same.

I seldom talk about my near-death experiences any more. The memories of them have so filled each cell of my body that to continue speaking of them seems somehow excessive and unnecessary. It is the after-effects that excite me and fill my life with unceasing wonder. Although not always comfortable or easy to handle, these after-effects prove to me that the so-called "impossible" is very possible, that life can improve and be a source of happiness, that love as a dimension of existence is quite practical and livable, that life itself is a glorious opportunity to learn and to grow. The real miracles are in the after-effects, ever unfolding as an active process of change without end. For me to consider any other way to live or to return to the lifestyle I once had would be unthinkable. I have no regrets.

But I am concerned about others. Certainly I could have denied my experiences but I could not have denied what happened to me because of them. And so it is with others. In addressing after-effects a whole potpourri of topics spring forth, things like: spirituality, religion, enlightenment, psychism, brain shift, altered states of consciousness, unconditional love, communication, relationships, the politics of authority and governance. I chose to address the entire spectrum of issues in this book, which is probably why so many people winced when they read earlier versions, and perhaps explains why it took five years to get it published. Yet these topics must be broached. No person who has ever gone through the experience or anything like it can avoid such a confrontation. Why, then, do professionals? Isn't the object of science open inquiry?

Barney Clark, one of the recipients of an artificial heart, is recorded to have had seven out-of-body experiences at times when drugs known to cause such "hallucinations" were *not* used. The press never mentioned that. Why? A number of hospitals have now instructed their staffs to address comatose patients during surgery as if they were wide awake, to explain all procedures and maintain decorum, because they tired of embarrassment afterwards when patients could accurately report everything the surgical staff said during surgery and describe each move of the surgeon—*from a position above the surgeon's head looking down.* No one ever mentions this publicly. Why?

And then there are those experiencers who are involuntarily committed to psychiatric wards and/or institutions simply because no one can deal with the after-effects.

Let me tell you about Mary Jane O'Connor of Saluda, Virginia. I use her story as an example, not because she is unique but rather because she is so typical:

> "I almost died in the accident. I was really angry with my parents for trying to suppress what I had to say. I told them a lot about my dreams, and my brothers were so upset. They told me, 'You can't do this.' I told them I wanted to be a director in films. I'd love to act, but why act when I can direct. I really told them things I really wanted to. I had traveled around quite a bit at that time and I had started writing a book. They said, 'You can't do that, you don't have the education.' I think the fact that I was scared about what had happened to me made me want to just let it all hang out. My family is very strict, staunch Roman Catholic. I told them I believe in God, but I don't believe I have to go to confession. I told them what I had been afraid to tell them half my life."

Mary Jane was twenty-one years old when the car accident nearly took her life. It happened a few hours after she and her fiancé canceled all wedding plans. She had been on her own for a couple of years, was employed, and of legal age. Her near-death experience consisted of an involved scenario followed later by several days in a semi-comatose state wherein she "walked and talked with Jesus." Throughout there were psychic episodes, such as hearing voices of people not present, reliving past lives, reading people's minds, remembering the future, suddenly knowing things, visionary dreams, and vivid manifestations.

She was in and out of doctor's offices but not hospitalized at first. She stayed with her parents for a while so she could recover. Confusion over psychic phenomena and a fear of sleeping lest she would never wake caused her to talk incessantly and refuse sleep. Past-life remembrances interspersed with present-life realities to the point that she insisted her name was Catherine. As part of her near-death scenario she had vividly seen her "Catherine-self" marry a man totally unlike her former fiancé, and do so in the historical motif of a past life. This wedding scene was important to her as she considered it a "sign" she would eventually recover from head and back injuries suffered in the accident and that indeed she would someday marry. It gave her hope. Because all this was as exciting as it was confusing and at times frightening, she shared what was happening with her family and friends, even waking up her parents at night to report "the latest." Her parents became so terrified of all this strange behavior and her "delusions" they took her to a psychiatrist. He labeled it an emotional breakdown and wrote out commitment papers.

> "The doctor committed me and the police took me away because I wouldn't go. I should have gone to a psychologist for help but the psychiatrist said 'Put her away,' so they did. They tranquilized me and drugged me and I wound up fighting all the way. I told them I didn't need to be there and leave me alone and don't give me drugs. I was sensitive to anything not healthy or lacking in good nutrition. With my head injuries the drugs made everything worse. I was tied down and they gave me injections. Megadoses. They violated my body. It was a horrible experience. I went from 108 pounds in April of 1980 to 184 pounds by that December. I just gave up and finally played the game they wanted me to."

For three years after being released from the institution, Mary Jane was forced to remain with her parents and undergo rehabilitation. She chose cosmetology school because, "My hair wouldn't come clean and I was all broken out. When you take drugs like I had to it comes out in your skin and hair." Today, Mary Jane is married, slender and beautiful, and very happy. She is openly psychic and becoming more so. She even claims to see UFOs. Incidentally, one of her brothers went on to become a stage performer as she had once considered doing, but Mary Jane herself married the man like "Catherine's beloved" in her near-death experience. Their meeting was as strange as all her other experiences, and he is supportive and respectful of the "different" kind of person she has become. In fact, he's a lot like her and just as open.

> "Before my accident, I was probably what you would have called a young little snob, stuck up. After

going through all the bad parts, getting fat and ugly and all that garbage I had to put up with, I really came down to earth and had to look at people and say, 'God, we are all human, you know.' We all have problems. All I wanted to do was help people after the accident. I went through a very compassionate time where I felt I had so much love to give. Even now, I still feel that somehow I'll help people because I think people in mental hospitals are really absolutely treated terribly. I want to help change that."

The sad part about what happened to Mary Jane is that because of all the drugs forced upon her not only while institutionalized but for years after, there is now evidence of nerve damage plus she has been warned against pregnancy as the risk of birth defects is high.

There has to be another way to guide and assist people recovering from the trauma of transformation—from a near-death experience—from the overwhelming impact of illumination or enlightenment. These people are *not* psychotic.

Stanislav and Christina Grof,[15] husband and wife team in the fields of psychiatry and psychotherapy, write:

"There exists increasing evidence that many individuals experiencing episodes of non-ordinary states of consciousness accompanied by various emotional, perceptual, and psychosomatic manifestations are undergoing an evolutionary crisis rather than suffering from a mental disease. If properly understood and treated as difficult stages in a natural developmental process, these experiences—'spiritual emergencies' or transpersonal crises—can result in emotional and psychosomatic healing, creative problem-solving, personality transformation, and consciousness evolution."

So convinced are Stanislav and Christina Grof of the reality of spiritual emergencies and the need to address such occurrences as part of a natural process, they are now conducting specific workshops in the United States and abroad to train people to become professional in giving "holotropic therapy"—a term coined from the Greek meaning "holos" (whole) and "trepein" (aim for or move in the direction of), and translated "aiming for wholeness" or "moving in the direction of totality." Their aim is to help the helpers so people such as Mary Jane can get the kind of treatment appropriate to their condition.

Holistic treatment, such as holotropic therapy, constitutes a practical and timely alternative to traditional psychiatry. This new type of counseling operates in a manner that facilitates growth and the integration of emerging levels of awareness. Diet is often used to stabilize and slow down after-effects. Treatment includes techniques such as controlled breathing, music, various forms of body work and massage, art, dialogue.

Results from this form of assistance are so amazing, especially considering that drugs are almost never used, that a number of doctors, counselors, and various clinics are now instituting regular holotropic-type services. In the resource section of this book under "Spiritual Emergencies" several groups are listed which maintain up-to-date directories of where help like this can be obtained. Any individual can call or write for information. The A.R.E. Clinic in Phoenix, Arizona, also offers programs of this nature, gearing their outreach toward the populace in general and those seeking to heal "dis-ease." The Clinic can be contacted through the Association for Research and Enlightenment, also listed in the resource section.

I am encouraged by the more humane and life-affirmative measures being practiced now, in almost every endeavor, everywhere. It's exciting, as are these times in which we live. People are demanding change, and getting it. But change has a "double edge"—what helps one may not help another. Maybe what's at issue here is something larger still—a challenge of more global proportions—*the conflict between mechanistic thinking and abstract thinking.* I see this challenging conflict described in the difference between Newtonian Physics and Quantum Physics:

Newtonian Physics	*Quantum Physics*
Uninvolved observation at a distance	Observation/participation simultaneous
Things happen regardless of thought	Things happen because of thought
The world exists irrespective of belief	The world exists in conjunction with belief

Empirical testing—"how it happens"	Participating consciousness—"what happens"
Correlates to Western teaching	Correlates to Eastern teachings
Deals with manifestation	Deals with pre-substance
Describes the visible world	Describes invisible worlds
Left-brain thinking	Right-brain thinking

This conflict is everywhere apparent and is, in my opinion, at the core of the deeper issues that divide people today. The true challenge, then, is to synergize, to bring together, to realize the real "war" is one of semantics and attitudes and nothing else. *Both* the Newtonian viewpoint and the Quantum viewpoint are valid and real. *Both* are needed to insure the health and healing of our times.

Perhaps Bucke and others like him are just a little off-base in their predictions of the evolving human and the "new" species now making its appearance. Perhaps what's really happening today is the beginnings of holism—for maybe it is not a new species that is being birthed but a whole one, a type of human willing and able to encompass and to utilize all the divisions of brain, all the possibilities of faculty, all the potential of mind. Maybe, at last, humanity is becoming *whole*!

It is this kind of wholeness that is the most noticeable with people who have shifted their consciousness. They operate more synergistically, more in step with natural rhythms and cycles. Because of this, they automatically deal with less stress and upset and are happier.

How many people have shifted their consciousness?

More than you could ever imagine!

It hasn't made front-page headlines because there is no hype involved, no big dollars or sleek sell. It is more a quiet undercurrent, a distant thunder. But it is a revolution. Make no mistake about that.

It is a revolution of consciousness.

AND IT IS TRULY GLOBAL.

Millions are choosing it. Millions more are being flung into it, ready or not, like the near-death survivor. It is happening, with or without anyone's permission.

Some see this revolution as the re-emergence of divinity, as a sweeping desire for the spiritual approach and a personal need to reconnect with God.

Regardless of how it is viewed or labeled, the revolution that is afoot is undeniable and growing. And with it come the "snake oil pitchmen," as we the people must somehow learn to tell the difference between the honeyed words of holy gurus who sell only promiscuity and subservience, and the blackmail demanded by egotistical, dogmatic ministers who openly pray for the death of imagined foes. Because of this, the spiritual quest is fast becoming a circus with more "animals" on display than performers!

I have two suggestions to offer:

1. *Use the near-death experience as a neutral prototype for studying the transformation of consciousness.*

   Anyone in any country from any research base can pursue research on this subject in any manner desired. It is neutral ground. It satisfies both the demands of Newtonian and Quantum viewpoints. If a lightflash is involved, it may well serve as a beacon for better understanding the core experience of enlightenment, which in turn would help to reconcile the religious with the spiritual.

2. *Use the after-effects of the near-death experience as a yardstick for measuring authenticity.*

   It is never the deed but our response to it that makes the difference. It is the consequences which determine value. And there always are consequences! Anyone can have a vision. Anyone can dream a dream. Anyone can be engulfed in rapture and ecstasy. Anyone can claim the blessings of God and become God's messenger. But the after-effects cannot be faked, and grow more prominent with the passing of time. "By their fruits ye shall know them," says the Bible, and that is true. Since the near-death experience is neutral ground, its after-effects can more easily be recognized and studied.

I am reminded here of words spoken long ago by the pragmatic philosopher, Ernest Holmes: "True teaching liberates the student from his teacher. He will find the teacher within himself. This will not make him arrogant or egotistical; rather, he will have a deep sense of humility, as we all should when we face the Great Reality."

I wonder, though, about the timing of our interest in the near-death experience. Plato wrote of it. History abounds with similar stories. But suddenly it is as if the modern world "invented" it. Certainly, because of recent technological breakthroughs more people are returning to life from the grips of death than ever before. Certainly, the possibility of one so saved having a "light" experience is greatly increased. But are these the only reasons?

As the microcosm reflects the macrocosm, I wonder about the mounting plethora of disaster warnings of late, and dire predictions about the future. Most vocal are fundamental religious leaders and outspoken psychics. Books about "coming earth changes" and "global catastrophes" are best sellers. Is the end coming? Are we all about to die?

At the end of each century there is traditionally a time of dire warnings. It has always been that way and it probably always will. But this time, as we approach the year 2000, the situation *is* different. An entire age is ending and another beginning. We are headed for "The Age of Aquarius," like it or not.

There are several ways of looking at this. Legend and myth, no matter the culture, biblical and religious texts as well, all point to the time period in which we now live as one of "great purgings and cleansings" on a massive scale. Some of these various predictions and warnings are detailed and explicit. But in this case, I find astrology to be simpler and more objective in putting forth a possible rationale. Astrology teaches that as an advancing age overlaps the age about to fade, a "cross-over" is created. Usually lasting one hundred fifty to two hundred years, this "cross-over" is said to be a time of great conflict, a "war" if you will between the old and the new, a time of extreme and accelerated change and radical polarizations between people. With The Age of Aquarius steadily advancing, it is due to be fully stabilized by the thirty-third visit of Halley's Comet in 2135–2136. That means we're in it, we are well into the cross-over between Ages. Regardless of what you think of astrology or any of the other predictions, take the time to read today's newspaper, or just look around you. Dramatic changes like at no other time in modern history are happening everywhere and affecting everyone.

Our world is shifting! We are shifting with it!

Are we preoccupied with near-death because we are afraid we will soon be facing full death on a massive scale? Are we learning not to fear death for a "reason?"

It would seem so, but let me remind you of something. Near-death is not the same as full death. It is a growth event, a transformation! It is literally an opportunity for us *to change our minds*!

Maybe that is why the near-death phenomenon is so important in today's news, for it is a symbol of life renewed, a second chance to start over, to relearn and redefine. *It proves the validity of hope and courage, and of promises fulfilled; it assures us that life will continue, no matter what.*

If I were to summarize the meaning of the near-death experience, I could do so in four words:

GOD IS, DEATH ISN'T.

Closing Statement

Back in the late 1800s, an American writer by the name of William Ellery Channing best described the philosophy of the average near-death survivor:

> "To live with small means, to seek elegance rather than luxury, and refinement rather than fashion; to be worthy, not respectable, and wealthy not rich; to study hard, think quietly, talk gently, act frankly; to listen to stars and birds, to babes and sages with an open heart; to bear all cheerfully, do all bravely, await occasions, hurry never. In a word to let the spiritual unbidden and unconscious grow up through the common. This is my symphony."

Resource Suggestions

What you are now is what you have been.
What you do now is what you will be.

Buddha

Coming back is complicated. Perhaps it shouldn't be but it is. Maybe the reason it is so complicated is because most of us have more to *unlearn* than to learn.

Coming back means returning to that space in time you left. It means picking up the pieces of whatever is there and beginning again, sometimes all over again. If there is a simple way to do this, I have yet to discover it.

Carl Gustav Jung, the famous psychoanalyst, once said, "There is no birth of consciousness without pain." Growth events, more often than not, are painful, and the near-death experience is no exception. It is painful to be jerked away from your security blanket, whatever that was, flung into a situation you did not ask for, and be returned only to discover that somehow everything changed while you were gone.

You come back, but in a very real sense there is no coming back. What you left isn't the same any more because you are not the same. You now have a basis of comparison unknown to you previously, and that is both wonderful and not so wonderful.

It is confusing at best!

Because of this, I feel *Coming Back to Life* would be incomplete without a section devoted to referrals, sources and resources where *anyone* can begin the process of looking around for ideas and inspiration. Thus, the following is a compilation of topics that seem pertinent, arranged by subject matter. This is not meant to be a comprehensive index, nor can I make any promises or guarantees about anything so presented; but I do offer it to you as a gesture of sharing some of the best of what is currently available. Any choices or results depend on you.

I intend to write two sequels to this book, the first, *Future Memory*, a further exploration of after-effects, and the second, *A Manual for Developing Humans*. The latter will be a "how-to-do-it" consisting of simple, practical suggestions and techniques for redefining and relearning life. Both books are meant as a celebration of life in all its fullness ... for everyone. Look for them if you are interested.

Thank you.

Near-Death

First of all, I want to introduce you to the *International Association for Near-Death Studies* (IANDS). Principle objectives are:

- To impart knowledge concerning near-death experiences and their implications.
- To encourage and support research dealing with the experience and related phenomena.
- To further the applications of such research findings in professional settings.

The organization has several publications: a scholarly magazine called *Journal of Near-Death Studies*, a general interest newsletter entitled *Revitalized Signs*, and a handy brochure every hospital and clinic on earth should stock called *Coming Back*. That brochure carries pertinent information needed to deal with the initial experience of near-death. Membership in this nonprofit organization is open to anyone; dues are annual. Reportings of near-death experiences are solicited and inquiries welcome.

IANDS, like many organizations of its kind, is currently reorganizing. Until the revamping process is finished, contact as follows:

For Research Information

IANDS
> University of Connecticut Health Center
> Department of Psychiatry
> Farmington, CT 06032

For General Information

IANDS
> Box 23
> Bryn Athyn, PA 19009

Books on Near-Death

> *Life After Life*, Raymond A. Moody, Jr., M.D. Covington, GA; Mockingbird Books, 1975.
>
> *Reflections on Life After Life*, Raymond A. Moody, Jr., M.D. New York, NY; Bantam, 1977.
>
> *Life at Death*, Kenneth Ring, Ph.D. New York, NY; Coward, McCann & Geoghegan, 1980.
>
> *Heading Toward Omega: In Search of the Meaning of the Near-Death Experience*, Kenneth Ring, Ph.D. New York; NY; William Morrow, 1984.
>
> *Return From Death*, Margot Grey. London, England; 1985.
>
> *Adventures in Immortality*, George Gallup, Jr. New York, NY; McGraw-Hill, 1982.
>
> *The Near-Death Experience: A Medical Perspective*, Michael B. Sabom. New York, NY; Harper & Row, 1982.
>
> *To Die Is Gain*, Johann Christoph Hampe. Atlanta, GA; John Knox Press, 1978.
>
> *Otherworld Journeys, Accounts of Near-Death Experience in Medieval and Modern Times*, Carol Zaleski. New York, NY; Oxford University Press, Inc., 1987.
>
> *The Near-Death Experience: Problems, Prospects, Perspectives*, Bruce Greyson, M.D. and Charles Flynn, Ph.D. (Eds.). Springfield, IL; C. C. Thomas, 1984.
>
> *After The Beyond*, Charles P. Flynn. Englewood Cliffs, NJ; Prentice-Hall, 1986.

A Collection of Near-Death Research Readings, Craig R. Lundahl. Chicago, IL; Nelson-Hall, 1982.

The Final Choice, Michael Grosso. Walpole, NH; Stillpoint, 1985.

Return From Tomorrow, George Ritchie. Waco, TX; Chosen Books, 1978.

I Saw Heaven, Arthur E. Yensen. Available from the author at P.O. Box 369, Parma, ID 83660.

Video on Near-Death "The Magnificent Journey: A Window on Life After Death," a detailed and fascinating account of Jayne Smith's near-death experience. Available from Starpath Productions, P.O. Box 90, Southeastern, PA 19399; Ph: (215) 293-0849.

Videos on Life and Death Transformations "Mandalas: Vision of Heaven and Earth" and "The Human Journey" both feature the transformational sculpture and poetry of Mirtala, set to music. Especially helpful in hospice and counseling situations, and with anyone seeking a deeper meaning to life. Available from Mirtala, P.O. Box 465, Belmont, MA 02178.

It is appropriate here to introduce **The International Foundation for Survival Research, Inc., an organization dedicated to the search for evidence of life after death.** Their booklet *Survival After Death—A Scientific View* is available without charge for the asking. For details about other important services contact the foundation at P.O. Box 291551, Los Angeles, CA 90029; Ph: (213) 857-5604.

Although this section deals with near-death, I would be remiss not to mention the best **manual on death education** I have yet found. Inexpensive and practical, it is:

A Manual of Death Education and Simple Burial, Ernest Morgan. Available from Celo Press, R #5, Burnsville, NC 28715.

Health and Healing

Many near-death survivors (and others so transformed) return unusually sensitive or allergic to most chemical

medications because of their brain shift. Such a shift
seems to render the physical body more vulnerable and
sensitive to any stimuli and is probably also responsible
for much of the uncontrollable or additional psychic phenomena so many report. This means that the physical body
and its care become extra important. I have seen good
nutrition make a demonstrable difference in comprehension levels and in the ability to control one's own psyche.
Once the physical body can be stabilized, it is much easier
to retrain the mind. There is no simple rule of thumb to
use, but the following suggestions may help you at least
begin the process of formulating an agenda for health
improvement.

Sources of Health and Nutrition Information

Medical Self-Care Magazine, P.O. Box 1000, Point Reyes,
CA 94956.

Prevention Magazine, Emmaus, PA 18098.

American Holistic Health Sciences Association, 1766
Cumberland Green, Suite 208, St. Charles, IL 60174
(Timely newsletter)

Center For Science In The Public Interest, 1501 16th
Street, N.W., Washington, DC 20036; Ph: (202) 332-9110.
(Many services)

**The best library of delightfully easy-to-read, well
illustrated books on health** I have yet found is the four-
teen-volume set of *The Prevention Total Health System*.
Excellent companion books are: *Your Emotions & Your
Health* (dealing with the healing power of the mind) and
The Right Dose (how to take vitamins and minerals safely).
The library plus these two books are available from: Rodale
Press, Emmaus, PA 18049.

Books on health and healing:

Food and Healing, Annemarie Colbin. New York, N.Y.;
Ballantine Books, 1986.

Shopper's Guide to Natural Foods, Editors of East West
Journal, 1987. Available from East West Journal Book-
shelf, P.O. Box 1200, Brookline Village, MA 02147.

Anatomy of an Illness, Norman Cousins. New York, NY; W.W. Norton & Co., 1979.

Confessions of a Medical Heretic, Robert Mendelsohn, M.D., Chicago, IL; Contemporary Books, 1979.

Love, Medicine & Miracles: Lessons Learned About Self-Healing From a Surgeon's Experience with Exceptional Patients, Bernie Siegel, M.D. New York, NY; Harper & Row, 1986.

Beyond Illness: Discovering the Experience of Health, Larry Dossey. Boston, MA; Shambhala Publications, 1984.

How Shall I Live, Richard Moss. Berkeley, CA; Celestial Arts, 1985.

Health for the Whole Person: The Complete Guide to Holistic Medicine, Edited by Arthur C. Hastings, Ph.D., James Fadiman, Ph.D., and James S. Gordon, M.D. Boulder, CO; Westview Press, 1980.

A Visual Encyclopedia of Unconventional Medicine: A Health Manual for the Whole Person, Ann Hill (Ed.). New York, NY; Crown Publishers, Inc., 1979.

The New Our Bodies Ourselves, The Boston Women's Health Book Collective. New York, NY; Simon and Schuster, 1984.

For personalized medical information that relates to a specific condition, you can now contact a service that will do the leg work for you. For a fee these people will either keep you abreast of the latest research and treatment or prepare specialized reports. Contact: The Health Resource, 209 Katherine Drive, Conway, AR, 72032; Ph: (501) 329-5272.

Included in **my criteria for what constitutes a good doctor** is the stipulation that the doctor be experienced in nutritional therapy and natural remedies in addition to any other degrees he or she may have. Although I respect allopathic medicine (the invasive type that most people are familiar with), I prefer treatment that emphasizes illness prevention and wellness. But, to quote from the *New England Journal of Medicine:* "Ninety percent of all illnesses that people bring to doctors are either self-limiting or beyond the medical profession's capabilities for cure." No matter how skilled or gifted a doctor may be, even a holistic practitioner, the real work, the real healing is up to the individual involved. If we can't get our act together, how can any doctor make much difference? A doctor can only do so much. The rest is up to the patient. Yes, the medical profession needs to change—but so do patients!

According to **Thomas A. Edison**: "The doctor of the future will give us no medicine, but will interest his patients in the care of the human frame, in diet, and in the cause and prevention of disease."

For those who prefer **holistic health care**, there exists now a registry of health care professionals who are nutritionally oriented. To receive referrals, send a brief letter specifying the geographical area in which you live and/or how far afield you would be willing to travel to receive such care. In your letter, include a legal-size, self-addressed stamped envelope for the reply. Send to: Price-Pottenger Nutrition Foundation, P.O. Box 2614, La Mesa, CA 92041.

The **People's Medical Society is an informational, advocacy-type organization working to insure freedom of choice in health care** and a more balanced and sensible health care system. They have already been instrumental nationally in reversing proposed legislation that would have strapped illness prevention and wellness movements. They are proving that we can have a more effective and inexpensive health care system if we refuse to accept otherwise! Two of their books, *Deregulating Doctoring* and *Take This Book to the Hospital With You*, are unusually outstanding. *People's Medical Society* is a groundswell movement of people like you and me who want to make a difference. To join up, write or call: People's Medical Society, 14 East Minor Street, Emmaus, PA 18049; Ph: (215) 967-2136.

Natural remedies are still classified as unconventional in today's society, yet the substances and ideas behind them are older than recorded history. Here are a few resources and contacts.

Herbs

Health Through God's Pharmacy, Maria Treben. Steyr, Austria; Wilhelm Ennsthaler, 1982 (can be ordered in

U.S.). Positively the clearest, easiest to use of all herbal references I have yet seen.

Herbal Medicine: The Natural Way to Get Well and Stay Well, Dian Dincin Buchman. New York, NY; McKay, 1979.

The Yoga of Herbs, Dr. Vasant Lad and David Frawley, 1986. Available from Lotus Press, Box 21607, Detroit, MI 48221.

Our Earth, Our Cure: A Handbook of Natural Medicine for Today, Raymond Dextreit. Secaucus, NJ; Citadel Press, 1986.

Essence of Flowers

Bach Flower Remedies
P.O. Box 320
Woodmere, NY 11598   Ph: (516) 825-2229

Flower Essence Society
P.O. Box 459
Nevada City, CA 95959   Ph: (916) 265-9163

Perelandra Rose and Garden Essences
Box 136
Jeffersonton, VA 22724   (no phone orders)

Homeopathy ("treating like with like")

Homeopathic Medicines at Home, Maesimund B. Panos, M.D., and Jane Heimlich. Los Angeles, CA; J. P. Tarcher, 1981.

Everybody's Guide to Homeopathic Medicines, Stephen Cummings and Dana Ullman. Los Angeles, CA; J. P. Tarcher, 1984.

Homeopathic Educational Services
2124 Kittredge Street
Berkeley, CA 94704   Ph: (415) 653-9270

National Center for Homeopathy
1500 Massachusetts Avenue, N.W.
Suite 41
Washington, DC 20005   Ph: (202) 223-6182

Whole Food Therapy

Kushi Foundation, Inc.
17 Station Street, Box 1200
Brookline, MA 02147   Ph: (617) 232-1000

Body Energy Meridians

American Association of Acupuncture
    and Oriental Medicine
50 Maple Place
Manhasset, NY 11030   Ph: (516) 627-0400

First-Aid/Natural Remedies

The Handbook of Alternatives to Chemical Medicine,
    Mildred Jackson, N.D. and Terri Teague, N.D. Oakland,
    CA; Lawton-Teague, 1975.
Available from Terri Teague Sherman, N.D., 38 Talister
    Court, Baltimore, MD 21237; or Bookpeople, 2940-7th
    Street, Berkley, CA 94710.

**Anyone can learn "laying-on-of-hands" healing
techniques.** Although still regarded as questionable, such
methods are quite safe, surprisingly effective, and becoming more and more popular worldwide. Caution is suggested here, as some teacher/practitioners claim to be
certified representatives of the "only" official technique
and, in that capacity, charge thousands of dollars for what
can be learned at a fraction of that cost. Before you commit
to any program of instruction, investigate thoroughly and
shop around. None are better or best. It all depends on what
you're looking for. Some sources to consider:

Therapeutic Touch

*Therapeutic Touch: How to Use Your Hands to Help or to
    Heal*, Dolores Krieger, Ph.D. Englewood Cliffs, NJ; Prentice-Hall, 1979.
Living The Therapeutic Touch: Healing as a Lifestyle,
    Dolores Krieger. New York, NY; Dodd, Mead & Company,
    1987.

Nurse Healers Professional Associates, Inc.
75 Fifth Avenue, Suite 3399
New York, NY 10010

Reiki Healing

Reiki Alliance
535 Cordova Road, Suite 419
Sante Fe, NM 87501
(505) 982-5331

Omega Dawn Foundation (Independent)
3712 3rd Avenue N Street
St. Petersburg, FL 33713
(813) 327-1881

Spiritual Healing Outreach

Institute of Healing
8306 Wilshire Boulevard, Suite #462
Beverly Hills, CA 90211
(800) 233-6520, ext. 31
Full-service training program and spiritual healing ministry, founded by near-death survivor Lona Peoples.

Mental Health

I know of no one who has done so much for so many as **Elisabeth Kübler-Ross, M.D.** Her methods for releasing pain and fear, and developing a more loving and grounded lifestyle, are incredible. Her books are classics. Her work with dying patients is legendary. But her best work, in my opinion, is the week-long, intensive, live-in workshops she and her staff offer. Although famous for work with death and dying, Elisabeth is now dedicated to the upliftment of life and the practice of unconditional love. To become a member of her Center or inquire of workshops and materials contact: The Elisabeth Kübler-Ross Center, South Route #616, Headwaters, VA 24442; Ph: (703) 396-3441.

On the topic of **mental and emotional health and how attitudes affect healing**, a small, inexpensive book by Louise L. Hay tops the list of anything else currently available in my opinion. After having cured herself of cancer, Louise set about to help others help themselves and, in so doing, compiled an alphabetical listing of probable mental causes for each physical illness plus metaphysical affirmations to help facilitate recovery. Entitled *Heal Your Body*, this important publication is available from Hay House, 3029 Wilshire Blvd., Santa Monica, CA 90404; Ph: (213) 828-3666. While you're at it, ask for a catalogue of other materials from Louise now available.

Several **more books on mental and emotional health:**

Who's the Matter With Me, Alice Steadman. Marina Del Ray, CA; DeVorss, 1977.

Make Anger Your Ally: Harnessing Our Most Baffling Emotion, Neil C. Warren. Garden City, NY; Doubleday, 1983.

I Want to Change But I Don't Know How, Tom Rusk, M.D., and Randy Read, M.D. Los Angeles, CA; Price Stern Sloan, 1986.

Love Is Letting Go of Fear, Gerald G. Jampolsky, M.D. Berkeley, CA; Celestial Arts, 1979.

During my own struggles to rebuild my life, I happened across **a very powerful and instructive litany** that made an immense difference in how I was able **to understand and handle fear**. The more I repeated it to myself the less fearful I became. The litany came from, of all places, a science fiction series about the planet Dune, There are now six books plus a major motion picture *Dune*, thanks to its author, Frank Herbert, and publishers, Berkley Books. Science fiction is not a particular favorite of mine, but the first book in the *DUNE* series contained the litany—and I owe a debt of thanks to Frank Herbert for it. With permission from Berkley Books, here now is the original version from *Dune* followed by what I memorized which made such a difference in my life:

Original:

> "I must not fear. Fear is the mind-killer. Fear is the little-death that brings total obliteration. I will face my fear. I will permit it to pass over me and through me. And when it has gone past I will turn the inner eye to see its path. Where the fear has gone there will be nothing. Only I will remain."

What I memorized:

Litany of Fear

Fear is the mind killer. It is the little death. I will face my fear. It will pass over me, around me and through me, and when it is gone—I *will* remain!

Religion

Any religion is a systematized approach to spiritual development based on set standards or dogmas, which may or may not alter as the religion evolves. Don't be distracted, however, by what appears restrictive, for the very purpose of religion is to provide the protection of community support and moral development, and the guidance of metaphors to describe what seems mysterious.

At the core of all religions is that moment of enlightenment, that mystical revelation and sacred teaching from which the religion itself grew and prospered. Sometimes called The Mysteries, Secret Teachings, or The Holy of Holies, this heart and soul of religion is exquisite and is as viable and true today as when first revealed. Most near-death survivors and others so transformed seem unaware of this undiluted, pure source of inspiration. This inner core is *not* dogmatic, egotistical, opinionated, or political. Although often veiled in cumbersome symbology, it is universally true and honest and uplifting.

There is not a religion you can name which does not have this mystical wellspring. Throughout history, this core was seldom revealed to the masses but kept, rather, for the privileged few. Today, you will still have to dig for it and be willing to ask many questions, but what you will find is well worth the effort. I challenge anyone to compare modern mysticism with this ancient heritage and determine which is more applicable or more important. For instance, reading the old Gnostic Gospels is just like reading modern-day Science of Mind. *Before we go too far forward, perhaps it would be wise to first go backward*, back to those original "grains of wisdom" that, in ways unique to each, fostered a revolution of consciousness in their time

and changed history. There is no simple way to do this, but I
urge you to try, nonetheless.

The Christian Bible translation I prefer was made
directly from Ancient Eastern Manuscripts by George M.
Lamsa. Lamsa was born and raised in a nomadic tribe of
the Holy Lands that still spoke the language of Jesus. He
was later educated by Christian missionaries and then
immigrated to the United Statees where he dedicated his
life to the direct translation of the Bible, finding in the
process over 1,200 errors made from previous translations.
In continuous publication since 1933, the twelfth printing
I have is entitled:

> *Holy Bible From the Peshitta: The Authorized Bible of
> the Church of the East,* translated by George M. Lamsa.
> A.J. Holman Co., Philadelphia, PA.

A study of Biblical idioms helps one to understand
why Biblical languages are so difficult to translate. One
person well experienced in this subject is Dr. Rocco A.
Errico, who was a student of the late George M. Lamsa. He is
a popular speaker and teacher. His three-tape program on
biblical idioms is entitled *Enlightment from the East,* and
can be obtained from The Three Arches Bookstore, P.O. Box
75127, Los Angeles, CA 90075; Ph: (213) 388-2181. Dr. Lamsa's original book on idioms first published in 1931 is once
again available:

> *Idioms in the Bible Explained and A Key to the Original
> Gospels,* by George M. Lamsa, D.D. New York, NY; Har-
> per & Row, 1985.

For more conventional approaches to the Holy Bible,
a particular favorite is the twelve-tape cassette program
called "The New Testament, King James Version," which is
narrated by Alexander Scourby. For both Old and New
Testament versions contact: Bible Tapes, P.O. Box 1700.
Tampa, FL 33601; Ph: (813) 935-0499.

In the Christian religion, the Holy Bible was changed,
altered, and subject to several highly political maneuver-
ings, not to mention various translations, before it
emerged in its present form. To gain some understanding of
its history and origins, I would recommend the following:

The Lost Books of the Bible and the Forgotten Books of Eden, (no editor listed). New York, NY; W. W. Norton & Co. Inc., 1948.

The Nag Hammadi Library, James M. Robinson (Ed.). New York, NY; Harper & Row, 1978.

The Secret Teachings of Jesus: Four Gnostic Gospels, Marvin W. Meyer. New York, NY; Random House, 1984.

The Other Bible, Willis Barnstone (Ed.). New York, NY; Harper & Row, 1984.

The Hidden Mystery of the Bible, Jack Ensign Addington. New York, NY; Dodd, Mead & Company, 1969.

The three most popular and well-grounded of the "New Thought" churches are:

Baha'i

The Baha'i Faith is founded on extensive writings and revelations of Bahá u llah, its principal prophet. It is predicated on the premise of unity in diversity. Baha'i people downplay the necessity of a physical "church" and emphasize the importance of family worship and community gatherings. For more information, contact: The National United States Baha'i Center, Wilmette, IL 60091; Ph: (312) 869-9039.

Church of Religious Science

Founded on principles laid out in *The Science of Mind*, New York, NY: Dodd, Mead & Company, and inspired by its author, Ernest Holmes, this church offers a full range of local centers, study groups, publications, prayer service, and educational programs. For more information, contact: The Church of Religious Science Headquarters, P.O. Box 75127, Los Angeles, CA 90075; Ph: (213) 388-2181 or 385-0209.

Unity Church of Practical Christianity

Inspired by healing miracles in the lives of Charles and Myrtle Fillmore, Unity Church has branched out into a large spiritual network predicated on prayer. The church offers local centers, extensive publications, and educational programs. For more information, contact: Unity, Unity Village, MO 64065; Ph: (816) 524-5104.

Helpful sources for **bridging older and newer views of Christianity are:**

Toward a New Age in Christian Theology, Richard H. Drummond. Los Angeles, CA; Orbis Books, 1985.
Lost Christianity: A Journey of Rediscovery, Jacob Needleman. New York, NY; Harper & Row, 1985.

Spirituality

Spirituality is based upon a personal, intimate experience of God. There are no standards or dogmas, only precedents, for individual knowing or gnosis is honored.

Because it is so personal, methodologies are often elusive or confusing at best. So here is a caution to remember: *There is no system of spiritual enlightenment that can guarantee spiritual attainment.* Just because someone thinks he or she is spiritual doesn't mean that person is. Always look to the results, the consequences, for after-effects cannot be faked. My own personal yardstick says, "If you can't live what you know to be true, then it isn't worth knowing."

The spiritual path is truly "The Inner Journey," deep within the depths of yourself, and it entails a thorough "house cleaning" on every level of your being. The challenge is to find the God within and reconnect, and that means a lifetime commitment. Spirituality is an ongoing process not a facade to hide behind.

It has been my experience that the two most powerful components to a positive, enriching spiritual life are prayer and meditation. Two halves of the same "whole," prayer is where we talk to God, meditation is where God talks to us. And that means learning how to listen in the "silence." New Thought churches often emphasize meditation and affirmative prayer, for they teach "as you believe it is done unto you." This affirmative method of prayer is based on practical results and demonstration. Since the spiritual path is so broad-ranging and diverse, approaches will vary according to individual needs and desires.

Meditation is a starting point, and the best, in my opinion. There are many methods and countless styles. One of my favorite teachers is the practical and humorous Eknath Easwaran. His book and record, *Meditation: Commonsense Directions for an Uncommon Life*, is excellent. Founder of the Blue Mountain Center for Meditation and a successful college professor, Easwaran has written many books which are available through: Nilgiri Press, Box 477, Petaluma, CA 94953; Ph: (707) 878-2369.

Other books on meditation are:

The Relaxation Response, Herbert Benson, with Miriam Z. Klipper. New York, NY; Avon, 1976.

How to Meditate: A Guide to Self-Discovery, Lawrence LeShan. New York, NY; Bantam, 1974.

Meditation, A Step Beyond With Edgar Cayce, M. E. Penny Baker. New York, NY; Doubleday & Co. Inc., 1976.

Meditation in The Silence, E. V. Ingraham. Available from Unity School of Christianity, Unity Village, MO 64065.

As part of the meditative experience, it is helpful to include reading materials which add "gems" to inspire and uplift. Here are two I especially enjoy:

Science of Mind Magazine, a monthly publication which contains daily guides to richer living in the middle of each issue. To subscribe, contact: Science of Mind Magazine, P.O. Box 75127, Los Angeles, CA 90075.

The Quiet Mind, a small book containing sayings of White Eagle, 1978. Available in bookstores or through: General Secretary, The White Eagle Lodge, New Lands, Ranke, Liss, Hampshire, GU33 7HY, England.

A study of the Chakras and the Kundalini system is essential to a healthy and knowledgable understanding of the overall effect of meditation. To meditate without some concept of how the technique affects the human body is not wise. Remember, however, that there is *no* one way of classifying Chakra/Kundalini translations. It is basically an Eastern approach, but the concept is universal in its importance and application. Any competent yoga instructor can get you started. There is a book I've come across which presents clear, simple techniques to understand and utilize the Chakra/Kundalini method. If you can overlook the author's need to worship a guru figure and concentrate on the text, it is well worth reading. The book is:

Energy, Ecstasy, and Your Seven Vital Chakras, Bernard Gunther. N. Hollywood, CA; Newcastle, 1983.

Meditation is a helpful way to facilitate and maintain the inner journey based on commitment and discipline. It is not some brand name sold upon an open market of pie-in-the-sky promises. There is no quick high to be had and no one has a monopoly on the subject. Meditative life consists of phases and cycles as the process assists with inner cleansing and inner purification. It changes as you change. In no way does it offer short cuts or magic. It is not a form of escapism.

There are many books out now on **affirmative prayer.** Here are two written in the Christian perspective:

Receptive Prayer and *A Manual of Receptive Prayer*, both by Grace Adolphsen Brame. Available from Science of Mind Publications. P.O. Box 75127, Los Angeles, CA 90075.

Of all materials researched and written on spirituality in this century, the work of one particular individual stands out from the rest for its unusual clarity, simplicity and inspiration. The individual concerned is Paul Brunton, Ph.D., a career journalist and editor, who, after a highly successful and event-filled life, retired to a life of self-imposed solitude in Switzerland. During his nearly thirty years of "quiet," he produced what has come to be called *The Notebooks of Paul Brunton*, a monumental achievement, in my opinion. These twenty-eight sections have been published by Larson Publications in over a dozen volumes and are available as a series from the Paul Brunton Philosophic Foundation, P.O. Box 89, Hector, NY, 14841; Ph: (607) 546-9342. His earlier books on spiritual and metaphysical topics have been reprinted by Weiser Press and are again available to the public through the Foundation or from Weiser Books, 132 East 24th Street, New York, NY 10010; Ph: (212) 777-6363.

Finding good **classes and courses in spiritual and holistic development** has always been difficult. There are none which are better or best, as it depends on the individual—for what is helpful to one may not be for another. Many times opportunities are local and can be found through traditional or conventional channels. Sometimes the best source of instruction is from someone you deeply admire. That someone could as easily be a sanitation worker as some "great" guru type. Truly balanced, loving people can be found in any area of life. For those of you who would like to expand your horizons and open yourself to other points of view, I have taken the liberty here of listing some places where you might begin. This is by no means a complete list nor is it meant to be in any way exclusive. Rather, I have merely included a cross-section of some organizations which have stood the test of time by consistently offering classes and workshop experiences that are responsible, pragmatic, and psychologically sound. Most offer catalogues. Feel free to query:

Ojai Foundation
  P.O. Box 1620, Ojai, CA 93023; Ph: (805) 646-8343.
The Love Project
  P.O. Box 7601, San Diego, CA 92107-0601; Ph: (619) 225-0133.
Institute of Human Development
  P.O. Box 1616, Ojai, CA 93023; Ph: (805) 646-4359.
John F. Kennedy University
  Graduate School of Consciousness Studies, 12 Altarinda Road, Orinda, CA 94563; Ph: (415) 254-0200.
The Bear Tribe
  P.O. Box 9167, Spokane, WA 99209; Ph: (509) 326-6561.

The Joy Lake Community
  P.O. Box 1328, Reno, NV 89504; Ph: (702) 323-0378.

School of the Natural Order
  P.O. Box 578, Baker, NV 89311; Ph: (702) 234-7304.

The Feathered Pipe Ranch
  Holistic Life Seminars, P.O. Box 1682, Helena, MT
  59624; Ph: (406) 442-8196.

Naropa Institute
  2130 Arapahoe, Boulder, CO 80302; Ph: (303) 444-0202.

Center for Spiritual Awareness
  P.O. Box 7, Lake Rabun Road, Lakemont, GA
  30552-9990, Ph: (404) 782-4723.

Sevenoaks Pathwork Center
  Route #1, Box 86, Madison, VA 22727; Ph: (703)
  948-6544.

Yes Education Society
  P.O. Box 5719, Takoma Park, MD 20912; Ph: (301)
  270-3887 or (301) 270-3808.

Kripalu Center For Yoga & Health
  Box 793, Lenox, MA 02140; Ph: (413) 637-3280.

Omega Institute
  Lake Drive, R#2, 377, Rhinebeck, NY 12572; Ph: (914)
  338-6030 before May 15th and (914) 266-4301 after May
  15th and through the summer session.

The Waldorf Institute
  260 Hungry Hollow Road, Spring Valley, NY 10977;
  Ph: (914) 425-0055.

New York Open Center
  83 Spring Street, New York, NY 10012; Ph: (212)
  219-2527.

Findhorn
  The Accommodation Secretary, Findhorn Foundation,
  Cluny Hill College, Forres, 1V36 ORD, Scotland; Ph:
  Forres (0309) 72288.

Moral Re-Armament
  The Conference Secretary, Mountain House, Ch-1824,
  Caux, Switzerland; Ph: 021-63-48-21.

The Course in Miracles is a controversial study which is difficult to grasp for many people, but it does offer a challenge to spiritual perception and in that regard is well worth approaching to see if it might be meaningful for you. Once a three-volume set, it has since been condensed into one book and should be available through any bookstore. If not, contact: The Foundation for Inner Peace, P.O. Box 635, Tiburon, CA 94920. Cassettes, books and poetry about *The Course in Miracles* can be ordered from Miracle Distribution Center, 1141 East Ash Avenue, Fullerton, CA 92631; Ph: (714) 738-8380.

Spiritual Emergencies

With spiritual development becoming increasingly popular and widespread, there is also developing the reality of *spiritual emergencies*. Various transpersonal processes can trigger a spiritual emergency. The awakening of Kundalini through intense meditation is an example. This process can mimic many psychiatric conditions, but the most common symptoms include intense physical shaking, emitting strange sounds, visions of geometric patterns, and waves of anxiety or other intense emotions. Another type is the state of possession, where the face or body of the person may go through contortions, and the voice may take on strange qualities. The person may try to control it through suppression and may become depressed or suicidal. Another type of spiritual emergency occurs when the psychic centers become opened, flooding the person with psychic impressions and phenomena which are confusing. To the traditional observer, the person involved may appear deluded. Activation of karmic patterns may arouse strong emotions and apparent confusions as the person responds simultaneously to past-life memories along with current life situations.

Christina and Stanislav Grof, husband-and-wife team in the fields of psychiatry and psychotherapy, have initiated **a program to identify counselors able to handle spiritual emergencies in a holistic manner,** which facilitates growth and helps the individual involved integrate new levels of awareness. To this end, they have established the **Spiritual Emergency Network,** which operates out of the California Institute of Transpersonal Psychology and over forty other spiritual emergency centers worldwide. Queries are welcome, especially from counselors willing to be included in the directory, or from individuals seeking alternatives to traditional psychiatry. *The Network phone is (415) 327-2776.* Or write: S.E.N., California Institute of Transpersonal Psychology, 250 Oak Grove Avenue, Menlo Park, CA 94025.

Foundation For Research on the Nature of Man is also offering the same service on the East Coast. To participate with their directory listing or to request aid, *call them at (919) 688-8241.* The Foundation also publishes the *Journal of Parapsychology.* For more information, write to them at P.O. Box 6847, Durham, NC, 27708-6847.

Originated by Gerald Jampolsky, M.D., there is now a worldwide movement to establish centers where people can join together to teach each other. Called **Attitudinal Healing Centers**, each is staffed by trained personnel plus experienced volunteers to offer a full range of services compatible with the special needs of those seeking to change or enrich their lives, or cope with difficult life situations. Attitudinal Healing Centers also *have the best program of growth and support* for near-death survivors and other people dealing with the consequences of spiritual emergencies than any other group or organization I have yet to discover. Please query any of the following for more information about the program, whether there's a center located in your area, and/or how to become a volunteer facilitator:

Center for Attitudinal Healing
   19 Main Street
   Tiburon, CA 94920; Ph: (415) 435-5022.

Center for Attitudinal Healing
   288 West T.C. Jester
   Houston, TX 77018; Ph: (713) 688-1734.

Center for Attitudinal Healing
4530 16th Street, N.W.
Washington, DC 20016; Ph: (202) 797-5522.

Here is a *Zen koan* which I feel best addresses the human quest for spirituality in context with the whole of life:

"After enlightenment—the laundry."

Intuition and the Psychic

Logic and intuition are equal partners. Without both working together harmoniously, we are neither healthy nor balanced. Logic, a product of conscious and deliberate thought, is considered a left-brain activity. Intuition, a product of subconscious abstractions, is most often associated with the right brain hemisphere. There has been enough scientific research now to prove the wisdom of *right-brain development* and the folly of exclusive dependence on left-brain linear thinking. A healthy brain is a whole brain, where all parts work together effectively and equally. Resources on the subject are:

The Right-Brain Experience: An Intimate Program To Free The Powers of Your Imagination, Marilee Zdenek. New York, NY; McGraw-Hill, 1983.

Whole-Brain Thinking: Working From Both Sides of the Brain to Achieve Peak Job Performance, Jacquelyn Wonder and Priscilla Donovan. New York, NY; William Morrow, 1984.

How Creative Are You, Eugene Raudsepp. New York, NY; Putnam, 1981.

As we expand our creative and intuitive potential, we develop solid, dependable skills and abilities with which to explore our inner life and dreamscapes. A question to ask is: How can we ever reach and endure transcended states of consciousness until we can first learn to utilize and integrate the inner realities of our own mind?

Visualization and dream interpretation are positive, safe ways to begin:

Creative Visualization, Shakti Gawain. New York, NY; Bantam, 1982.

Visualization: Directing the Movies of Your Mind, Adelaide Bry and Marjorie Bair. New York, NY; Harper & Row, 1979.

Imagineering For Health, Serge King. Wheaton, IL; Theophysical Publishing House, 1981.

How To Interpret Your Own Dreams: An Encyclopedic Dictionary, Tom Chetwynd. New York, NY; P. H. Wyden, [1980] c1972.

The Dream Dictionary, Jo Jean Boushahla and Virginia Reidel-Geubtner. New York, NY; Pilgrim, 1983.

Lucid Dreaming: The Power of Being Awake and Aware in Your Dreams, Stephen LaBerge, Ph.D. Los Angeles, CA; J. P. Tarcher, 1985.

The Inner Eye: Your Dreams Can Make You Psychic, Joan Windsor. Englewood Cliffs, NJ; Prentice-Hall, 1985.

In 1985, when I had the hysterectomy, I used **visualization techniques** and **affirmative thoughts** beginning two weeks before, imaging a successful surgery, my scar thin and straight, and no negative side-effects from any chemical used. During my hospital stay, I visually performed *every* physical maneuver in my mind *before* actually doing it, affirming that each movement would be done easily and without harm or pain. So successful were these techniques that every doctor and nurse on the floor came to ask what was causing my remarkable healing. To my way of thinking, every hospital and clinic should have this kind of training available for their patients. Savings in pain, effort, time, and money would be tremendous!

The dynamics of inner realities are really the same thing as psychic abilities. The only real difference is one of semantics. **The psychic and the intuitive are the same!** But when we start discussing psychism, people immediately associate it with voodoo, occult, magic, sorcery, witchcraft, and the devil. Psychic powers are simply extensions of natural sensing faculties. It is all a matter of usage and purpose. Perhaps the best way to think of this and keep everything in a healthy perspective is to concentrate on developing ourselves to be the best we can, to emphasize virtue, responsibility, joy, and service. All else will assume its rightful proportions.

Psychic ability developed just for the sake of being psychic boomerangs!

Forgive me if I seem to be repeating myself here, but this issue is so important. Notice, for instance, how many *psychics* lead miserable lives and/or drink excessively, smoke heavily, or are hooked on drugs and sex. *Being "accurate" is not necessarily a sign of competence.* Psychic abilities developed out of context from our practical and spiritual natures represents the negative aspect of inner growth, in my opinion; but, psychic abilities developed as part of a balanced, wholesome life are invaluable. Skills of the inner life are just as valid and desirable as skills of the outer life. And anything you can already do you can always learn to do better!

The best established organization that serves as a guidepost for the safe, constructive exploration of psychism as it relates to wholesome, spiritual development is the *Association for Research and Enlightenment.* Highly diversified, they offer a complete range of books, tapes, class and seminar opportunities, therapeutic departments, several health clinics, list of cooperating doctors, summer camps, study groups throughout the world, libraries, Atlantic University for the study of consciousness, ongoing research projects, and much more. Their magazine, *Venture Inward,* is the best in its field. Introductory packets with book catalogue are free for the asking. Contact them at: A.R.E., P.O. Box 595, Virginia Beach, VA 23451; Ph: (804) 428-3588. Located on the corner of 67th and Atlantic Avenue, their program for beginners is excellent.

Another reliable organization, which is more of a movement than a fixed-base operation, is *Spiritual Frontiers Fellowship.* Although not as large as the A.R.E., nor offering the same programs for beginners, they do have a challenging and very stimulating summertime seminar program at various college campuses across the country. Attracting some of the finest talent in the field, their seminars are lively and enjoyable as well as diverse. Their quarterly journal is excellent. S.F.F. also maintains a library, local study groups, and various educational programs. Queries are welcome. Contact them at: S.F.F., 10715 Winner Road, Independence, MO 64052; Ph: (816) 254-8595.

Two of the most constructive and practical manuals for psychic development are not available in bookstores at this writing. Contact the authors directly:

Harold Sherman's Great ESP Manual, Harold Sherman, Highway 5 South, Mountain View, AR 72560.
Practical ESP: A Step by Step Guide for Developing Your Intuitive Potential, Carol Ann Liaros, Blind Awareness Project, 5201 S.W. 22nd Terrace, Ft. Lauderdale, FL 33312.

Other excellent books on the subject:

Stalking the Wild Pendulum: On the Mechanics of Consciousness, Itzhak Bentov. New York, NY; E. P. Dutton, 1977.
A Cosmic Book: On the Mechanics of Creation, Itzhak Bentov and Mirtala. New York, NY; E. P. Dutton, 1982.
The Mind Race: Understanding and Using Psychic Abilities, Russell Targ and Keith Harary. New York, NY; Ballantine, 1985.
Venture Inward, Hugh Lynn Cayce. New York, NY; Harper & Row, 1985.
Psychic Studies: A Christian's View, Michael Perry. San Bernadino, CA; Borgo Press, 1987.
The Secret of the Golden Flower: A Chinese Book of Life, Richard Wilhelm (translator) and commentary by Carl Gustav Jung. San Diego, CA; Harcourt Brace Jovanovich, 1970.

The Secret Teachings of All Ages, Manley P. Hall. Los Angeles, CA; The Philosophical Research Society, Inc., 1978.

Magazines on the subject:
Metapsychology—contact: *Metapsychology*, Box 3295, Charlottesville, VA 22903.
Fate—contact: *Fate* magazine, P.O. Box 249, Highland Park, IL 60035.
Body, Mind Spirit—formerly "Psychic Guide". Contact them at P.O. Box 701 Providence, RI 02901.

Video on levels of consciousness:

The cosmology of Itzhak Bentov is presented by his widow, Mirtala, on this video entitled "From Atom to Cosmos." Available from MACROmedia, P.O. Box 1223, Brookline, MA 02146.

Dowsing is the most constructive way I know to explore and expand intuitive/psychic abilities. And it's fun! Anyone from a four-year-old to great-grandparents can do it. Contrary to some notions, dowsing is not a "special" gift but is readily teachable as a practical skill to access octaves beyond the electromagnetic spectrum. *Dowsers are the doers of PSI. The bottom line is always demonstration and results!* One of the best books written on the subject is:

The Divining Hand, Christopher Bird. Black Mountain, NC; New Age Press, 1985.

The largest and most established organization devoted to dowsing is The American Society of Dowsers headquartered in Vermont. They sponsor a large, well-attended conference each mid-September, a full line of books and tapes, plus local chapters scattered across the country. Queries always welcome. Contact: The American Society of Dowsers, Danville, VT 05828-0024; Ph: (802) 684-3417.

Music

Earth music to a survivor of death often sounds like so much noise! These people usually prefer silence or the sounds of nature, tuning inward rather than outward. If commercial music can be tolerated, preferences change. For those who alter consciousness naturally or because of a growth event, the idea of music usually centers around that which is melodic and gentle. Even if the music's upbeat there will be a certain "naturalness" to it, a harmony and a flow. For those who artificially force altered states, musical preferences invariably focus more on loud, heavy beats which can numb the brain and overstimulate lower chakras. (This overemphasizes issues of security, sex, and energy.) Tests have shown that melodious music nourishes and promotes plant and animal growth in a healthy, positive manner. The only plant I know of which thrives on harsh rock-beats and heavy metal is marijuana.

Since music becomes such an issue for survivors and others like them, I would like to suggest two companies which specialize in *a broad selection of uplifting, inspirational sound.* Catalogs are free for the asking.

Vital Body Marketing, P.O. Box 1067, Manhasset, NY 11030; Ph: (800) 221-0200, in New York, dial (516) 365-4115.

Narda, 1845 N. Farwell Avenue, Milwaukee, WI 53202; Ph: (800) 862-7232.

When you play music you literally "play" people. Our endocrine system, major organs, and brain waves are easily entrained by what we hear and sense from sound and rhythm. For this reason, people can actually be "brainwashed" by music and not know it. For near-death survivors and others like them, it is almost as if we no longer "listen" to music but rather "become" it. We enter "into" music and spread out with every note and vibration. Music which is gutteral and hard, like some rock, becomes painful and disturbing; music that is natural and flowing, such as creations from The Paul Winter Consort or Kiri Te

Kanawa, or sounds from harp and flute, become nourish-
ment for the soul.

The different effects from sound and vibration are
no small issue. For this reason, I recommend personal
explorations of the subject. Here are some resource books
which may help:

*Sound Health: The Music and Sounds That Make Us
Whole,* Steven Halpern and Louis Savary. New York, NY;
Harper & Row, 1985.

*The Secret Power of Music: The Transformation of Self
and Society Through Musical Energy,* David Tame.
Rochester, VT; (Destiny Books) Inner Tradition, 1984.

The only earthplane music I have yet found that best
typifies music heard while on "The Other Side" is hoomi
singing. Originated in Mongolia, **hoomi or harmonic singing** is a way of using the body and vocal cords to refract
sound. This vibratory technique produces "overtones" or a
series of notes from a single tone, creating, in the process,
an imitation of nature's finest without the use of instrumentation. *The Harmonic Arts Society* has revived this
ancient skill. Their albums are available through "New
Age" music outlets or can be ordered directly from the
Harmonic Arts Society, 25 Claremont Avenue, #4C, New
York, NY 10027; Ph: (212) 222-2138. This kind of music is so
hauntingly beautiful I hesitate to call it music. For me, it is
like "the soul's heartsong reaching out to God."

There are now a number of experienced and innovative
teachers who offer classes and workshops in **the creative
use of great music and how to tune and tone the human
body.** One of these is Rhoda Beryl Semel, a distinguished
opera and concert artist, who presently offers outstanding
programs in "Sound, Voice and Spirit," which combine the
vibrations of sound with color. Contact her at 285 Watch-
ung Avenue, Bloomfield, NJ 07003; Ph: (201) 338-3917.
There are many other leaders in this new field, so look for
announcements of local opportunities.

A classic in **the exploration of human sound** is the
book, *Toning: The Creative Power of the Voice,* by Laurel

Elizabeth Keyes. Although small in size, it is dynamic in presentations of how to more effectively utilize the kind of sound each of us can create. Purchase from DeVorss & Co., P.O. Box 550, Marina del Rey, CA 90291.

Expanding Worldviews

Those who have altered their consciousness see the world differently. They tend to prefer cooperation instead of competition, conservation instead of consumerism, caring instead of apathy. They are not easily swayed by public opinion or the antics of Madison Avenue. They seem rather to walk to the tune of a different drummer. And they are curious. Extremely curious! Invariably their worldview will expand. The following resources provide a starting place. Use your own judgment concerning these selections, and make your own decisions.

Books

Chaos; Making a New Science, James Gleick. New York, NY; Viking, 1987.

The Body Electric: Electromagnetism and the Foundation of Life, Robert O. Becker, M.D. & Gary Shelden. New York, NY; William Morrow, 1985.

A New Science of Life: The Hypothesis of Formative Causation, Rupert Sheldrake. Los Angeles, CA; J. P. Tarcher, 1981.

The Aquarian Conspiracy: Personal and Social Transformation in the 1980's, Marilyn Ferguson. Los Angeles, CA; J. P. Tarcher, 1981.

The Medium, the Mystic and the Physicist, Lawrence LeShan. New York, NY; Ballantine, 1982.

The Tao of Physics, Fritjof Capra. New York, NY; Bantam, 1977.

The Dancing Wu-Li Masters: An Overview of the New Physics, Gary Zukav. New York, NY; Bantam Books, 1979.

Gaia, A New Look at Life on Earth, James E. Lovelock. New York, NY; Oxford University Press, 1982.

The Living Economy: A New Economics in the Making,

Paul Elkins. Available from Technology Development Group, P.O. Box 337, Croton-on-Hudson, NY 10520

When Society Becomes an Addict, Anne Wilson Shaef. New York, NY; Harper & Row, 1987.

Faces of The Enemy, Sam Keen. New York, NY; Harper & Row, 1987.

Vital Lies, Simple Truths: The Psychology of Self-Deception, Daniel Goleman, Ph.D. New York, NY; Simon & Schuster, 1985.

We're All Doing Time, Bo Lozoff. Available from Human Kindness Foundation, R#1, Box 201-N, Durham, NC 27705.

For Your Own Good: Hidden Cruelty in Child-Rearing and the Roots of Violence, Alice Miller. New York, NY; Farrar, Straus & Giroux, 1983.

The Secret Life of the Unborn Child, Thomas Verny & John Kelly. New York, NY; Dell, 1986.

Exploring the Crack in the Cosmic Egg, Joseph C. Pearce. New York, NY; Pocket Books, 1982.

Tesla, Man Out of Time, Margaret Cheney. Englewood Cliffs, NJ; Prentice-Hall, 1981.

The Bone Peddlers: The Selling of Evolution, William R. Fix. New York, NY; Macmillan, 1984.

A Life in the Day of an Editor (the story behind Eco-Agriculture), Charles Walters, Jr. Available from Halcyon House Publishers, Box 9547, Kansas City, MO 64133.

The Lives of a Cell: Notes of a Biology Watcher, Lewis Thomas. New York, NY; Viking Press, 1974.

Kinship With All Life, J. Allen Boone. New York, NY; Harper & Row, 1976.

The Immense Journey, Loren Eiseley. New York, NY; Random House, 1957.

The Road Less Traveled: A New Psychology of Love, Traditional Values and Spiritual Growth, M. Scott Peck, M.D. New York, NY; Simon & Schuster, 1980.

The Silent Pulse: The Search for the Perfect Rhythm That Exists in Each of Us, George Leonard. New York, NY; E. P. Dutton, 1986.

Initiation, Elisabeth Haich. Palo Alto, CA; Seed Center, 1974.

The Man Who Tapped the Secrets of the Universe, Glenn Clark. Available from The University of Science and Philosophy, Swannanoa Palace, P.O. Box 520, Waynesboro, VA 22980.

The Bridge Across Forever: A True Love Story, Richard Bach. Thorndike, ME; Morrow, 1984.

Builders of the Dawn: Community Lifestyles in a Changing World, Corinne McLaughlin and Gordon Davidson. Walpole, NH; Stillpoint Press, 1985.

The Re-Enchantment of the World, Morris Berman. Ithaca, NY; Cornell University, 1981.

The Hour Glass: Sixty Fables for This Moment In Time, Carl Japikse (for children of all ages). Ariel, OH; Ariel Press, 1984.

Hope for the Flowers, Trina Paulus (for children of all ages). New York, NY; Paulist Press, 1972.

You—A Source of Strength in Our World, Eleanor Rost (for grade-school-age children). Available from Coleman Publishing, 99 Milbar Blvd., Farmingdale, NY 11735.

Mister God, This Is Anna, Fynn. New York, NY; Holt, Rinehart & Winston, 1975.

The Magic of Findhorn, Paul Hawken. New York, NY; Harper & Row, 1975.

To Hear The Angels Sing: An Odyssey of Co-Creation With the Devic Kingdom, Dorothy Maclean. Middletown, WI; Lorian Press, 1983.

The Perelandra Garden Workbook: A Complete Guide to Gardening with Nature Intelligences, Machaelle Small Wright. Available from Perelandra Ltd., Box 136, Jeffersonton, VA 22724.

Permaculture: A Designer's Handbook, Bill Mollison. Stanley, Australia; Tagaari, 1981.

The Wandering Taoist, Deng Ming-Dao. New York, NY; Harper & Row, 1983.

Jesus, The Son of Man, Kahlil Gibran. New York, NY; Knopf, 1928.

Magazines, Newsletters and Materials

East West Journal—magazine of both better health *and* spiritual development. East West Subscription Dept.,

P.O. Box 6769, Syracuse, NY 13217–9990. Editorial Offices at 17 Station St., Brookline, MA 02146; Ph: (617) 232-1000.

Interspecies Communication—a cassette recording honoring human communication with other species. Interspecies Communication, 273 Hidden Meadow Lane, Friday Harbor, WA 98250.

Acres U.S.A.—a newspaper dedicated to humane methods of agriculture. Acres U.S.A., P.O. Box 9547, Kansas City, MO 64133; Ph: (816) 737-0064.

Sonic Bloom—a revolutionary "new" way to insure healthy and abundant plant growth. Scientific Enterprises, 708–119th Lane, Blaine, MN 55434; Ph: (612) 757-8274.

Lindisfarne—workshop experience in sacred architecture at Lindisfarne Mountain Retreat, P.O. Box 130, Crestone, CO 81131. Publications in sacred architecture from Lindisfarne Press, Route #2, West Stockbridge, MA 01266. Centers around the work of people like Keith Critchlow, 2 Larkall Lane, London SW4 6SP, England, an innovative architect specializing in the harmonics of spiritual forms.

New Alchemy Institute—designs and produces appropriate technology in keeping with environmental needs. Extensive programs, tours, and training classes. New Alchemy Institute, 237 Hatchville Road, East Falmouth, MA 02536; PH: (617) 563-2655.

Earth Star—new concept of earth-energy grid lines as depicted on a cardboard model which is accompanied by plastic overlay and explanatory article formerly published in *Pursuit* magazine. Request from Conservative Technology, 105 Wolpers Road, Park Forest, IL 60644; Ph: (312) 481-6168.

Choices & Connections—resources catalog for contacts and suggestions in support of expanding growth and awareness. Choices & Connections Network, 10002 Walnut Street, Boulder, CO 80302; Ph: (303) 938-9960.

Tranet—directory and networking service of transformation on a worldwide basis. Tranet, P.O. Box 567, Rangeley, ME 04970; Ph: (207) 864-2252.

Utne Reader—the reader's digest of the alternative press. Utne Reader Subscription Dept., P.O. Box 1974, Marion, OH 43305. Editorial Offices at 2732 West 43rd Street, Minneapolis, MN 55410; Ph: (612) 929-2670.

New Options—newsletter of humane politics. New Options Inc. P.O. Box 19324, Washington, DC 20036; Ph: (202) 234-0747.

Hospice Movement

Adults—
National Hospice Organization
1311A Dolly Madison Blvd.
McLean, VA 22101
Ph: (703) 356-6770

Children—
Children's Hospice International
1101 King Street
Alexandria, VA 22314
Ph: (703) 684-0330

**The Hopi word for "family" translates—
to breathe together.
Think about that.**

Notes

"Most of the shadows of this life are caused by standing in one's own sunshine."

Ralph Waldo Emerson

1. Should any of you wish to contact the holistic, naturopathic doctor who successfully assisted me after the three "death" experiences I survived, he is available, but no longer maintains a full schedule. You may call or write: William G. Reimer, N.D., Health Care Clinic, 466 West Idaho, Ontario, OR 97914; Ph: (503) 889-6556.

2. Naturopathy employs a variety of wholistic techniques to stimulate the body's ability to heal itself. Various recommendations on diet, massage, herbs, vitamins and exercise are made. Naturopathic doctors are not allowed to prescribe drugs, nor would they want to. Should you wish to investigate this healing art further, query:

The National College of Naturopathic Medicine
510 S.W. Third Avenue
Portland, OR 97204   Ph: (503) 226-3745

The John Bastyr College of Naturopathic Medicine
1408 N.E. 45th Street
Seattle, WA 98105   Ph: (206) 632-0165

3. The Bear Tribe Medicine Society originated because of a vision by Sun Bear, a Chippewa Medicine Man. Because of this, the Society specializes in Native American teachings and sponsors a diverse range of opportunities for learning, including "Medicine Wheel Gatherings" held in various places across the United States and in foreign countries. They publish extensively including the excellent magazine *Wildfire* and operate a mail-order catalog service. Contact: The Bear Tribe Medicine Society, P.O. Box 9167, Spokane,WA 99209; Ph: (509) 326-6561.

4. The Neuropsychology of Achievement is a home study course available from SyverVision Systems, Inc., 2450 Washington Avenue, Dept. 270, San Leandro, CA 94577; Ph: 1-800-227-0600.

5. Arthur E. Yenson has self-published a number of books, including *I Saw Heaven*, the story of his near-death experience. His article, *Saying Goodbye to Alice*, about his wife's death and her pioneer burial is most unusual and interesting and well worth obtaining a copy of. For more information about his various publications, you may reach him by writing: Arthur E. Yenson, P.O. Box 369, Parma, ID 83660.

6. *Cosmic Consciousness*, Richard Maurice Bucke, M.D. First published in book form by Innes & Sons in 1901. Now under reprint rights with the Citadel Press. I want to thank the Citadel Press for their generosity in allowing me to discuss and quote from this book.

7. From a series of articles by Michael Eldridge, with this particular quote appearing in the September, 1983, issue of *The Aquarian Age* mini-magazine, P.O. Box 55214, Indianapolis, IN 56205.

8. *A Sociable God*, Ken Wilbur. New York, NY; McGraw-Hill, 1982. Check on other books by Ken Wilbur. He has written many fine volumes on spirituality and has a remarkable depth of understanding on the subject.

9. *A Search In Secret Egypt*, Paul Brunton, New York: E. P. Dutton, 1936. Available in reprint from Weiser Book Store, 132 East 24th Street, New York, NY 10010; or from The Paul Brunton Philosophic Foundation, P.O. Box 89, Hector, NY 14841.

10. *Threshold To Tomorrow*, Ruth Montgomery. New York, NY; Putnam, 1983.

11. *Messengers of Hope*, Reverend Carol W. Parrish-Harra; New Age Press, 1983. Available through Light of Christ Community Church, P.O. Box 1274, Tahlequah, OK 74465.

12. *Brain and Psyche: The Biology of the Unconscious*, Jonathan Winson. New York, NY; Doubleday, 1985.

13. Dr. Richard Cytowic's work was originally reported in the June 1983 issue of *Omni Magazine*, P.O. Box 5700, Bergenfield, NJ 07621. Capital Neurology Lab where he works is located at 8700 Central Avenue, Landover, MD 20785.

14. Charles C. Wise, Jr., is especially noted for authoring the thought provoking books *Magian Gospel* and *Picture Windows on the Christ*. A brochure describing all his publications is available by writing: The Magian Press, P.O. Box 117, Penn Laird, VA 22846.

15. Christina and Stanislav Grof are internationally renowned for their pioneering discoveries concerning the effects of hallucinatory drugs and altered states of consciousness. They are among the few in their field who realize that alternatives to traditional therapy must be found in cases of spiritual emergencies. Stanislav's latest book is *Brain, Birth, Death and Transcendence in Psychotherapy*, Stanislov Grof. Albany, NY; State U. NY, 1985. To learn more about their work, write them in care of Esalen Institute, Big Sur, CA 93920.

16. The lines by Reverend Gene Emmet Clark on page 109 are from the September 8, 1983, "Daily Guide to Richer Living" section of *Science of Mind Magazine*, P.O. Box 75127, Los Angeles, CA 90075.

Index